P9-DDD-796

*Choose for yourselves this day whom
you will serve. . . . As for me and my
house, we will serve the Lord.*

JOSHUA 24:15 NKJV

Copyright © 2005 Thomas Nelson, Inc.

The quoted ideas expressed in this book (but not Scripture verses) are not, in all cases, exact quotations, as some have been edited for clarity and brevity. In all cases, the author has attempted to maintain the speaker's original intent. In some cases, quoted material for this book was obtained from secondary sources, primarily print media. While every effort was made to ensure the accuracy of these sources, the accuracy cannot be guaranteed.

All rights reserved. No portion of this book may be reproduced, stored in a retrieval system, or transmitted in any form or by any means—electronic, mechanical, photocopy, recording, scanning, or other—except for brief quotations in critical reviews or articles, without the prior written permission of the publisher.

Published in Nashville, Tennessee, by Thomas Nelson®. Thomas Nelson is a trademark of Thomas Nelson, Inc. Thomas Nelson, Inc., titles may be purchased in bulk for educational, business, fund-raising, or sales promotional use. For information, please e-mail SpecialMarkets@ThomasNelson.com.

Scripture quotations marked (KJV) are taken from the King James Version of the Bible.

Scripture quotations marked (NKJV) are taken from NEW KING JAMES VERSION. Copyright © 1982 by Thomas Nelson, Inc. Used by permission. All rights reserved.

Scripture quotations marked (MSG) are taken from *The Message* by Eugene H. Peterson © 1993, 1994, 1995, 1996, 2000. Used by permission of NavPress Publishing Group. All rights reserved.

Scripture quotations marked (NASB, ASB, or ASV) are from the NEW AMERICAN STANDARD BIBLE®. © The Lockman Foundation, 1960, 1962, 1963, 1968, 1971, 1972, 1973, 1975, 1977, 1995. Used by permission.

Scripture quotations marked (NIV) are from the HOLY BIBLE, NEW INTERNATIONAL VERSION®. Copyright © 1973, 1978, 1984 by Biblica, Inc.™ Used by permission of Zondervan. All rights reserved worldwide. www.zondervan.com.

Scripture quotations marked (NLT) are taken from *Holy Bible*, New Living Translation © 1996. Used by permission of Tyndale House Publishers, Inc., Wheaton, Illinois, 60189. All rights reserved.

Scripture quotations marked (RSV) are taken from the REVISED STANDARD VERSION of the Bible. © 1946, 1952, 1971, 1973 by the Division of Christian Education of the National Council of the Churches of Christ in the U.S.A. Used by permission.

Scripture quotations marked (NRSV) are taken from the NEW REVISED STANDARD VERSION of the Bible. © 1989 by the Division of Christian Education of the National Council of the Churches of Christ in the U.S.A. All rights reserved.

Scripture quotations marked (NCV) are taken from the New Century Version®. © 2005 by Thomas Nelson, Inc. Used by permission.

The Chosen Path © 2005
Compiled by Patti M. Hummel
The Benchmark Group, Nashville, Tennessee
Project Editor: Alice Sullivan

ISBN-13: 978-1-4041-7473-3 Released 2012

Printed in China

12 13 14 15 WAI 5 4 3 2 1

www.thomasnelson.com

365-Day Devotional

The Chosen Path

Encouragement for Your Daily Walk

THOMAS NELSON
Since 1798

NASHVILLE   DALLAS   MEXICO CITY   RIO DE JANEIRO

WHEN I AM WEAK HE IS STRONG!

*And he said unto me, My grace is sufficient for thee:
for my strength is made perfect in weakness.*

*Most gladly therefore will I rather glory in my infirmities,
that the power of Christ may rest upon me. Therefore I take pleasure
in infirmities, in reproaches, in necessities, in persecutions, in
distresses for Christ's sake: for when I am weak, then am I strong.*

2 CORINTHIANS 12:9–10 KJV

It might sound like an expression of false humility, but it has been my life, truly it has. When God is big and I am small, I have seen Him do great and mighty things. I read a story this week about a couple of little boys—Kevin, 5, and Ryan, 3—they are sitting down to breakfast. Their mom is bringing pancakes. She brings them the first pancake and they both grab for it. The mom decides this is a great moment to teach them a moral lesson. She says, "If Jesus were here, He would give His brother the first pancake. Then He'd sit and wait patiently." So Kevin looks at his little brother and says, "Ryan, you be Jesus." The question is who's going to be Jesus for the millions of lost people in our world? Who is going to make the unselfish choice to reach out to those that have not yet heard the GOOD NEWS. Who's going to make the unselfish choice to serve, to give, and to go? Our number one weakness in the church today is selfishness. If we can see our weakness and turn to Christ, He is strong and faithful to give us the power to make the right choices.

~DOUG MILLAR (1957–) CANCUN, MEXICO

PLAYING CHURCH

Blows that hurt cleanse away evil,
As do stripes the inner depths of the heart.

PROVERBS 20:30 NKJV

There is no greater hindrance to revival than a comfortable pastor settled and satisfied, coasting along until he reaches retirement, who does not want his flock disturbed or the status quo upset. He resents any intrusion into the complacency of a sleeping church, and interprets the prophet's call to repentance as an indictment of his own preaching. He is determined not to get excited, assumes a philosophical tolerance of things as they are, and he may speak facetiously of the prophet's seriousness. Sometimes his own people may get under conviction, and put him to shame by a concern he does not seem to feel. This makes it exceedingly difficult for any revivalist calling Christians to repentance, but what a delight when pastor and prophet stand together! Most pastors understand that the traveling prophet can say things the pastor cannot say—that he fills a different role and follows an utterly different pattern. They complement each other. One plants, another waters, but God gives the increase. The teacher plants the seed, the pastor cultivates the crop, the evangelist gathers it, but the prophet must first break up the fallow ground. Breaking up the ground is never a pleasant, comfortable business, and churches sometimes resent the plow of plain preaching. Blessed is the pastor who knows this, and stands behind the lonely prophet who calls the church to repentance.

~VANCE HAVNER (1901–1986)

THE CHOSEN PATH

UNEXPECTED GUARDIANS

Don't be afraid, for those who are with us
outnumber those who are with them.

2 KINGS 6:16 HCSB

You are my highly prized fellow Believer and Southern Baptist with confidence in a God without limits and boundaries and you are able to understand the unusual. That gives me freedom to tell of things that even I would have accepted with honest reservations. These events occurred in 1965 as I served as a missionary physician in Indonesia during the Marxist dictatorship of Sukarno and his coup to remove his military and religious opposition, Baptist missionaries and the many Indonesian believers included. We declined the placing of a Communist slogan over our gate as Independence Day decoration so the Party staged a demonstration against us five days later on August 21. Their 4–7,000 demonstrators were advised that we were a "nest of subversives" and that we should be killed and the Kediri Baptist Hospital should be burned. They arrived waving machetes and carrying jerry cans of gas with the vocalized intent to destroy us. The signal to attack was ignored and we watched from within as they became quiet and then left without incident. My pastor, Sukirman, was at the Nurses' Dormitory 100 yards in front of the 2-story Clinic and Administration building with its roof of clay tiles resting on 1 ½ inch bamboo slats. There were two men in white clothing walking back and forth on a tile roof that couldn't possibly support their weight. Our five days of prayer had been heard and answered. We finally understood why God had not given us permission to leave. We would have missed the blessing of a hundred lifetimes!

~JIM CARPENTER (1927–) SENECA, SC

GLORY IS THE VISION OF GOD!

. . . Christ in you, the hope of glory.
COLOSSIANS 1:27 KJV

Glory is the vision of God. The old theologians talked of the beatific vision, the sight that makes happy. To see the king in His beauty this is indeed the vision splendid. We know how a beautiful sight delights the soul beyond words to tell. It may be the majesty of spring, the warm light of summer sunshine, or the gold and purple splendors of setting day, or the simple grace of a fair and fragile flower, or the beauty of a human face, lit with purity and love and peace. We have seen things that make us glad. But who shall say that anything can make a soul so glad as to see God? This is the vision promised in the gospel of Christ. Our human language stumbles and fails in its poor endeavor to express the glory of that vision. Theologians have discussed whether we shall see three persons or only one, whether we shall see only Jesus in His glorified form, or even whether we shall see anything that corresponds to the material sight. All such discourses are futile. There is no need to try to analyze by our poor process of reason, or to express in our weak and imperfect language all that can be meant by seeing God. Surely we know that the vision itself will far surpass in beauty and in joy every image of it that we now can form. To the thinker, puzzled with problems, the ultimate good will then appear. To the artist, striving for the ideal, perfect beauty will then appear. To the simple soul that knows naught but to look and love, the face of infinite love will be seen. That is glory.

~E. C. DARGAN (1852–1930)

INSPIRATION OF SCRIPTURE

And when he had said this, he breathed on them,
and saith unto them, Receive ye the Holy Ghost.

JOHN 20:22 KJV

"We believe that the Holy Bible was written by men divinely inspired, and is a perfect treasure of heavenly instruction; that it has God for its author, salvation for its end, and truth without any mixture of error for its matter; that it reveals the principles by which God will judge us; and therefore is, and shall remain to the end of the world, the true center of Christian union, and the supreme standard by which all human conduct, creeds, and opinions shall be tried." This is the first Article of Faith of a great many Baptist churches in our Southland. This brings us at once to the subject of the inspiration of the Scriptures. The word inspiration is derived from the Latin word *inspiro*, which means to breathe on or to breathe into. That is the literal meaning of the word. The theological meaning is to breathe on or to breathe into for the purpose of conveying the Holy Spirit, in order that those inspired may speak or write what God would have spoken or written. A Scriptural example of this is found in John 20:22: "And when he said this he breathed on them and saith unto them, Receive ye the Holy Ghost." Following that, verse 23 gives the result: "Whosoever sins ye forgive, they are forgiven unto them; whosoever sins ye retain, they are retained." That is, an inspired man can declare exactly the terms of remission of sins, and the terms upon which sins cannot be remitted, because he is speaking for God. The book that a man, so breathed on, writes is called theopneustos, a Greek word meaning "God-inspired." The Holy Bible!

~B. H. CARROLL (1843–1914)

VANITIES

*I am the light of the world: he that followeth me shall
not walk in darkness, but shall have the light of life.*

JOHN 8:12 KJV

The teaching of Christ is more excellent than all the advice of the saints, and he who has His spirit will find in it a hidden manna. Now, there are many who hear the Gospel often but care little for it because they have not the spirit of Christ. Yet whoever wishes to understand fully the words of Christ must try to pattern his whole life on that of Christ. What good does it do to speak learnedly about the Trinity if, lacking humility, you displease the Trinity? Indeed it is not learning that makes a man holy and just, but a virtuous life makes him pleasing to God. I would rather feel contrition than know how to define it. For what would it profit us to know the whole Bible by heart and the principles of all the philosophers if we live without grace and the love of God? This is the greatest Wisdom—to seek the kingdom of heaven through contempt of the world. It is vanity, therefore, to seek and trust in riches that perish. It is vanity also to court honor and to be puffed up with pride. It is vanity to follow the lusts of the body and to desire things for which severe punishment later must come. It is vanity to wish for long life and to care little about a well-spent life. It is vanity to be concerned with the present only and not to make provision for things to come. It is vanity to love what passes quickly and not to look ahead where eternal joy abides.

~**THOMAS À KEMPIS** (1380–1471)

IT'S EITHER, OR

"Enter by the narrow gate; for wide is the gate and broad is the way
that leads to destruction, and there are many who go in by it."

MATTHEW 7:13 NKJV

Jesus was an either/or teacher. There was no middle ground when He taught His disciples moral and spiritual truths, and there must be no middle ground today. You say, "That sounds mighty narrow." Yes it is, but Jesus taught in Matthew 7:13–15 that there are only two ways to live: the narrow way that leads to life, and the broad way that leads to destruction. Not much wiggle room; it's either/or. A little further in the chapter, He continues to be intolerant by contrasting life styles as being either good or bad. Ask most people you know about their behavior and they will say, "I think I'm a good person." None of us want to think we are "bad," because bad people should be punished. What makes a good life style? It begins with the choice to follow Jesus, and give Him control of our lives. Finally Jesus addresses the wise and the foolish. It makes infinite sense to choose the wise course and build our lives on substance, on The Rock. The wise choice is to follow Jesus. When He declared, "I am the way, the truth and the life, no one comes to the Father except through Me," He marked Himself and all His followers as EITHER/OR people. This makes people either children of light or children of darkness, destined for either life or for death.

~G. W. STROTHER (1933–) CLAYTON, GA

FAITH OR EXPERIENCE?

. . . the Son of God, who loved me, and gave himself for me.

GALATIANS 2:20 KJV

We should battle through our moods, feelings, and emotions into absolute devotion to the Lord Jesus. We must break out of our own little world of experience into abandoned devotion to Him. Think who the New Testament says Jesus Christ is, and then think of the despicable meagerness of the miserable faith we exhibit by saying, "I haven't had this experience or that experience!" Think what faith in Jesus Christ claims and provides; He can present us faultless before the throne of God, inexpressibly pure, absolutely righteous, and profoundly justified. How dare we talk of making a sacrifice for the Son of God! We are saved from hell and total destruction, and then we talk about making sacrifices! We must continually focus and firmly place our faith in Jesus Christ, not a "prayer meeting" Jesus Christ, or a "book" Jesus Christ, but the New Testament Jesus Christ, who is God Incarnate, and who ought to strike us dead at His feet. Our faith must be in the One from whom our salvation springs. Jesus Christ wants our absolute, unrestrained devotion to Himself. We can never experience Jesus Christ, or selfishly bind Him in the confines of our own hearts. Our faith must be built on strong determined confidence in Him. It is because of our trusting in experience that we see the steadfast impatience of the Holy Spirit against unbelief. All of our fears are sinful, and we create our own fears by refusing to nourish ourselves in our faith. How can anyone who is identified with Jesus Christ suffer from doubt or fear! Our lives should be an absolute hymn of praise resulting from perfect, irrepressible, triumphant belief.

~OSWALD CHAMBERS (1874–1917)

AND CAN IT BE?

AND can it be, that I should gain an interest in the Saviour's blood?
Died he for me, who caused his pain? For me, who him to death pursued?
Amazing love! How can it be that thou, my God, shouldst die for me?

'Tis mystery all! The Immortal dies! Who can explore his strange design?
In vain the first-born seraph tries to sound the depths of love divine!
'Tis mercy all! Let earth adore, let angel-minds inquire no more.

He left his Father's throne above, (so free, so infinite his grace!)
Emptied himself of all but love, and bled for Adam's helpless race:
'Tis mercy all, immense and free, for, O my God, it found out me!

Long my imprisoned spirit lay fast bound in sin and nature's night;
Thine eye diffused a quickening ray, I woke, the dungeon flamed with light;
My chains fell off, my heart was free, I rose, went forth, and followed thee.

No condemnation now I dread, Jesus, and all in him, is mine!
Alive in him, my living Head, and clothed in righteousness divine,
Bold I approach the eternal throne, and claim the crown,
through Christ my own.

~**JOHN WESLEY (1707–1788)**

THE CHOSEN PATH

HAVING A HUMBLE OPINION OF SELF

. . . he that followeth me shall not walk in darkness,
but shall have the light of life.

JOHN 8:12 KJV

Every man naturally desires knowledge; but what good is knowledge without fear of God? Indeed a humble rustic who serves God is better than a proud intellectual who neglects his soul to study the course of the stars. He who knows himself well becomes mean in his own eyes and is not happy when praised by men. If I knew all things in the world and had not charity, what would it profit me before God Who will judge me by my deeds? Shun too great a desire for knowledge, for in it there is much fretting and delusion. Intellectuals like to appear learned and to be called wise. Yet there are many things the knowledge of which does little or no good to the soul, and he who concerns himself about other things than those which lead to salvation is very unwise. Many words do not satisfy the soul; but a good life eases the mind and a clean conscience inspires great trust in God. The more you know and the better you understand, the more severely will you be judged, unless your life is also the more holy. Do not be proud, therefore, because of your learning or skill. Rather, fear because of the talent given you. If you think you know many things and understand them well enough, realize at the same time that there is much you do not know. Hence, do not affect wisdom, but admit your ignorance. Why prefer yourself to anyone else when many are more learned, more cultured than you?

~THOMAS À KEMPIS (1380–1471)

THE ULTIMATE SELF-ESTEEM

*But ye are a chosen generation, a royal priesthood, an holy nation, a
peculiar people; that ye should shew forth the praises of him who hath
called you out of darkness into his marvellous light.*

1 PETER 2:9 KJV

Contained in these two verses is all the self-esteem you will ever
need in this life or the life to come. To know that you have been plucked
out of the obscurity of the world and held in such regard by the Creator
of the universe, to be taken out of a darkened world of fear and
trepidation and shown the marvelous light of salvation through faith in
Jesus Christ. To know that God, Himself, has showered you with mercy
and grace through His Son, that you are now a part of a chosen
generation, a generation that has set aside fear and doubt and
embraced faith and hope. And by embracing that faith and hope you
are now a royal priesthood! Do you understand who you are as a
Christian? Do you understand that in whatever position or situation
you find yourself in, that you are a holy priest of God? Oh, if we could
only get a handle on the most basic concept of this reality, why, it would
revolutionize our lives. No longer would we have to bolster ourselves
through self-destructive behaviors and relationships. No matter where
we find ourselves on the social or economic ladder, to be able to answer
the question of who and what we are by the affirmation, "I am a royal
priest of the most high God," is all the self-esteem you will ever need!

~RUSSELL C. LAMBERT (1955–) AIRWAY HEIGHTS, WA

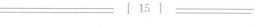

THE CHOSEN PATH

IT IS GOD WHO KEEPS US FROM FALLING . . .

Now unto him that is able to keep you from falling . . .

JUDE V. 24 KJV

This is a most precious promise. The revised translation is both accurate and suggestive. It is not merely from falling that He wants to keep us, but from even the slightest stumbling. We are told that Abraham staggered not at the promise (Romans 4:20). God wants us to walk so steadily that there will not even be a quiver in the line of His regiments as they face the foe. It is the little stumblings of life that most discourage and hinder us, and most of these stumblings are over trivialities. Satan would much rather knock us down with a feather than with a gun. It is much more to his honor and delight to defeat a child of God by some insignificant matter than by some great temptation. Beloved, let us be on guard against the banana peels that trip us on our pathway, the little foxes that destroy the vines and the dead flies that spoil a whole vessel of precious ointment. "Trifles make perfection," and as we get farther on in our Christian life, God will hold us much more closely to obedience in things that seem insignificant.

~ A. B. SIMPSON (1844–1919)

THE POSSUM DEFENSE (PART 1)

I press on toward the goal . . .
PHILIPPIANS 3:14 NIV

As I drive home tonight, I struggle with fearful and anxious thoughts from recent events. I have asked God for help but have been emotionally paralyzed. False hope tells me that I can passively keep on doing what I am doing until the storm passes. Startled back to the present by the sight of a possum on the road, I swerve and miss the motionless creature! Instinctively, I pull off the road to see if the animal is mortally wounded. A visual check and a poke confirm the creature's final demise, so I start back to my car. Suddenly, movement catches my eye causing me to spin around and see the "deceased" possum scurrying off the road! Laughing, I now understand what "playing dead" means, but somberly realize the possum's defense mechanism against fear of my approaching headlights almost killed it tonight. The words *defense mechanism . . . fear . . . killed . . .* replay in my mind. A whisper with substance, like a gentle laser, cuts into my soul and says, "You have been doing the same thing as the possum." I know it is from God by the peace and life changing remorse that comes with it. I've been freezing in fear. The very thing the possum needs to do (keep on moving), it does just the opposite and freezes. This explains why there are dead possums and seemingly dead "Christian possums" lying all over the roads . . . of life. Scripture takes front-stage in my thinking, as a child of God, I have the eternal true Words of God to guide and comfort me! The only hitch— I must truly believe His Words and keep pressing on toward the goal or be run-over by life.

~BRIAN KEAY (1963–) ASHEVILLE, NC

THE POSSUM DEFENSE (PART 2)

And he said, Come.

MATTHEW 14:29 KJV

Then Peter got down out of the boat, walked on the water, and came toward Jesus. But when he saw the wind, he was afraid and, beginning to sink, cried out, "Lord, save me!" Immediately Jesus reached out his hand and caught him. "You of little faith," he said, "why did you doubt?" (Matthew 14:29–31 NIV) Doubt and fear are mutually exclusive with faith. Peter froze and became a rock in the water. He focused on the wind and waves. The possum's waves are headlights. What are your waves? We cannot please God without faith (Hebrews 11:6) and anything that doesn't come from faith is missing the mark (Romans 14:23). How are you handling fear and worry today? Is your Father speaking to you through His Word and in the apparently insignificant? Are you trying to use the world's remedies which have no true power? (2 Corinthians 10:3–5). The next time you notice your defense mechanisms against fearful events and worrisome thoughts coming on, ask God to show you, "What happened today that made me lose my peace?" And two, "What am I perceiving wrongly, from a human perspective?" Believe that the enemy of mankind wants you paralyzed and ineffective in your knowledge of Christ (1 Peter 5:8; 2 Peter 1:8). Satan does not want the witness of your peace and faith through difficult times pointing others to Christ! Quote a scripture to yourself that counteracts your fear and believe it. The Holy Spirit will bring to your memory the truth of Christ in your time of need so you can escape The Possum Defense.

~BRIAN KEAY (1963–) ASHEVILLE, NC

FAITH SHARING 101

"Go therefore and make disciples of all the nations . . ."
MATTHEW 28:19 NASB

Remember the name Helen Keller? Helen was born blind and deaf. Her life was extremely difficult because of her inability to communicate with the outside world. Her parents loved her dearly, but knew all too well the frustrations her condition brought. Anne Sullivan had been employed to teach her. Hours turned into days that turned into weeks. The whole experiment met with such frustration. And then on one fateful day everything changed. At the water pump in the yard, Anne was able to hold Helen's hands under the water and while holding her hands, flesh to flesh, she was able to spell out the word *water*, over and over again until the message was finally received. There are some messages that are so important and so precious, they can only be conveyed when human warmth and compassion shares that important message with someone else . . . face to face, flesh to flesh, heart to heart. Important to your development as a Christian is the discipline of giving away your faith; the discipline of sharing your heart story with someone else. When Christ challenged the disciples to share their faith, He used one key word . . . the word *Go*. The imperative word *Go* does not imply a one-time and one-time-only event. In fact, in its Greek form the word implies continual action. More correctly translated it should read, "As you are going . . . be a witness." That's the challenge that we must accept. We must have a willingness to be used of God, to speak for God, as He prods us to do so during the day-to-day routines of our lives. As you are going, as you travel, as you live, as the moment arises, share your faith. The message is that important.

~JON R. ROEBUCK (1960–) FRANKLIN, TN

WE WILL SERVE THE LORD!

As for me and my house, we will serve the LORD.

JOSHUA 24:15 KJV

It is true indeed, visit our churches, and you may perhaps see something of the form of godliness still subsisting amongst us; but even that is scarcely to be met with in private houses. So that were the blessed angels to come, as in the patriarchal age, and observe our spiritual economy at home, would they not be tempted to say as Abraham to Abimilech, "Surely the fear of God is not in this place?" (Genesis 20:11 KJV). How such a general neglect of family-religion first began to overspread the Christian world, is difficult to determine. As for the primitive Christians, I am positive it was not so with them: No, they had not so learned Christ, as falsely to imagine religion was to be confined solely to their assemblies for public worship; but, on the contrary, behaved with such piety and exemplary holiness in their private families, that St. Paul often styles their house a church: "Salute such a one, says he, and the church which is in his house." And, I believe, we must for ever despair of seeing a primitive spirit of piety revived in the world, till we are so happy as to see a revival of primitive family religion; and persons unanimously resolving with good old Joshua, in the words of the text, "As for me and my house, we will serve the Lord."

~GEORGE WHITEFIELD (1714–1770)

ABSOLUTISM VS. INDIVIDUALISM

The highway of the upright is to depart from evil;
He who keeps his way preserves his soul.

PROVERBS 16:17 NKJV

The student of history cannot fail to observe that through the long years two ideas have been in endless antagonism—the idea of absolutism and the idea of individualism, the idea of autocracy and the idea of democracy. The idea of autocracy is that supreme power is vested in the few, who, in turn, delegate this power to the many. That was the dominant idea of the Roman Empire, and upon that idea has found world-wide impression in the realms both civil and ecclesiastical. Often have the two ideas, absolutism versus individualism, autocracy versus democracy, met in battle. Autocracy dared, in the morning of the twentieth century, to crawl out of its ugly lair and proposed to substitute the law of the jungles for the law of human brotherhood. For all time to come, the hearts of men will stand aghast upon every thought of this incomparable death drama, and at the same time they will renew the vow that the few shall not presumptuously tyrannize over the many; that the law of the jungle shall be given supremacy in all human affairs. And until the principle of democracy, rather than the principle of autocracy, shall be regnant in the realm of religion, our mission shall be commanding and unending.

~G. W. TRUETT (1867–1944)

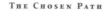

THE CHOSEN PATH

RESISTING THE URGE TO DIRGE
(PART 1)

Rejoice in the Lord always. I will say it again: Rejoice!

PHILIPPIANS 4:4 NIV

Life has a way of delivering some gut-wrenching blows that brings us to our knees. The betrayal of a friend, death of a loved one, a rebellious child, an unfaithful spouse, the loss of a job or a terminal illness can leave you paralyzed with pain. When life hurts, our natural response is to dirge. A dirge is a sad song performed at funerals. It is a natural part of the grieving process, whenever we experience a sense of loss. Those in Christ grieve, but our grieving is not without hope (1 Thessalonians 4:13). Christ calls His own to respond with an attitude of gratitude. Paul says, "Rejoice in the Lord always" (Philippians 4:4 NIV). Our rejoicing is not in the situation; instead, our rejoicing is in The Lord. Our joy is the byproduct of our trust in the Lord Jesus Christ. Trusting He will care for us no matter what. Paul's command "to have joy" is the direct result of trusting in the care of a loving God. Therefore don't worry about anything; instead, pray about everything. Tell God what you need, and thank Him for all He has done. If you do this, you will experience God's peace, which is far more wonderful than the human mind can understand (Philippians 4:6–7).

~WILLIAM M. BLACKFORD, IV (1969–) LOUISVILLE, KY

RESISTING THE URGE TO DIRGE
(PART 2)

Be joyful always; pray continually; give thanks in all circumstances
1 THESSALONIANS 5:16–18 NIV

Pastor Paul encourages you and I to "Rejoice in the Lord always." But it's hard to encourage someone to rejoice when they are going through tough times. To "Rejoice in the Lord" is the most encouraging thing we can share with someone that's struggling. Paul's emphasis is on "The Lord" and not their circumstances. The impact of what Paul is saying is revealed in the nature of God. God Is Sovereign: The Sovereignty of God means He has the absolute right to do all things according to His own good pleasure (Daniel 4:25, 35; Romans 9:15–23; 1 Timothy 6:15; Revelation 4:11). God's Power covers everything and nothing goes beyond what His power can cover. God Is Good: God uses His power for our good. The Bible says, "And we know that in all things God works for the good . . ." (Romans 8:28). God transforms the manure in our lives into fertilizer that helps us grow. Finally, God cares for you. The Bible says, "Cast all your anxiety on him because he cares for you" (1 Peter 5:7). He cares when the marriage ends, when the biopsy is positive, and when the layoff comes. He is there and He cares. God is bigger than all of our problems so cancel the pity party and have a praise party. Take your focus off of the problem and place it on the "Problem Fixer" and He will turn your situation around. "Rejoice in the Lord always. I will say it again: Rejoice!" (Philippians 4:4 NIV).

~**WILLIAM M. BLACKFORD, IV** (1969–) LOUISVILLE, KY

VICTORY OVER THE WORLD THROUGH FAITH

For whatsoever is born of God overcometh the world: and this
is the victory that overcometh the world, even our faith.

1 JOHN 5:4 KJV

A man certainly does not overcome the world unless he gets above being engrossed and absorbed with its concerns. The man who gains the victory over the world must overcome not one form only of its pursuits, but every form—must overcome the world itself and all that it has to present as an allurement to the human heart. Overcoming the world implies overcoming the fear of the world . . . and a state of worldly anxiety. The victory under consideration implies that we cease to be enslaved and in bondage to the world in any of its forms. There is a worldly spirit and there is also a heavenly spirit; and one or the other exists in the heart of every man and controls his whole being. Those who are under the control of the world of course have not overcome the world. No man overcomes the world till his heart is imbued with the spirit of heaven. "To me," said Paul, "it is a small thing to be judged of man's judgment." So of every real Christian; his care is to secure the approbation of God; this is his chief concern, to commend himself to God and to his own conscience. No man has overcome the world unless he has attained this state of mind. Almost no feature of Christian character is more striking or more decisive than this—indifference to the opinions of the world. Men who are not thus dead to the world have not escaped its bondage. The victorious Christian is in a state where he is no longer in bondage to man. He is bound only to serve God.

~CHARLES FINNEY (1792–1875)

THE CHOSEN PATH

THE GUIDING PILLAR

So it was alway; the cloud covered [the tabernacle]
by day, and the appearance of fire by night.

NUMBERS 9:16 KJV

The children of Israel in the wilderness, surrounded by miracle, had nothing which we do not possess. They had some things in an inferior form; their sustenance came by Manna; ours comes by God's blessing on our daily work, which is better. Their guidance came by this supernatural pillar, ours comes by the reality of which that pillar was nothing but a picture. And so, instead of fancying that men thus led were in advance of us, we should learn that these, the supernatural manifestations, visible and palpable, of God's presence and guidance were the beggarly elements: "God having provided some better thing for us, that they without us should not be made perfect." It is easiest to do our duty when we are first sure of it. It then comes with an impelling power which carries us over obstacles on the crest of a wave, while hesitation and delay leave us stranded in shoal water. If we would follow the pillar, we must follow it at once. A heart that waits and watches for God's direction, that uses common sense as well as faith to unravel small and great perplexities, and is willing to sit loose to the present, however pleasant, in order that it may not miss the indications which say, "Arise! This is not your rest"—fulfills the conditions on which, if we keep them, we may be sure that He will guide us by the right way, and bring us at last to the city of habitation.

~ALEXANDER MACLAREN (1826–1910)

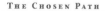

THE CHOSEN PATH

IMITATION OF CHRIST:
PRUDENCE IN ACTION (PART 1)

*You shall not go about as a talebearer among your people; nor shall
you take a stand against the life of your neighbor: I am the LORD.*

LEVITICUS 19:16 NKJV

Do not yield to every impulse and suggestion but consider things
carefully and patiently in the light of God's will. For very often, sad to
say, we are so weak that we believe and speak evil of others rather than
good. Perfect men, however, do not readily believe every talebearer,
because they know that human frailty is prone to evil and is likely to
appear in speech. Not to act rashly or to cling obstinately to one's
opinion, not to believe everything people say or to spread abroad the
gossip one has heard, is great wisdom. Take counsel with a wise and
conscientious man. Seek the advice of your betters in preference to
following your own inclinations. A good life makes a man wise
according to God and gives him experience in many things, for the
more humble he is and the more subject to God, the wiser and the more
at peace he will be in all things.

~THOMAS À KEMPIS (1380–1471)

IMITATION OF CHRIST:
READING THE HOLY SCRIPTURE
(PART 2)

You shall not go about as a talebearer among your people; nor shall
you take a stand against the life of your neighbor: I am the LORD.

LEVITICUS 19:16 NKJV

Truth, not eloquence, is to be sought in reading the Holy Scriptures; and every part must be read in the spirit in which it was written. For in the Scriptures, we ought to seek profit rather than polished diction. Likewise, we ought to read simple and devout books as willingly as learned and profound ones. We ought not to be swayed by the authority of the writer, whether he be a great literary light or an insignificant person, but by the simple truth. We ought not to ask who is speaking, but mark what is said. Men pass away, but the truth of the Lord remains forever. God speaks to us in many ways without regard for persons. Our curiosity often impedes our reading of the Scriptures, when we wish to understand and mull over what we ought simply to read and pass by. If you would profit from it, therefore, read with humility, simplicity, and faith, and never seek a reputation for being learned. Seek willingly and listen attentively to the words of the saints; do not be displeased with the sayings of the ancients, for they were not made without purpose.

~THOMAS À KEMPIS (1380–1471)

THE CHOSEN PATH

IMITATION OF CHRIST:
UNBRIDLED AFFECTIONS (PART 3)

*You shall not go about as a talebearer among your people; nor shall
you take a stand against the life of your neighbor: I am the LORD.*

LEVITICUS 19:16 NKJV

When a man desires a thing too much, he at once becomes ill at
ease. A proud and avaricious man never rests, whereas he who is poor
and humble of heart lives in a world of peace. An unmortified man is
quickly tempted and overcome in small, trifling evils; his spirit is weak,
in a measure carnal and inclined to sensual things; he can hardly
abstain from earthly desires. Hence it makes him sad to forego them; he
is quick to anger if reproved. Yet if he satisfies his desires, remorse of
conscience overwhelms him because he followed his passions and they
did not lead to the peace he sought. True peace of heart, then, is found
in resisting passions, not in satisfying them. There is no peace in the
carnal man, in the man given to vain attractions, but there is peace in
the fervent and spiritual man.

~THOMAS À KEMPIS (1380–1471)

FINISH WELL

I have fought the good fight, I have finished the course, I have kept the faith.
2 TIMOTHY 4:7 NASB

Why is it that rock shows and Super Bowls all shoot for the big ending? Because it's the ending that everyone remembers! I've seen, on too many occasions, the sprinter lose the otherwise perfectly run race, just as he reaches the finish line because he didn't run through the tape. At sporting events and concerts, we know when the ending is near. Not true about life. We should be living our ending every moment of every day. In March of 2001, I found myself preaching the funeral of my son's best friend. Ryan was eighteen years old and on his way with his girlfriend, Lynley, to a Saturday afternoon showing of Carman's movie *The Champion*. They were both tragically killed, along with two other teenage boys, in a head on collision. Over two thousand people crammed into our worship center for the memorial service. I heard several testimonies shared how these two young teenagers had influenced others' lives. Even the patrolman working the accident remarked to me, "Andy, we are usually picking up beer bottles at the scene. Today, we are picking up Bibles." Eight Bibles were found in Ryan's pick-up! I had everyone stand that had come to Christ through Ryan's ministry . . . sixty-four stood to his or her feet. Another twelve had received Christ the week before at a prison where Ryan spoke. In addition, seven stood indicating the desire to receive Christ as I gave an invitation. Many people run the race but few finish well; Ryan did!

~ANDY DIETZ (1950–) BORGER, TX

SUNDAY SAYINGS

Let's quit fiddling with religion and do
something to bring the world to Christ.

If you want to drive the devil out of the world,
hit him with a cradle instead of a crutch.

I'm against sin. I'll kick it as long as I've got a foot, and I'll fight it as long
as I've got a fist. I'll butt it as long as I've got a head. I'll bite it as long as
I've got a tooth. And when I'm old and fistless and footless and toothless,
I'll gum it till I go home to Glory and it goes home to perdition!

Live so that when the final summons comes, you will leave something more
behind you than an epitaph on a tombstone or an obituary in a newspaper.

The Lord is not compelled to use theologians. He can take snakes, sticks or
anything else, and use them for the advancement of his cause.

I believe that a long step toward public morality will have
been taken when sins are called by their right names.

Your reputation is what people say about you.
Your character is what God and your wife know about you.

If you took no more care of yourself physically than spiritually,
you'd be just as dried up physically as you are spiritually.

~BILLY SUNDAY (1862–1935)

BORN OF GOD

Are you brought out of the dark dungeon of this world into Christ? Have you learned to cry, My Father? All God's children are criers. Can you be quiet without you having a belly-full of the milk of God's word? Can you be satisfied without you having peace with God? Pray you consider it, and be serious with yourselves. If you have not these marks, you will fall short of the kingdom of God, you shall never have an interest there; there is no intruding. They will say, "Lord, Lord, open to us," and he will say, "I know you not." We sometimes give something to those that are not our children, but not our lands. O do not flatter yourselves with a portion among the sons, unless you live like sons. If you be risen with Christ, set your affections on things above, and not on things below. When you come together, talk of what your Father promised you; you should all love your Father's will, and be content and pleased with the exercises you meet with in the world. If you are the children of God, live together lovingly. If the world quarrels with you, it is no matter; but it is sad if you quarrel together. If this be amongst you, it is a sign of ill-breeding, it is not according to rules you have in the Word of God. Dost thou see a soul that has the image of God in him? Love him, love him; say, This man and I must go to heaven one day. Serve one another, do good for one another; and if any wrong you, pray to God to right you, and love the brotherhood.

~JOHN BUNYAN (1628–1688)

WE'VE MADE IT BY BITS AND PIECES

And the rest, some on boards, and some on broken pieces of the ship.
And so it came to pass, that they escaped all safe to land.

ACTS 27:44 KJV

The apostle Paul was shipwrecked along with other passengers aboard a vessel headed to Rome. They found themselves having to abandon ship because it was breaking up. Some on boards, some on broken pieces of the ship, but all made it to shore safely. They made it by bits and pieces. As life goes on, and we review our journey, we too can summarize that we made it by bits and pieces. God had assured Paul that no lives would be lost, only the ship. Sometimes it is the fragments of life that cause us to go on to do things we think impossible and succeed. All we need to do is trust in His deliverance power. God is always true to His promise. He always makes a way where we can't see a way. His deliverance is sometimes hard to understand or accept. But He promised that He would be with us even to the end of the age. The testimony of Paul is our example of faith and trust in God. He told the ship's crew that God had promised that no lives would be lost, so all that can swim, let them swim. But those who can't, take boards or broken pieces of the ship, and you will make it. When our anticipated mode of deliverance fails, don't become discouraged. God is still at work. Discover what He is doing and join Him. It might not be comfortable or what you thought He would do, but He will deliver.

~D. D. ALEXANDER (1945–) INGLEWOOD, CA

GRACE (PART 1)

Of all the temptations that ever I met with in my life, to question the being of God, and the truth of His gospel, is the worst, and the worst to be borne; when this temptation comes, it takes away my girdle from me, and removed the foundations from under me. Sometimes, when, after sin committed, I have looked for sore chastisement from the hand of God, the very next that I have had from Him hath been the discovery of His grace. Sometimes, when I have been comforted, I have called myself a fool for my so sinking under trouble. And then, again, when I have been cast down, I thought I was not wise to give such way to comfort. With such strength and weight have both these been upon me. I have wondered much at this one thing, that though God doth visit my soul with never so blessed a discovery of Himself, yet I have found again, that such hours have attended me afterwards, that I have been in my spirit so filled with darkness, that I could not so much as once conceive what that God and that comfort was with which I have been refreshed. I have sometimes seen more in a line of the Bible than I could well tell how to stand under, and yet at another time the whole Bible hath been to me as dry as a stick; or rather, my heart hath been so dead and dry unto it, that I could not conceive the least drop of refreshment, though I have looked it all over. Of all tears, they are the best that are made by the blood of Christ; and of all joy, that is the sweetest that is mixed with mourning over Christ.

~JOHN BUNYAN (1628–1688)

THE CHOSEN PATH

GRACE (PART 2)

Oh! It is a goodly thing to be on our knees, with Christ in our arms, before God. I hope I know something of these things. I find to this day seven abominations in my heart: Inclinings to unbelief. Suddenly to forget the love and mercy that Christ manifests. A leaning to the works of the law. Wanderings and coldness in prayer. To forget to watch for that I pray for. Apt to murmur because I have no more, and yet ready to abuse what I have. I can do none of those things which God commands me, but my corruptions will thrust in themselves, "When I would do good, evil is present with me." These things I continually see and feel, and am afflicted and oppressed with; yet the wisdom of God doth order them for my good. They make me abhor myself. They keep me from trusting my heart. They convince me of the insufficiency of all inherent righteousness. They show me the necessity of flying to Jesus. They press me to pray unto God. They show me the need I have to watch and be sober. And provoke me to look to God, through Christ, to help me, and carry me through this world. Amen.

~JOHN BUNYAN (1628–1688)

COMPLETE CONFIDENCE

The Lord Will Provide.
GENESIS 22:14 NASB

Pastoring in Steamboat Springs, Colorado, brings with it many unexpected and wonderful Privileges, I'm often reminded, after having been here for five and one-half years. One of the many things I get to do is go on cattle round-ups with local ranchers. Imagine riding on a 9,500-acre cattle and buffalo ranch. Once you leave the houses, the barns, and corrals the land looks just as it did when this part of Colorado was settled back in the 1800s. All through the summer months and into the fall, I make weekly forays into the wide-open valleys and in the mountains of Northwest Colorado. Invariably, during these times, we find ourselves riding through some intimidating terrain. Many times I have found myself looking straight down into a "draw" (a steep descending trail) that must be ridden. If a cow can do it, so can I, or should I say my horse can. It is the kind of ride that is so steep that I let go of the reigns and lean as far back on the horse as possible while still staying in the saddle. My feet, still in the stirrups, are up around the horse's shoulders. The horse has complete control and I am just along for the ride. I must place my complete confidence in the knowledge of this animal hoping he will get me where we are supposed to be—safely! In Genesis 22, Abraham found himself in a situation where he had to place his complete confidence in God. Jehovah-Jireh is the place where God Provides. He will provide for you as well, as you place your complete confidence in Him.

~KEVIN KING (1962–) STEAMBOAT SPRINGS, CO

THE CHOSEN PATH

THE CERTAINTY OF
THE ANSWER TO PRAYER

Ask, and it shall be given you; seek, and ye shall find; knock,
and it shall be opened unto you: For every one that asketh receiveth;
and he that seeketh findeth; and to him that knocketh it shall be opened.

MATTHEW 7:7–8 KJV

Next to the revelation of the Father's love, there is, in the whole course of the school of prayer, not a more important lesson than this: Every one that asketh, receiveth. In the three words the Lord uses, ask, seek, knock, a difference in meaning has been sought. If such was indeed His purpose, then the first, ASK, refers to the gifts we pray for. But I may ask and receive the gift without the Giver. SEEK is the word Scripture uses of God Himself; Christ assures me that I can find Himself. But it is not enough to find God in time of need, without coming to abiding fellowship: KNOCK speaks of admission to dwell with Him and in Him. Asking and receiving the gift would thus lead to seeking and finding the Giver, and this again to the knocking and opening of the door of the Father's home and love. One thing is sure: the Lord does want us to count most certainly on it that asking, seeking, knocking, cannot be in vain: receiving an answer, finding God, the opened heart and home of God, are the certain fruit of prayer.

~ANDREW MURRAY (1828–1917)

FROM THE MOUTHS OF CHILDREN?

Even so the tongue is a little member, and boasteth great things.
Behold, how great a matter a little fire kindleth!

JAMES 3:5 KJV

How often do you realize exactly what you say? A lady one day came to visit a minister's family and found herself sitting at the kitchen table. She promptly saw an open Bible and began to make a few comments. She didn't believe that God's Word was a special book or that it held a special place. Her comments were directed at how it was surely a good book, and she even enjoyed reading it from time to time. However, It was just another book, like Shakespeare. The minister's wife was rather taken with the comments, but unsure how to respond. She shared her belief in this book and proclaimed this to be God's spoken Word. The visitor, however, was not shaken by her persistence; she again proclaimed this is just a book. All of a sudden to the surprise of both the visitor and the minister's wife, another voice chimed in the conversation. It was a six-year-old little boy who had been listening carefully to both sides of this debate. He picked up the Bible, smiled, and said, "This is God's Word." The visitor smiled and stated again that it's just a book. The little boy smiled and stated, "You could go to hell for that!" Behold, how great a matter a little fire kindleth! The honesty of a six-year-old got a message through that the wisdom of a minister's wife struggled to find. Truth spoken in Love is the real message of Jesus and it often comes through the mouths of children. Listen from your heart!

~TIMOTHY RAY PITTMAN (1959–) SHIFFIELD, VA

SANCTIFICATION BY FAITH

Do we then make void the law through faith? God forbid:
yea, we establish the law.

ROMANS 3:31 KJV

When obedience to the law is held forth to the sinner as the condition of life, immediately it sets him upon making self-righteous efforts. In almost every instance, the first effort of the awakened sinner is to obey the law. He thinks he must first make himself better, in some way, before he may embrace the gospel. He has no idea of the simplicity of the gospel plan of salvation by faith, offering eternal life as a mere gratuitous gift. Alarm the sinner with the penalty of the law, and he naturally, and by the very laws of his mind, sets himself to do better, to amend his life, and in some self-righteous manner obtain eternal life, under the influence of slavish fear. And the more the law presses him, the greater are his pharisaical efforts, while hope is left to him, that if he obeys he may be accepted. What else could you expect of him? He is purely selfish, and though he ought to submit at once to God, yet, as he does not understand the gospel terms of salvation, and his mind is of course first turned to the object of getting away from the danger of the penalty, he tries to get up to heaven some other way. I do not believe there is an instance in history, of a man who has submitted to God, until he has seen that salvation must be by faith, and that his own self-righteous strivings have no tendency to save him.

~CHARLES FINNEY (1792–1875)

MASTER WASH MY FEET
(JOHN 13)

At Calvary He died for all my sins.

At the Cross forgiveness I received.

He washed my white as snow.

I walked in the world today

Dirt and garbage is all around.

I fall, get dirty, Lord, please wash my feet.

You lay aside Your garment,

You have a towel in hand.

You have poured out the water of Your word

Into the Master's hands

Again I place my feet,

Wash me and I shall be clean.

Humble me, Jesus, fill my heart with love

So I will go forth and wash

My neighbor's feet.

~LINDA K. SMITH (1948–) SENECA, SC

RELIGIOUS AFFECTIONS

. . . to humble thee, and to prove thee, to know what was in thine heart . . .

DEUTERONOMY 8:2 KJV

It is God's manner of dealing with men, to "lead them into a wilderness, before he speaks comfortably to them," and so to order it, that they shall be brought into distress, and made to see their own helplessness and absolute dependence on his power and grace, before he appears to work any great deliverance for them, it is abundantly manifested by the Scripture. Before God delivered the children of Israel out of Egypt, they were prepared for it, by being made to "see that they were in an evil case," and "to cry unto God, because of their hard bondage" (Exodus 2:23, 5:19). And before God wrought that great deliverance for them at the Red Sea, they were brought into great distress, the wilderness had shut them in, they could not turn to the right hand nor the left, and the Red Sea was before them, and the great Egyptian host behind, and they were brought to see that they could do nothing to help themselves, and that if God did not help them, they should be immediately swallowed up; and then God appeared, and turned their cries into songs. So before they were brought to their rest, and to enjoy the milk and honey of Canaan, God "led them through a great and terrible wilderness, that he might humble them and teach them what was in their heart, and so do them good in their latter end" (Deuteronomy 8:2, 16).

~JONATHAN EDWARDS (1703–1758)

CONVERSION

And he shewed me Joshua the high priest standing before the angel of the LORD, and Satan standing at his right hand to resist him. And the LORD said unto Satan, The LORD rebuke thee, O Satan, even the LORD that hath chosen Jerusalem rebuke thee: is not this a brand plucked out of the fire?

ZECHARIAH 3:1–2 KJV

The conversion of a soul is by far the most remarkable event in the history of the world. It is the object that attracts the eyes of the holy angels to the spot where it takes place. It is the object which the Father's eye rests upon with tenderness and delight. This work in the soul is what brings greater glory to the Father, Son, and Spirit, than all the other works of God. There is nothing that can equal it. Ah! Brethren, if you think little of it, or laugh at it, how little have you of the mind of God! Conversion is as a victory of Christ over the devil—"Is not this a brand plucked out of the fire?" The world is a great battle-field. "I will put enmity between thee and the women, and between thy seed and her seed, it shall bruise thy head, and thou shalt bruise his heel." Satan has the world bound in strong fetters. But there is a great One gone forth, sitting on a white horse, and having on his head many crowns, and ever and anon he is cutting the strong chains with which sinners are bound, and saying, as he does so, to Satan, "Is not this a brand plucked out of the fire?"

~R. M. McCheyne (1813–1843)

FROM THE CRADLE, TO THE GRAVE, TO ETERNITY

Deliver me in thy righteousness, and cause me to escape:
incline thine ear unto me, and save me.

PSALM 71:2 KJV

David had but one hope, one trust, and one faith and they were not in him: not in the strength of his body, or the intellect of his mind, not in his advisors, the economy or his armies. David had but one Rock, one Fortress, and that was the Lord God. His faith started in his youth, and as he walked hand-in-hand with the Lord through life's adversities it had grown stronger. David understood that the Lord had been with him from the time of his conception, watched over him as a child, and stood with him against the bears, lions, and giants of his life. Yes, from the cradle to the grave the Lord was with David. Yet, even as David praises God, you can see a hint of fear creep into his prayer, the fear of growing old. These are fears we will all face. I, like the psalmist, have learned to trust in the righteousness of the Lord, for my salvation, from the cradle, to the grave, to eternity.

~RUSSELL C. LAMBERT (1955–) AIRWAY HEIGHTS, WA

BLESSED IS THE MAN

Blessed is the man . . .
PSALM 1:1 KJV

Three things are notable about this blessed man: 1. His company. He walketh not in the counsel of the ungodly, nor standeth in the way of sinners, nor sitteth in the seat of the scornful. 2. His reading and thinking. His delight is in the law of the Lord; and in his law doth he meditate day and night. 3. His fruitfulness. And he shall be like a tree planted by the rivers of water, that bringeth forth his fruit in his season; his leaf also shall not wither; and whatsoever he doeth shall prosper. The river is the Holy Spirit; the planting, the deep abiding life in which, not occasionally but habitually, we absorb Him. The fruit is not once in a while, but continual and appropriate to each changing season. His life is also prosperous and his spirit fresh, like the unfading leaf. Such a life must be happy. Indeed, happiness is a matter of spiritual conditions. Put a sunbeam in a cellar and it must be bright. Put a nightingale in the darkest midnight, and it must sing.

~A. B. SIMPSON (1844–1919)

THE DEPTH OF THE CROSS

Father, into thy hands I commend my spirit.

LUKE 23:46 KJV

That is where the Christian's dying begins. He does not have to taste death; it has been tasted for him. He does not have to bear the separation from God; it has been borne for him. He has accepted the finished salvation through the merit of Jesus Christ, and when he comes to the end he finds it just the beginning. Death is separation from God. But the Christian when he dies is departing to be with God. "The time of my departure is at hand," says Paul; and Paul got so enthusiastic over the idea that he was almost extravagant, for you remember that the word "departure" is a nautical term. It carries with it the idea of lifting anchor and spreading sail, and going out of the land-locked harbor into the open sea. Paul was not thinking about contraction, but expansion; and through the gate of Christ I am going to begin to live. I am going to lay aside this garment we call the body, and enter into the spiritual world with a freedom I cannot have in this. In the autumn of 1912, Nonconformists met at Smithfield and recalled the deeds of the martyrs, who were obedient unto death, even the death of the stake. We glorify them, almost canonize them; and the spirit that went to the flames was the spirit of the Cross. In 1662, two thousand preachers left their churches and their livings. Why? They were willing to be "obedient unto death, even the death of the Cross." What a challenge to us today.

~A. C. DIXON (1854–1925)

FAMINE IN THE LAND

Behold, the days come . . . I will send a famine in the land.

AMOS 8:11 KJV

We have hurricanes in Florida, a drought in the Southwest, and wildfires in California, but have you heard about the nationwide famine we are suffering? It is the same kind of deadly famine that the prophet Amos spoke about in the Old Testament when he wrote, "Behold, the days come, saith the Lord GOD, that I will send a famine in the land, not a famine of bread, nor a thirst for water, but of hearing the words of the LORD: And they shall stagger from sea to sea, and from the north even to the east, they shall run to and fro to seek the word of the LORD, and shall not find it" (Amos 8:11–12). What is this famine? It's certainly not a lack of printed Bibles. We have more Bibles printed and placed around us then any other time in history. It's not a lack of knowledge. We have exponentially more knowledge than any previous generation. What is it then? We are in a famine of "hearing God's Word." With all the religion and all the Bibles we have, many people are still starving to hear wise answers to the problems people are facing today. Our generation has been taught that there are no absolutes and that the best way to approach a problem is to ask, "What would be right to do in this situation?" From coast to coast, people are "staggering" under the burden of foolish decisions. Feeding ourselves regularly with the truth of the Bible, and sharing its wisdom with others, is the only solution to this national crisis!

~**JIM DOWNS** (1950–) **GREEN BAY, WI**

A PROMISE FOR EVERY DAY

As thy days, so shall thy strength be.

DEUTERONOMY 33:25 KJV

Over against our weakness, there in that promise is the promise of strength. "As thy days, so shall thy strength be." How heartening that promise is, in the face of our weakness! And our weakness will be discovered to us, in any one of many directions that we may take. Take our own duty, whatever it is—and who has not cried out time and again, as he faced his duty and grappled with it—be he preacher, or parent, or professional man, or other toiler. Whoever he is—who has not cried out saying, "Who is sufficient for these things? How can I get through this task?" Now, over against our sense of weakness and weariness and faintness, here is this promise of strength. "As thy days, so shall be thy strength." Whose is the promise? It is the promise, in essence, which God makes to His friends, times without number, here in this Holy Book, by direct statement, and by implication. That is the unending promise of God all through this Book. There are promises human. They are often frail; they often come short; they often break. But this is God's promise, and when we know it is God's promise we can rest upon it with all the tranquility and peace with which a child lies back upon its mother's heart. Yes, it is God's promise. He comes to us, saying: "You cling to me, and follow as I point the way, and your strength shall be meted out to you. Whatever your doubt or duty or difficulty, whatever your sin or sorrow or suffering, so shall be your strength, if you will only cling to me."

~G. W. TRUETT (1867–1944)

NOT WHAT WE HAD IN MIND

FROM EXODUS 3:1–15

God has his own purposes, which are to give us a future that will not be evil but good, yet not necessarily—indeed not likely—the future we have in mind. You and I are also sometimes startled to meet God in strange places intruding into what was supposed to have been an ordinary conversation, looking over the shoulder of our child, sitting down next to us in the same old church, where we haven't met him for ages. We ask for help, and he changes our lifestyles. We pray for strength, and he puts us in a position where we have to trust in him. We ask for more meaning and purpose in our lives, and he sends us down the path that Jesus walked. He calls us to go, still, to people who might not listen, to stand against evil that might not yield, that they might receive the freedom that they don't know they need, but without which they will perish. All of these things do not come from our whims, our dreams, or even our passionate religious ideals. They come from the mind and heart of Holy God. They are not hidden from us but revealed in His written word. It is left for us, by His grace, to say yes and to walk in the path he has chosen.

~DAVID F. RASMUSSEN (1952–) GREENCASTLE, PA

BROKEN DOWN ALTARS

He repaired the altar of the LORD that was broken down.

1 KINGS 18:30 KJV

God sent His messenger to warn the people of the judgment which they were bringing on themselves because of sin and iniquity. The old Tishbite bobbed up before weak-kneed Ahab with all the abruptness of a thunderclap out of a clear sky, and without banners or bands or furbelows or salaam, spoke out in the first breath in a way that brought a deadly pallor upon the cheeks of the miserable wretch Ahab: "As the LORD of hosts liveth, before whom I stand," cried the prophet (1 Kings 18:15). That ought to be the preacher's cry ever by time he walks into the pulpit. That kind of faith makes the devil get up and dust every time! Such confidence in God as the prophet had as he stood before Him would make granite out of soapstone. And to know God as Elijah knew Him, and to have the same unbroken sense of His presence, is better preparation for a great career in the ministry than a degree from any college you can name. I am not discounting the value of education. I consider a mind without education as something like marble in a quarry, which shows none of the inherent beauty until the skill of the polisher fetches out the color and discovers every ornamental vein that runs through the marble. Education draws out many virtues and perfections which otherwise would never come to the surface and never be seen. I believe in education, but education alone cannot make character—never! It takes acquaintance with God to do that. It takes purity of heart as well as brilliancy of intellect to make one great for God.

~BILLY SUNDAY (1862–1935)

BEN

Your eyes saw my substance, being yet unformed.
And in Your book they all were written, the days fashioned for me,
when as yet there were none of them.

PSALM 139:16 NKJV

My husband and I have taken strong stands on the value of life, both born and unborn. God brought to task our convictions with the adoption of four children. The first three, less challenging than the last. Benjamin was born with a cleft lip and palate and a heart murmur. He suffered mental retardation, physical challenges, and an early death. Benjamin's new siblings took little time learning to love him, this child God obviously destined to be ours. Benjamin's life consisted of doctors, hospitals, and monumental diagnosis of the problems inherited from a drug and alcohol addicted birth mother. The damage in-utero left Ben without the full faculties needed to grow, mature, learn, and thrive. In spite of demanding tests, his disposition was sweet and his life a blessing. He never walked, talked, or tasted food, and never spoke a word, but the impact Ben made on the world was great. His life brought our family to a unified love over our gift called Ben. Our church, where my husband was the pastor, made enormous sacrifices to visit and to sit with Ben. The body of Christ ministered to Ben as well as to our whole family, and we all learned from this "little man" whose presence in our home made us aware of God's love and compassion. Our community marveled at the love exhibited on many avenues. Our convictions are strong, having been forged by fire. Our lives have been changed forever because of the beauty of a life the world would classify as disposable. Every life is valuable. Like Ben, they are all a gift from God.

~CAROL HENSCHELL (1951–) ELLERSLIE, GA

THE CHOSEN PATH

CAN'T I JUST PRAY HARDER?

For you are saved by grace through faith, and this is not from yourselves;
it is God's gift—not from works, so that no one can boast.
EPHESIANS 2:8–9 HCSB

One of seven students I had in an Easy English Bible Study was Korean. There was a countenance about her that made me think she would be open to the gospel. She had attended a Christian school in Korea, but had not personally committed herself to Jesus. This particular day was my birthday. Being a Southern Baptist Missionary, I knew there would be thousands of Baptist Women praying for me. I asked God to allow me to speak to one of three people that day. God is so good! The Korean student was one of my three. That day she was the only person who came to class. As we studied how sin entered the world in the garden, she asked how someone could really know they had been forgiven. "Can't I just pray harder?" she asked. English class ceased immediately, and I shared a careful point by point explanation of how someone could receive forgiveness and become a child of God. My student had been trying harder and harder through Buddhist chanting to reach God and His forgiveness. She now understood that all she needed to do was to confess her sin and receive God's forgiveness through Jesus. She did that very thing on my birthday.

~DAVID BALDWIN (1943–) ANCHORAGE, AK

SHARING IN THE CHUTES

*But you shall receive power when the Holy Spirit has come upon you;
and you shall be witnesses to Me in Jerusalem, and in all Judea
and Samaria, and to the end of the earth.*

ACTS 1:8 NKJV

Like my granddaddy used to say, "You can't tell it like it is, if you don't believe it like it was." I have studied the liberal, neorthodox, as well as conservative views, and stand where my granddaddy stood: the Bible is the infallible, inerrant Word of God! And yet when I read this verse, I often seem to not be living in its promise. There are times, however, when God moves in such a way that the promise of Acts 1:8 is unmistakable. The city of Steamboat, where I pastor, is host to a rodeo series each year, and I've been privileged to lead a prayer service for the cowboys. We've held these prayer meetings in the bucking chutes for the past several events. One Saturday in late July, the cowboys weren't interested in praying before the rodeo, but I remained in my place for a while and a young cowboy approached me. He sat down next to me and it was obvious that this was a divine encounter. He had been struggling, not only as a professional cowboy, but also in life. It was just before the bulls would be loaded in the chutes to start the rodeo, as I shared with this young man the difference that Christ made in my life and how Christ could transform his, God's power was unmistakable. He prayed to receive Christ as Savior that night. I was a witness to the unmistakable power of God, where a lost sinner met His savior . . . in the chutes, and before the bulls!

~KEVIN KING (1962–) STEAMBOAT SPRINGS, CO

FEAR OF THE LORD;
THE BEGINNING OF WISDOM

Come unto me, all ye that labour and are heavy laden,
and I will give you rest.

MATTHEW 11:28 KJV

As Jesus sent the disciples, He sent us also to tell the harassed and helpless lost sheep of Indonesia His Love. Many times we experienced His Power, Healing, Protection, Total Faithfulness, and in the end, Revival. My doctor husband, Jim, and I were in Kediri, Java, Indonesia, from 1962 through 1969 where He was one of the physicians in our 50-bed Baptist hospital. Jim felt called to Indonesia because it was the last Muslim nation still open to the gospel. For years, President Sukarno had been secretly leading the country toward Communism. His slogan was RELIGION, NATIONALISM, AND COMMUNISM, all working together. His real plan was to kill all religious leaders. For three years, wherever we traveled we were aware of impending danger. We experienced much anti-Americanism and anti-Christianity. Fear lingered over the whole country. While in the capital city of Djakarta, and after an executive meeting, Jim wanted me, and our three daughters, to leave for our safety and fly to Singapore. A decision was made that we would remain and stay together. We agreed God would take care of us as we reclaimed Romans 8:28–39, verses God had given us as our stake to staying in Indonesia.

~JOYCE S. CARPENTER (1931–) SENECA, SC

THE CHOSEN PATH

LESSONS FROM THE MINISTRY OF ELIJAH

Behold, the word of the LORD came to him,
and he said unto him, What doest thou here, Elijah?

1 KINGS 19:9 KJV

This is the summit of Elijah's exaltation. He seemed to have everything before him. The people had shouted their enthusiastic approval of him and renewed their allegiance to God. The rain had come down in torrents to refresh the long wasted earth. The prophet, victorious but weary, comes to the capital of the kingdom. With what a glow of rejoicing, with what exaltation of spirits, he must have reached the city. His fidelity has been rewarded, his glowing zeal has found response, his faith in God has been justified. We can imagine his joy and triumph in this hour. Nothing sweeter ever comes to a man than the hour in which his long and painful advocacy of righteous things seems to come to its fruition. In greater or less degree, all leaders have such moments. These victorious hours in the midst of an arduous career are resting places for faith and confidence. Yet there ever lurks here a hidden peril, a peril which grows out of the reaction of the soul that has been strained to a tense and exalted experience, through the weariness of body and exhaustion of nerve that must follow such tension; and the peril is increased when it must be remembered that no such victory as that of Elijah could ever be complete. The forces of evil, silenced for a moment, are not put out of existence. Popular applause does not always signify a real change in the habits of thought or in the moral character of the people.

~E. C. DARGAN (1852–1930)

JUST AS I AM

Just as I am, without one plea, but that Thy blood was shed for me,
And that Thou bidst me come to Thee,
O Lamb of God, I come, I come.

Just as I am, and waiting not to rid my soul of one dark blot,
To Thee whose blood can cleanse each spot,
O Lamb of God, I come, I come.

Just as I am, though tossed about with many a conflict, many a doubt,
Fightings and fears within, without, O Lamb of God, I come, I come.

Just as I am, poor, wretched, blind; sight, riches, healing of the mind,
Yea, all I need in Thee to find, O Lamb of God, I come, I come.

Just as I am, Thou wilt receive, wilt welcome, pardon, cleanse, relieve;
Because Thy promise I believe, O Lamb of God, I come, I come.

Just as I am, Thy love unknown hath broken every barrier down;
Now, to be Thine, yea, Thine alone, O Lamb of God, I come, I come.

Just as I am, of that free love, the breadth,
length, depth, and height to prove,
Here for a season, then above, O Lamb of God, I come, I come!

~CHARLOTTE ELLIOT (1789–1871)

THE CHOSEN PATH

LORD, SAVE ME!

Lord, Save me.
MATTHEW 14:30 KJV

Sinking times are praying times with the Lord's servants. Peter neglected prayer at starting upon his venturous journey, but when he began to sink, his danger made him a suppliant, and his cry, though late, was not too late. In pain and mental anguish, we find ourselves as naturally driven to prayer as the wreck is driven upon the shore by the waves. The tried believer hastens to the mercy seat for safety. Heaven's great harbor of refuge is all-prayer, and the moment a storm comes on, it is wise for us to make for it with all sail. Short prayers are long enough. There were but three words in the petition which Peter gasped out, but they were sufficient for his purpose. If our prayers had less of the tail feathers of pride and more wing they would be all the better. Verbiage is to devotion as chaff to the wheat. Precious things lie in small compass, and all that is real prayer in many a long address might have been uttered in a petition as short as that of Peter. Our extremities are the Lord's opportunities. Immediately a keen sense of danger forces an anxious cry from us, the ear of Jesus hears, and with Him, ear and heart go together, and the hand does not long linger. At the last moment we appeal to our Master, but His swift hand makes up for our delays by instant and effectual action. Are we nearly engulfed by the boisterous waters of affliction? Let us then lift up our souls unto our Savior, and we may rest assured that He will not suffer us to perish. When we can do nothing Jesus can do all things.

~C. H. SPURGEON (1834–1892)

A CALL TO A DEVOUT LIFE

Take no thought, saying, What shall we eat? or,
What shall we drink? or, Wherewithal shall we be clothed?
(For after all these things do the Gentiles seek.)

MATTHEW 6:31–32 KJV

It is very observable, that there is not one command in all the Gospel for public worship; and perhaps it is a duty that is least insisted upon in Scripture of any other. Our blessed Savior and His Apostles are wholly taken up in doctrines that relate to common life. They call us to renounce the world, and differ in every temper and way of life, from the spirit and the way of the world: to renounce all its goods, to fear none of its evils, to reject its joys, and have no value for its happiness: to be as new-born babes, that are born into a new state of things: to live as pilgrims in spiritual watching, in holy fear, and heavenly aspiring after another life: to take up our daily cross, to deny ourselves, to profess the blessedness of mourning, to seek the blessedness of poverty of spirit: to forsake the pride and vanity of riches, to take no thought for the morrow, to live in the profoundest state of humility, to rejoice in worldly sufferings: to reject the lust of the flesh, the lust of the eyes, and the pride of life: to bear injuries, to forgive and bless our enemies, and to love mankind as God loveth them: to give up our whole hearts and affections to God, and strive to enter through the straight gate into a life of eternal glory.

~WILLIAM LAW (1686–1781)

THE CHOSEN PATH

INFLUENCED OF GOD'S SPIRIT

Ask that you may be filled with the knowledge of
His will in all wisdom and spiritual understanding.

COLOSSIANS 1:9 NKJV

Although it is with relation to the Spirit of God and his influences, that persons and things are called spiritual; yet not all those persons who are subject to any kind of influence of the Spirit of God, are ordinarily called spiritual in the New Testament. They who have only the common influences of God's Spirit, are not so called, in the places cited above, but only those who have the special, gracious, and saving influences of God's Spirit; as is evident, because it has been already proved, that by spiritual men is meant godly men, in opposition to natural, carnal, and unsanctified men. And it is most plain, that the apostle, by "spiritually minded," Romans 8:6, means graciously minded. And though the extraordinary gifts of the Spirit, which natural men might have, are sometimes called spiritual, because they are from the Spirit; yet natural men, whatever gifts of the Spirit they had, were not, in the usual language of the New Testament, called spiritual persons. For it was not by men's having the gifts of the Spirit, but by their having the virtues of the Spirit, that they were called spiritual; as is apparent by Galatians 6:1: "Brethren, if any man be overtaken in a fault, ye which are spiritual, restore such a one in the spirit of meekness." Meekness is one of those virtues which the apostle had just spoken of, in the verses next preceding, showing what are the fruits of the Spirit. Those qualifications are said to be spiritual in the language of the New Testament, which are truly gracious and holy, and peculiar to the saints.

~JONATHAN EDWARDS (1703–1758)

THE CHOSEN PATH

GOD'S CONNECTIONS

He that heareth my word, and believeth on him that sent me,
hath everlasting life, and shall not come into condemnation;
but is passed from death unto life.

JOHN 5:24 KJV

Back in early 1970s, I met one of my husband's patients in the post office. We will call her "Lady A." She is German and a few years younger than I. We struck up a conversation, then we went our separate ways. The Lord immediately impressed upon me that somehow she was my responsibility. We became friends and spent times together. Even though she showed absolutely no interest in spiritual things we continued to be friends. I could not get away from the fact that the Lord put her on my heart. About two months ago "Lady A" was invited to go to a new Bible study with me. To my utter surprise she said, "Yes." "Well!" I said to myself. "Lord, You are working!" After the second week she decided the lesson was just too hard. The Christian terms and Bible were too difficult to understand. On the phone she said she just didn't think she would be able to continue. "Don't stop. I'll be right over and give you some basics to make the study easier for you," I encouraged. Oh my! I couldn't let her quit when I knew her heart was being drawn to the Lord. I eagerly went over and gave her "The Basics—the plan of Salvation." After about an hour and many scriptures later she was ready and without hesitation gave the Lord her life. After all these years of waiting and praying, I saw the miracle of His working in her life. Now Bible study is easier and she is growing in her faith.

~JOYCE S. CARPENTER (1931–) SENECA, SC

THE CHOSEN PATH

1 JOHN 1

What was from the beginning, what we have heard, what we have seen with our eyes, what we have observed, and have touched with our hands, concerning the Word of life—that life was revealed, and we have seen it and we testify and declare to you the eternal life that was with the Father and was revealed to us—what we have seen and heard we also declare to you, so that you may have fellowship along with us; and indeed our fellowship is with the Father and with His Son Jesus Christ. We are writing these things so that our joy may be complete. Now this is the message we have heard from Him and declare to you: God is light, and there is absolutely no darkness in Him. If we say, "We have fellowship with Him," yet we walk in darkness, we are lying and are not practicing the truth. But if we walk in the light as He Himself is in the light, we have fellowship with one another, and the blood of Jesus His Son cleanses us from all sin. If we say, "We have no sin," we are deceiving ourselves, and the truth is not in us. If we confess our sins, He is faithful and righteous to forgive us our sins and to cleanse us from all unrighteousness. If we say, "We have not sinned," we make Him a liar, and His word is not in us.

HCSB

1 JOHN 2:7–17

Dear friends, I am not writing you a new command, but an old command that you have had from the beginning. The old command is the message you have heard. Yet I am writing you a new command, which is true in Him and in you, because the darkness is passing away and the true light is already shining. The one who says he is in the light but hates his brother is in the darkness until now. The one who loves his brother remains in the light, and there is no cause for stumbling in him. But the one who hates his brother is in the darkness, walks in the darkness, and doesn't know where he's going, because the darkness has blinded his eyes. I am writing to you, little children, because your sins have been forgiven on account of Jesus' name. I am writing to you, fathers, because you have come to know the One who is from the beginning. I am writing to you, young men, because you have had victory over the evil one. I have written to you, children, because you have come to know the Father. I have written to you, fathers, because you have come to know the One who is from the beginning. I have written to you, young men, because you are strong, God's word remains in you, and you have had victory over the evil one. Do not love the world or the things that belong to the world. If anyone loves the world, love for the Father is not in him. For everything that belongs to the world— the lust of the flesh, the lust of the eyes, and the pride in one's lifestyle—is not from the Father, but is from the world. And the world with its lust is passing away, but the one who does God's will remains forever.

HCSB

BIBLE INFUSION

Let the word of Christ richly dwell within you.
COLOSSIANS 3:16 NASB

I had an interesting conversation a couple of years ago with one of the team physicians for the Tennessee Titans. He told me that the Titans, like all NFL teams, use a lot of energy in the course of playing each game. Players can lose a lot of fluids, and the challenge on the training staff is to help them replace it quickly. At times, simply drinking fluids doesn't work quickly enough to replenish the fluids that are lost. Therefore, they take an I.V. bag and they run a line into a player's arm during halftime to help rehydrate the player. In fact, on a hot day it is not unusual to have 15 to 20 players hooked up to an I.V. bag during the half to get them ready to return to the field. Wouldn't it be great if we could take the Bible and all of its truth and wisdom, all of its testimony of God, and somehow put it in a bag that we could suspend above our heads and let it slowly drip into our veins? How easy . . . it would require no real effort. It would be quick and painless. Who wouldn't buy a "Bible bag"? But Bible wisdom doesn't come that way. Bible study is a discipline. It takes dedication and determination to let God's Word slowly fill your soul. Becoming a student of God's Word begins with the simple decision to read each day. Find a translation you can understand. Find a schedule you can keep. Find a place where you can quietly read. Let God's Word find a dwelling place in your life.

~JON R. ROEBUCK (1960–) FRANKLIN, TN

THE CHOSEN PATH

GOD HAS A PURPOSE
FOR HIS CHILDREN

I pray not that thou shouldest take them out of the world,
but that thou shouldest keep them from the evil.

JOHN 17:15 KJV

God wants us here on earth for some higher purpose than mere existence. That purpose is to represent Him to the world, to be the messengers of His gospel and His will to men and women, and by our lives to exhibit to them the true life and teach them how to live it. He is representing us in heaven, and our one business is to represent Him on earth. We are just as truly sent into this world to represent Him as if we had gone to China as the ambassador of the United States government. Although we may be engaged in the secular affairs of life, it is simply that we may represent Christ here, carry on His business and use our means to further His cause. He came here from another realm with a special message, and when His work was done, He was called to go home to His Father. Lord, help me to represent Thee worthily . . . and carry music in our heart through busy street and wrangling mart; plying our daily task with busier feet, because our souls a heavenly strain repeat.

~A. B. SIMPSON (1844–1919)

TRUTH!

*Jesus said to him, "I am the way, and the truth, and the life;
no one comes to the Father but through Me."*

JOHN 14:6 NASB

It must happen to all of us . . . at least I think it does. Even after years of experiencing God in your life, those times come when you wonder, where is the life? It happened to me in a more profound way than ever before in 1991. I found myself asking that question, "Where is the life?" I had four wonderful teenagers and a beautiful wife, a growing and rewarding student ministry, but no life! My wife, Becky, and I began to discover that we had both been asking this question of God. He had first begun to reveal the answer to Becky, and then to me, as we studied together the well-known passage from John 14:6. God began to show us that this verse was progressive. "The way" was, of course, representative of salvation through Christ. Then God revealed to us that we had to go through "Truth" to get to "Life!" Truth with God: admitting to Him, who and what we really were . . . He already knew it. The Truth of God's Word: always applying God's word to Satan's lies. Truth in Relationships: clearing up any past or present wrongs. Finally, we should be speaking the Truth, living the Truth, praying the Truth, and believing the Truth! We have a saying, "What is the Truth about that?" In counseling sessions, I've heard people repeat untruths such as, "I can't do anything right!" and I'll reply, "What is the Truth about that?" Then I quote Truth: "I can do all things through Christ who strengthens me." You see, many people choose to believe Satan's lies rather than God's truth. Examine your thoughts. Are you believing the Truth?

~ANDY DIETZ (1950–) BORGER, TX

THE CHOSEN PATH

TO SUBMIT OR TO ASSERT

For I myself am a man under authority, with solders under me.
I tell this one, "Go," and he goes; and that one, "Come," and he comes.
I say to my servant, "Do this," and he does it.

MATTHEW 8:9 NIV

Sometimes the holder of the mantel of authority depends upon the situation. When Jesus healed the Centurion's slave, He demonstrated amazing grace. Those of the centurion's ilk were the same ones who nearly beat Him to death and then nailed Him on a cross . . . and Jesus knew it would be that way. Let that sink in for a moment. The centurion was very aware of authority structures; so much so that He recognized Jesus' authority in the situation and submitted himself to it. The results were miraculous. How much more, then, will we as God's chosen children reap the rewards of submitting ourselves to Christ's authority in our lives? The centurion described how he was on both sides of authority. There were those under him and those over him. As a result he understood both submission (to those over him) and responsibility (to those under him). Almost everyone has both issues to deal with in their lives, and when it comes to spiritual matters it is no different. Be spiritually responsible for those under your spiritual authority and be spiritually submissive to those who you understand to be over you spiritually. Try jotting down a few people on both sides of that coin and pray for guidance and grace to know in what new ways to approach them.

~SCOTT TAYLOR (1960–) MARIETTA, SC

GOD, MY HELPER!

"It is but a small thing for Me, thy God, to help thee. Consider what I have done already. What! not help thee? Why, I bought thee with My blood. What! not help thee? I have died for thee; and if I have done the greater, will I not do the less? Help thee! It is the least thing I will ever do for thee; I have done more, and will do more. Before the world began I chose thee. I made the covenant for thee. I laid aside My glory and became a man for thee; I gave up My life for thee; and if I did all this, I will surely help thee now. In helping thee, I am giving thee what I have bought for thee already. If thou hast need of a thousand times as much help, I would give it thee; thou requirest little compared with what I am ready to give. 'Tis much for thee to need, but it is nothing for me to bestow. 'Help thee?' Fear not! If there were an ant at the door of thy granary asking for help, it would not ruin thee to give him a handful of thy wheat; and thou art nothing but a tiny insect at the door of My all-sufficiency. 'I will help thee.'" O my soul, is not this enough? Dost thou need more strength than the omnipotence of the United Trinity? Haste, gather up thy wants, and bring them here—thine emptiness, thy woes, thy needs. Behold, this river of God is full for thy supply; what canst thou desire beside? Go forth, my soul, in this thy might. The Eternal God is thine helper!

~C. H. SPURGEON (1834–1892)

A TRUE FRIEND (PART 1)

And Jonathan Saul's son arose, and went to David
into the wood and strengthened his hand in God.

1 SAMUEL 23:16 KJV

Someone has said that there is nothing which moves the heart like the approach of a friend. There is a mutual conscious attraction, an enhancement of feeling. It is as the approach of magnet and iron, as the coalescing of points of light into a warmer and fuller glow. Sometimes nothing needs to be said or done. My friend comes! That itself suffices. It tells me more than words can say; it counts for more than money can buy. Yet this need not mean the failure of words nor the omission of deeds; for with himself the friend may also bring a gift. Notice what this gift of friendship was. Jonathan strengthened David's hand in God. What did he bring to his friend? Something to eat? News of other friends? Perhaps; but the thing most needed he brought was that he strengthened his hand in God. The highest gift of friendship is to give to our friend a new grip on God. This is more than earthly friendship, more than affection's kindly words, more than admiration's finest compliments. The man who helps me to God is the best friend I can have. The man who strengthens my faith in the time of my deepest need is indeed my friend. And so on the other hand I am best friend to another when I help him to renew and strengthen his grasp upon God.

~E. C. DARGAN (1852–1930)

A TRUE FRIEND (PART 2)

And Jonathan Saul's son arose, and went to David
into the wood, and strengthened his hand in God.

1 SAMUEL 23:16 KJV

The sweetest friendship in this world is the friendship that brings the friend to the Great Friend. For a man to claim to be another man's friend and drag that man to hell is awful travesty and tragedy. You are not a friend to the man whom you debauch, and the man who would lead you astray from paths of virtue is your worst enemy. The man who grasps your hand and strengthens you in God is the best friend you have in this world. When you need a savior, a man who can bring you up out of the dark, that man is your friend. But it is a travesty upon the name of friendship when friends drag their friends to evil. The man that helps you to God, that stands by you when your virtue is tried, that stands by you when you are tempted to evil, that man is your friend, the man who comes to you in the woods and strengthens your hand in God. The kind of friendship we ought to show is to help our friends to be better than they are, not by criticism, but by kindness. The truest friend is the friend who helps us in the way of righteousness, in the way of salvation.

~E. C. DARGAN (1852–1930)

TAKE IT TO HEART

*And now, O ye priests this commandment is for you. If ye will not hear,
and if ye will not lay it to heart, to give glory unto my name, saith the
LORD of hosts, I will even send a curse upon you, and I will curse your
blessings: yea, I have cursed them already, because ye do not lay it to heart.*

MALACHI 2:1–2 KJV

Each and every Christian wants to receive the blessings of God. We
want peace and tranquility. We want direction and guidance. We want
to have the power of the Holy Spirit upon us to do mighty works for the
kingdom, and strength to resist the wiles of the enemy. Yet it is sad to
say that most of us are defeated in our everyday lives, just making
heaven by the skin of our teeth. We seem to be facing the same
problems today as the priest of old. We fail to take the responsibility of
our priesthood, our Christianity, our salvation to heart. You see, just as
certain of the Jews of old were born unto the priesthood, you as a
Christian have been born again into the priesthood of believers.
Certain responsibilities come with your new-elevated status, the
responsibility to study the word of God, to serve Jesus Christ and
witness of Him, and pray. In turn, you will receive those blessings you
were seeking after and live a victorious life in your Lord. But the
prerequisite is that you take it to heart, after all, He did when He went
to the cross for you.

~RUSSELL C. LAMBERT (1955–) AIRWAY HEIGHTS, WA

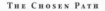

DINNER WITH SINNERS

*"Those who are well don't need a doctor, but the sick do
need one. I didn't come to call the righteous, but sinners."*

MARK 2:17 HCSB

While He was reclining at the table in Levi's house, many tax collectors and sinners were also guests with Jesus and His disciples, because there were many who were following Him. When the scribes of the Pharisees saw that He was eating with sinners and tax collectors, they asked His disciples, "Why does He eat with tax collectors and sinners?" This passage reminds us of an issue that seems to have gotten increasingly difficult. We are called to seek the lost, reach out to them, and love them without condoning their actions. Jesus reached out to the lost during His life and ministry here on earth. Likewise we must get out of our churches, our homes, and familiar "Christian" places so that we have an audience with the lost sinners of our time. It is often uncomfortable for born again Christians to be around the lost. We don't live the way they live, like the things they like or seek the things they seek. Concern for what others may think may also discourage us. There were those who looked down on Jesus. He was breaking social and religious taboos by being with Levi's friends, some of whom may even have been excommunicated from Jewish fellowship. That didn't faze Jesus at all. He compared it to a doctor going to the sick; they needed Jesus, so He went. Let's take our example from Levi who, when called to follow Jesus, immediately invited his friends to a dinner with Jesus in hope that they too would follow.

~JOE JONES (1964–) GOODYEAR, AZ

CHRIST'S EXCELLENCY

Weep not: behold, the Lion of the tribe of Judah, the Root of David,
hath prevailed to open the book, and to loose the seven seals
thereof . . . stood a Lamb as it had been slain.

REVELATION 5:5–6 KJV

Christ never so eminently appeared for divine justice, and yet never suffered so much from divine justice, as when he offered up himself a sacrifice for our sins. In Christ's great sufferings, did his infinite regard to the honor of God's justice distinguishingly appear, for it was from regard to that that he thus humbled himself. And yet in these sufferings, Christ was the mark of the vindictive expressions of that very justice of God. Revenging justice then spent all its force upon him, on account of our guilt, which made him sweat blood, and cry out upon the cross, and probably rent his vitals—broke his heart, the fountain of blood, or some other blood vessels—and by the violent fermentation turned his blood to water. For the blood and water that issued out of his side, when pierced by the spear, seems to have been extravasated blood, and so there might be a kind of literal fulfillment of Psalm 22:14, "I am poured out." And this was the way and means by which Christ stood up for the honor of God's justice, namely, by thus suffering its terrible executions. For when he had undertaken for sinners, and had substituted himself in their room, divine justice could have its due honor no other way than by his suffering its revenges. In this, the diverse excellencies that met in the person of Christ appeared through his infinite regard to God's justice, and such love to those that have exposed themselves to it, as induced him thus to yield himself a sacrifice to it.

~JONATHAN EDWARDS (1703–1758)

I'VE JUST GOT TO TELL IT

For we cannot but speak the things which we have seen and heard.

ACTS 4:20 NKJV

"I don't want anyone pushing their religion off on me!" Have you ever heard someone make that statement? So what is it that makes a Christian feel compelled to talk to others about their religion as if they want everyone to believe just like them? Don't they realize that they might upset some people? Consider this analogy. Suppose that you and I live in the same neighborhood but I know absolutely nothing about you. One Saturday morning, I go for an early jog through the neighborhood, and I notice smoke pouring from the roof of your house. I am confident now that I have a very important warning for you, and being so early, I know that you and your family may still be in bed asleep. I am compelled because of my concern for you, and I know that I should run to your door and shout, "Wake up, your house is on fire!" On the other hand, I don't know if you are usually a grumpy person in the mornings or not, and I don't think you are going to be too happy about the news of your burning house. In spite of the risk of offending you, my zeal about warning you of the danger comes from my belief that you desperately need what I have to tell you. Most of the world believes that any old religion will do. Since the Bible teaches that Jesus is the ONLY way to heaven, it's only a matter of time before others will thank you for trying to warn them of their impending danger, no matter how grumpy they may be right now!

~**JIM DOWNS** (1950–) **GREEN BAY, WI**

SET FREE

But now that you have been set free from sin and have become
slaves to God, the benefit you reap leads to holiness.

ROMANS 6:22 NIV

Do you ever wonder why it's impossible to finish everything on your to-do list or why you never get around to studying God's word? Why are Sunday mornings so hectic? Do you find it hard to carve out enough time for a daily quiet time? When will you ever have time to witness to the new neighbor? You barely have enough time to say hello. In Mark 5, we read how Satan was controlling a man using demons. Today, he puts things in our lives to trap us, sins of selfishness, pride, gossip. . . . He seeks to distract us from knowing and following Christ, filling our lives with too many tasks and activities. Jesus' goal was to set free the demon possessed man, free from sin and Satan's control. Jesus offers this same freedom today. Jesus willingly died on the cross, was buried, and rose again to set us free. Yes, free from sin and free from Satan's "busyness" schemes. After being freed from the power of Satan, the man asked to follow Jesus. But Jesus had another plan and sent him to tell his story to his family. As Christians, we too have experienced Jesus' freeing power just like this man. As we accept the call to follow Jesus, we must be eager to follow His agenda for our lives and seek to accomplish what is on His to-do list. Have you accepted God's gift of grace through faith in Jesus Christ? What in your life is distracting you from doing God's will? What has been your response to God's call on your life? Who's to-do list will you seek to complete today?

~TERESA N. SHAW (1966–) ALABASTER, AL

THE WORD OF THE LORD

The words of the LORD are pure.

PSALM 12:6 KJV

"The words of the Lord are pure words"—there is NOT AN ERROR OF ANY SORT in the whole compass of them. These words come from him who can make no mistake, and who can have no wish to deceive his creatures. If I did not believe in the infallibility of the Book, I would rather be without it. If I am to judge the Book, it is no judge of me. If I am to sift it, like the heap on the threshing-floor, and lay this aside and only accept that, according to my own judgment, then I have no guidance whatever, unless I have conceit enough to trust to my own heart. The new theory denies infallibility to the words of God, but practically imputes it to the judgments of men; at least, this is all the infallibility which they can get at. I protest that I will rather risk my soul with a guide inspired from heaven, than with the differing leaders who arise from the earth at the call of "modern thought." You may lean your whole weight upon any one of the words of God, and they will bear you up. In your darkest hour, you may have no candle but a single promise, and yet that lone light shall make high noon of your midnight. Glory be to his name, the words of the Lord are WITHOUT EVIL, WITHOUT ERROR, AND WITHOUT FAILURE!

~C. H. SPURGEON (1834–1892)

THE CHOSEN PATH

DEATH HAS BEEN SWALLOWED UP IN VICTORY (PART 1)

So when this corruptible shall have put on incorruption, and this mortal
shall have put on immortality, then shall be brought to pass the saying that
is written, Death is swallowed up in victory.

1 CORINTHIANS 15:54 KJV

Does the Lord speak directly to us? In 1980, our only child, a nineteen-year-old, was killed in an auto accident. In our grief and pain, my wife and I never questioned God or blamed Him. We knew our son was a Christian and was with Him. One night, two months later, I was walking in the yard. A voice in my mind said clearly, "He lives!" We all talk to ourselves and know our own voices. This was not my voice. The wonderful peace and assurance that came from those two words was overwhelming. I told my wife of the experience and she, too, had a comparable one. In her grief, walking in the house, she felt "someone" give her a physical hug. Of course our pain continued, but we both received greatly added strength. Additionally, we renewed our faith in a loving Lord who heals the broken hearted. What a mighty God we serve!

~JOSEPH WILLIS STROTHER (1933–) CLAYTON, GA

THE CHOSEN PATH

DEATH HAS BEEN SWALLOWED UP IN VICTORY (PART 2)

JOEY

Almost nineteen . . . I told him goodbye
Heard the door close . . . and he was gone
He's been gone twenty-four years. I miss him . . .
it should have been me.
Across the valley towards the mountains
The view is blurred . . . unfocused.
The sun is gone, shadow forms emerge
The sky kneels down and drapes my world,
The woods . . . a mist-soaked drawing.
I withdraw like a hurt thing
Into the gray.
In the gray, a crow, sightless, calls to his kin
And I know his fear . . . loneliness.
Then the gray lightens
A south wind sends it down the valley
It, too, clears my mind.
A wren sings
The crow, his eyes returned, flies to his kin
Life restarts . . . I know he lives!
Praise you, Lord Jesus!

~JOSEPH WILLIS STORTHER (1933–) CLAYTON, GA

THE LORD'S MUSIC

The trumpeters and singers joined in unison, as with one voice,
to give praise and thanks to the LORD. Accompanied by trumpets,
cymbals and other instruments, they raised their voices in praise
to the LORD and sang: "He is good; his love endures forever."

2 CHRONICLES 5:13 NIV

At the center of our church service is a sermon. It is the longest portion of the service and is usually supported before and after by prayer, music, song, and fellowship. Through inspiration and plain hard work, the pastor tries to help us connect or reconnect to the Lord. Scripture is woven into a good sermon like wool into a favorite sweater. For new Christians this is new guidance. For the more experienced, it is a reminder, or refresher course, in how God wants us to live. A good sermon gives me feelings of peace and contentment in the Lord. Sometimes it helps me get "back on track" and motivated once again. But this doesn't always happen. If I've had a hard week or just can't "tune in" because of personal, health, or work problems, the best sermon goes right over my head. This is where music often helps. Sometimes music, a good hymn or a choir selection, will move me when the sermon won't. It can be a release. My emotions come to the surface, tears may be shed, and thankfully, I feel my burdens lifted. When this happens it feels like I am in the presence of God. My love for Him and His for me are renewed. I feel hope, faith, and motivated again. In my life, music, hymns, singing, and song are an important part of worship. Every now and then, they are the most important part.

~DAVID SCHOLTON (1951–) SANFORD, NC

THE CHOSEN PATH

DESPERATION

You shall love the LORD your God with all your heart,
with all your soul, and with all your might.

DEUTERONOMY 6:5 NASB

"Now the bad, you die!" Dying had crossed my mind many times in my relatively short forty-eight years but actually meeting death face-to-face was an entirely different experience. I was returning through Budapest, Hungary, from a trip to Moscow, Russia, where I had delivered six thousand dollars for the building of a new church. It was my fifth time to Budapest and I had, unfortunately, become too comfortable with being there. Because of my familiarity with the city and the limited time I had, I chose to eat at a restaurant that I knew nothing about. Long story short, the restaurant was mafia owned and preyed on unsuspecting lone clientele. As my eyes adjusted to the dark of the cold and quiet room, I noticed no one else but a "waitress" and me. Over the simple mix up of my drink order, mafia began to emerge from nowhere! I was told I owed 92,500 forint (460 U.S. dollars) and if I didn't pay, I would die! After an eight-hour ordeal of negotiating and manipulating, I finally escaped the eight men, two woman entourage to the safety of a good ol' American Burger King where I summoned the police. This experience taught me to be as desperate for God as I was to live that day!

~ANDY DIETZ (1950–) BORGER, TX

THE CHOSEN PATH

LISTEN AS YOU PREPARE

*But unto the wicked God saith, What hast thou to do to declare my
statutes, or that thou shouldest take my covenant in thy mouth? Seeing
thou hatest instruction, and castest my words behind thee.*

PSALM 50:16–17 KJV

Preach to yourselves the sermons which you study, before you
preach them to others. When your minds are in a holy, heavenly frame,
your parishioners are likely to partake of the fruits of it. Your prayers,
and praises, and doctrine will be sweet and heavenly to them. They will
likely feel when you have been much with God: that which is most on
your hearts, is like to be most in their ears. We are the nurses of Christ's
little ones. If we forbear taking food ourselves, we shall famish them; it
will soon be visible in their leanness, and dull discharge of their several
duties. If we let our love decline, we are not like to raise up theirs. If we
abate our holy care and fear, it will appear in our preaching: if the
matter show it not, the manner will. If we feed on unwholesome food,
either errors or fruitless controversies, our hearers are like to fare the
worse for it. Whereas, if we abound in faith, and love, and zeal, how
would it overflow to the refreshing of our congregations, and how
would it appear in the increase of the same graces in them! O brethren,
watch therefore over your own hearts: keep out lusts and passions, and
worldly inclinations; keep up the life of faith, and love, and zeal: be
much at home, and be much with God.

~RICHARD BAXTER (1615–1691)

WHAT WILL YOU DO WITH JESUS?

Choose for yourselves this day whom you will serve. . . .
But as for me and my household, we will serve the LORD.

JOSHUA 24:15 NIV

All throughout the Gospels we read about people who had to make the decision of what to do with Jesus. One example is that of Pontius Pilate, the Roman governor. Pilate was responsible for administering justice and keeping peace. But his decision of what to do with Jesus did not bring him peace. Jesus was brought before Pilate falsely accused of several crimes. Pilate had the authority to sentence Jesus to death as the Jewish leaders were requesting. During the trial, however, Pilate announced that Jesus was innocent. But Pilate was influenced by what other people thought. He chose to please the crowd and sentenced Jesus to death on a cross. First, we must realize that a decision must be made by all. We must decide what to do with Jesus. God has extended to us a gift—a right relationship with Him available only through His Son. We must decide to accept or reject God's gift. No one else can make that decision for us. Second, we must understand that when we put aside God's word and make decisions based on feelings or common practices, we fall into the "gray area." Right and wrong seems blurred; convictions seem to change to fit the situation. God often speaks through others, but our true authority is found in God's word and through the guiding of the Holy Spirit. One will never contradict the other. What is your response to God's gift? Are you choosing to do right or compromise so that no one is offended? Who or what is your final authority?

~TERESA N. SHAW (1966–) ALABASTER, AL

THE CHOSEN PATH

ANGELS WATCHING OVER US
(PART 1)

*Are they not all ministering spirits, sent out to render
service for the sake of those who will inherit salvation?*

HEBREWS 1:14 NASB

The word angel or angels appears 287 times in the Bible. Dr. Billy Graham explains in his book *Angels: God's Secret Agents* that he believes in angels because the Bible says there are angels. I also believe in angels because I have sensed their presence in my life on special occasions. Returning from a mission trip to Honduras where I had been unable to sleep, I became extremely tired and sleepy and later found myself waking in the aisle of the plane that was landing in Atlanta under a medical emergency . . . yours truly being the emergency! It was determined that I had suffered a seizure. A friend traveling with our team is convinced to this day that I actually died on the plane that day. I stopped breathing and there were no apparent vital signs for several minutes. Christians on the plane gathered in prayer groups and began to cry out to God for His help. I awoke from my experience and walked off the plane. After spending some time in the hospital and undergoing several tests, I was released. The amazing thing was something I was unaware of until two weeks later. A woman wearing a pair of blue jeans, a brown leather jacket, and a baseball cap stood near my side on the plane. No one seemed to know who she was or where she came from. She never said a word to anyone on the plane and simply stood silently near my side. Who was this woman? Perhaps just a busybody who felt she had to get involved . . . or, was she on a mission? A mission ordained by God!

~JAMES RUDY GRAY (1953–) SENECA, SC

ANGELS WATCHING OVER US
(PART 2)

*Are they not all ministering spirits, sent out to render
service for the sake of those who will inherit salvation?*

HEBREWS 1:14 KJV

As the mysterious lady left the plane, she told someone waiting to meet some of the mission travelers that I had had a seizure but would be "ok" and she said that I had spoken with my wife who would be making her way to Atlanta. She called my wife by name, Anne, and referred to the town where we lived. When the woman spoke these words it was not yet known that Anne would, in fact, be coming to Atlanta because she had a severe back problem and could not drive that distance. It wasn't until several hours later that Anne decided to make the trip with a friend doing the driving. Once admitted to the hospital, it was thought I had suffered a heart attack or there was some serious problem with my brain. As I laid in that hospital room with continuous medical attention, an enormous sense of peace literally flooded my soul. I have never experienced anything quite like it. Deep inside my heart, I heard this message, "It's ok!" I did not understand that to mean I would live or die, but simply that whatever happened would be "ok." A stream of tests continued through the night, but by morning, the cardiologist came in and informed me that he was discharging me. Confused by what we had been told, Anne inquired about my heart and was told, in amazement, "His heart is in good shape. He will be ok!" Are you aware that there are angels watching over us? Well, they are! The Bible tells us so, and I believe the inspired Word of God.

~JAMES RUDY GRAY (1953–) SENECA, SC

WHO IS THIS?

Blessed is he that cometh in the name of the LORD;
Hosanna in the highest.

MATTHEW 21:9 KJV

And the multitudes that went before, and that followed, cried, saying, "Hosanna to the son of David; Blessed is he that cometh in the man of the Lord; Hosanna in the highest." And when he was come to Jerusalem, all the city was moved saying, "Who is this?" Who was this unusual man? Who was this mysterious man? Some say he was a good man . . . others say he wasn't. In the Gospels, Matthew, Mark, Luke, and John presented Jesus in different ways. Matthew introduced him as a king (Matthew 2:2; 21:5; 22:11; 25:34; 27:11, 37, 42). Mark presented Jesus as the tireless servant of God and man (Mark 1:35–37; 3:20; 3:21; 6:31–34). Luke laid out the universal grace of God in Christ (Luke 2:32; 3:6; 24:47). John inspired faith in Jesus as the Son of God (John 20:31). Jesus was man enough to attend a wedding, God enough to turn water into wine. He slept and rested as a man, and yet was God enough to multiply five loaves and fish to feed thousands. Jesus was crucified and buried as a man and God enough to rise from the dead. Who was this Jesus? My Savior, my friend, my Master.

~E. K. SHEPHERD (1913–2002)

ETHICAL TEACHINGS OF JESUS

Then He said to them, "Follow Me, and I will make you fishers of men."
MATTHEW 4:19 NKJV

The words of Jesus to the young ruler, "Sell all thou hast and give to the poor, and thou shalt have treasure in heaven; and come, follow me," are often spoken of as if he had enjoined this upon all who propose to follow him. Yet there is no record of his laying such requirement upon any one else, except that Matthew the publican and the two sons of Zebedee left their business to follow him as permanently attached disciples. The "one thing" lacked by the young ruler was that he should not only care much for eternal life, but care more for it than all things else. The test was, whether he would sacrifice what he valued most in this world, out of supreme devotion to Jesus. That which he valued most was his vast wealth, and this test he could not stand. The test for another man would be whether out of devotion to Jesus he could abandon sinful pleasures, or relinquish worldly ambitions. The principle involved is that the service of God must be supreme. In a certain sense, "religion must be everything, or it is nothing." One who retains or acquires wealth, one who pursues ambition or indulges in pleasures, must subordinate all to his Christian discipleship, or he is no disciple.

~JOHN A. BROADUS (1827–1895)

HOW DESPERATE MUST WE BE?

*He who has found his life will lose it, and he who
has lost his life for My sake will find it.*

MATTHEW 10:39 NASB

The most intense hours of my life and the prospect of death brought to me, real soul searching. I knew that the God of this universe had spared me for something and that I needed to find out what that was! On the long thirteen-hour plane flight home, God revealed to me that as desperate as I was to live, I needed to be that desperate to know him! I was reminded of a young minister who had interned under a renowned scholar. The young minister knew of the scholar's revival experiences and had asked him on their numerous walks through the woods, "How do you experience revival?" The old scholar replied each time, "Someday I'll tell you." Nearing the last days of his internship, the young minister began once again to ask that same question but this time the old man drove the intern's face into the chilly waters of the mountain stream they were crossing, holding him under until he began taking water into his lungs. The old man finally lifted the intern's head out of the water as he gasped for air. "When you desire revival as much as you desired your next breath," said the old man, "you will experience it!" God is not asking us to have a casual acquaintance with Him as we would with a taxi driver or store clerk. . . . He desires a relationship that goes beyond even our family or our spouse, one that totally consumes us!

~ANDY DIETZ (1950–) BORGER, TX

GROWING BY HIS CARE

Now if any of you lacks wisdom, he should ask God, who gives to all generously and without criticizing, and it will be given to him.

JAMES 1:5 HCSB

My dad was a serious checker player. As a boy, I often saw him with a friend or relative, around a checkerboard, deep in thought. It wasn't unusual to find him studying checker strategies. One of the most amazing things I ever saw was my dad playing checkers with his back to the board. He had a photographic memory. His opponent would tell my dad which checker he moved. My dad would instruct which of his checkers to move, never looking at the board. I never remember him losing a game that way. Sometimes Dad would play checkers with me. Often winning, I felt pretty proud. But one day I realized, "He's letting me win." I remember the mixed feelings I felt. I was a little angry to think that he would trick me like that. I also realized that he was doing it to encourage me to keep playing. I said to my dad, "I don't care if I never win another game. Don't LET me win anymore." I never beat him at checkers again. It was another day that my dad let me GROW UP a little more. Our heavenly Father is always concerned about our growth. Sometimes He separates us from the difficulties we face. His grace and mercy overlooks our inadequacies. We often miss difficulties, as part of God's plan. At other times, He lets us walk right into a difficult situation. He knows it's time for us to learn . . . to grow up a bit. Never ceasing to watch over and care for us, His love leads us toward maturity.

~RANDOLPH (RANDY) ALAN McCOLLUM (1952–) BLOOMINGTON, IN

HIMSELF

Once it was the blessing; now it is the Lord.

Once it was the feeling; now it is His Word.

Once His gifts I wanted; now the Giver own.

Once I sought for healing, now Himself alone.

Once 'twas painful trying; now 'tis perfect trust.

Once a half salvation; now the uttermost.

Once 'twas ceaseless holding; now He holds me fast.

Once 'twas constant drifting; now my anchor's cast.

Once 'twas busy planning; now 'tis trustful prayer.

Once 'twas anxious caring; now He has the care.

Once 'twas what I wanted, now what Jesus says.

Once 'twas constant asking; now 'tis ceaseless praise.

Once I tried to use Him; now He uses me.

Once it was my working; His it hence shall be.

Once the power I wanted, now the Mighty One.

Once for self I labored, now for Him alone.

Once I hoped for Jesus; now I know He's mine.

Once my lamps were dying; now they brightly shine.

Once for death I waited; now His coming hail.

And my hopes are anchored safe within the veil.

~A. B. SIMPSON (1844–1919)

THE CHOSEN PATH

WHAT IS THIS I HEAR FOLLOWING ME?

Surely goodness and mercy shall follow me all the days of my life.

PSALM 23:6 KJV

Many years ago, a pastor explained how he used the Bible when counseling his parishioners. He recalled that a distraught member came to him and told him that he heard footsteps behind him all the time, but when he turned to look no one was there. The pastor read to him Psalm 23:6, "Surely goodness and mercy shall follow me all the days of my life." The pastor implied that the church member left his office cured of his paranoia forever. Although we would rightly be skeptical that reading one verse in a ten-minute counseling session would cure someone of a serious mental problem, there is a kernel of truth in this story. It does indeed make a huge difference in our outlook on life when we realize that God's goodness and mercy are constantly pursuing us. (The Jerusalem Bible translation is powerful: "Ah, how goodness and kindness pursue me every day of my life.") No, the psalmist is not naïve, seeing life as just a bed of roses, because he speaks about "the valley of the shadow of death" and about "enemies." Life is tough and suffering, disappointments, and loss often abound in our everyday lives. But what a profound difference it makes when we believe that God's presence is with us in the midst of these difficulties. God is indeed the "Hound of Heaven" who pursues us with His goodness and kindness.

~JOHN A. WOOD (1938–) WACO, TX

A MIGHTY FORTRESS IS OUR GOD

A mighty fortress is our God, a bulwark never failing;
Our helper He, amid the flood of mortal ills prevailing:
For still our ancient foe doth seek to work us woe; His craft and power are
great, and, armed with cruel hate, on earth is not his equal.

Did we in our own strength confide, our striving would be losing;
Were not the right Man on our side, the Man of God's own choosing:
Dost ask who that may be? Christ Jesus, it is He; Lord Sabaoth, His Name,
from age to age the same, and He must win the battle.

And though this world, with devils filled, should threaten to undo us,
We will not fear, for God hath willed His truth to triumph through us:
The Prince of Darkness grim, we tremble not for him; His rage we can endure,
for lo, his doom is sure, one little word shall fell him.

That word above all earthly powers, no thanks to them, abideth;
The Spirit and the gifts are ours through Him Who with us sideth:
Let goods and kindred go, this mortal life also; The body they may kill: God's
truth abideth still, His kingdom is forever.

~**MARTIN LUTHER (1483–1546)**

THE CHOSEN PATH

THE ACCEPTABLE SACRIFICE

*The sacrifices of God are a broken spirit; a broken
and a contrite heart, O God, thou wilt not despise.*

PSALM 51:17 KJV

This Psalm is David's penitential psalm. It may be fitly so called because it is a Psalm by which is manifest the unfeigned sorrow which he had for his horrible sin, in defiling of Bathsheba, and slaying Uriah her husband; a relation at large of which you have in the 11th and 12th of the second of Samuel. Many workings of heart, as this psalm showeth, this poor man had, so soon as conviction did fall upon his spirit: one while he cries for mercy. Then he confesses his heinous offences. Then he bewails the depravity of his nature; sometimes he cries out to be washed and sanctified. And then again he is afraid that God will cast him away from his presence and take his Holy Spirit utterly from him: and thus he goes on till he comes to the text, and there he stayeth his mind. Finding in himself that heart and spirit which God did not dislike: "The sacrifices of God," says he, "are a broken spirit." I thank God I have that. "A broken and a contrite heart," saith he. "O God, thou wilt not despise;" as if he should say. I thank God I have that . . . that the high and lofty One, the God that inhabiteth eternity, and that has a high and holy place for his habitation, should choose to dwell with, and to be a companion of the broken in heart, and of them that are of a contrite spirit: yea, and here is also great comfort for such.

~JOHN BUNYAN (1628–1688)

OUR INTERNATIONALS' GIFTS

The field is the world; the good seed are the children of the kingdom.
MATTHEW 13:38 KJV

The Lord has blessed my husband and me in special ways. Instead of our going to the world, the world has come to us. We live only five miles from Clemson University in South Carolina. Each year hundreds of international students come to the university. Each year we look forward to meeting the ones the Lord has brought to be part of our family. It's amazing to experience His matchmaking. We have fallen in love with students from China, Formosa, Germany, India, Indonesia, and Japan. Most of the students we have hosted have only been in the States a few weeks and are eager to learn all they can about this new, strange place. Some speak very good English. Others struggle in the beginning because they have not had opportunities of conversing with "real" Americans. How excited and overwhelmed they are that we desire to spend time with them. They become "our" children while they are here. When they leave we try to keep in touch. As we welcome them into our home, there is much laughter and sharing of different cultures when our students come together with our immediate family of twenty plus. They are interested in what we believe and about our Faith and we're happy to share. Two of our students who came from Germany and India were already believers and we learned about their Christian experience and the church life in their respective countries. Annie, our Indian friend, comes from the area where the apostle Thomas went sharing the Lord Jesus. Her home church was founded by him.

~**JOYCE S. CARPENTER (1931–) SENECA, SC**

A MOUNTAIN CHOIR

*Sing, O heavens; and be joyful, O earth; and break forth
into singing, O mountains: for the LORD hath comforted
his people, and will have mercy upon his afflicted.*

ISAIAH 49:13 KJV

So sweet are the comforts of the Lord, that not only the saints themselves may sing of them, but even the heavens and the earth may take up the song. It takes something to make a mountain sing; and yet the prophet summons quite a choir of them. Lebanon, and Sirion, and the high hills of Bashan and Moab, He would set them all singing because of Jehovah's grace to His own Zion. May we not also make mountains of difficulty, and trial, and mystery, and labor become occasions for praise unto our God? "Break forth into singing, O mountains!" This word of promise, that our God will have mercy upon His afflicted, has a whole peal of bells connected with it. Hear their music—"Sing! Be joyful! Break forth into singing." The Lord would have His people happy because of His unfailing love. He would not have us sad and doubtful; He claims from us the worship of believing hearts. He cannot fail us: why should we sigh or sulk as if He would do so? Oh, for a well tuned harp! Oh, for voices like those of the cherubim before the throne!

~C. H. SPURGEON (1834–1892)

THE CHOSEN PATH

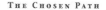

THE LORD OUR RIGHTEOUSNESS

THE LORD OUR RIGHTEOUSNESS.

JEREMIAH 23:6 KJV

Whoever is acquainted with the nature of mankind in general, or the propensity of his own heart in particular, must acknowledge, that self-righteousness is the last idol that is rooted out of the heart: being once born under a covenant of works, it is natural for us all to have recourse to a covenant of works, for our everlasting salvation. And we have contracted such devilish pride, by our fall from God, that we would, if not wholly, yet in part at least, glory in being the cause of our own salvation. We cry out against popery, and that very justly; but we are all Papists, at least, I am sure, we are all Arminians by nature; and therefore no wonder so many natural men embrace that scheme. It is true, we disclaim the doctrine of merit, are ashamed directly to say we deserve any good at the hands of God; therefore, as the Apostle excellently well observes, "we go about," we fetch a circuit, "to establish a righteousness of our own," and, like the Pharisees of old, "will not wholly submit to that righteousness which is of God through Jesus Christ our Lord." Christ not only died, but lived, not only suffered, but obeyed for, or instead of, poor sinners. And both these jointly make up that complete righteousness, which is to be imputed to us, as the disobedience of our first parents was made ours by imputation. In this sense, and no other, are we to understand that parallel which the apostle Paul draws, in the 5th of the Romans, between the first and second Adam. This is what he elsewhere terms, "our being made the righteousness of God in him."

~GEORGE WHITEFIELD (1714–1777)

A DADDY'S LOVE

Sons are a heritage from the LORD, children a reward from him.
PSALM 127:3 NIV

I played golf with my four-year-old son not too long ago. He brought his tiny golf clubs with him and rode in the golf cart with me. He was able to tee-off and putt while I played. After a few holes, he was hooked (like my drives) and did not want to go home with my wife. We had the best time as we drove the cart to each hole. He wanted to get so close to me that he just had to sit on my lap. I remember wanting to be near my dad that way; it did not matter what he was doing, I just wanted to be there. What joy! Now, I love to golf and it's one of the things that I love to do with my dad. I enjoy sitting in the cart next to him, receiving the cheers, the lessons, and the high fives. But most of all I love the TIME. When golfing with my dad, there is always time to talk (especially about the things of God), ask questions, discuss and solve the issues of the world, etc. I long for those days with my son—they are coming quickly. Yesterday was one of the finest days to be a daddy! The joy that I had of having my son close to me, holding him, teaching him, and cheering him on—I know God experiences when we are close to Him. Everyday God desires the most important part of our lives: TIME. That day was one of the finest days to be a daddy, but once again caught a glimpse into the depths of Abba Father's love.

~MILES ROHDE (1972–) MARSHALL, MN

THE CHOSEN PATH

NATURAL AND UNNATURAL

Call unto me, and I will answer thee, and show
thee great and mighty things, which thou knowest not.

JEREMIAH 33:3 KJV

Prayer is both natural and unnatural at times. It is the vital element of a thriving relationship with God and it is a lifeline in day to day living. Knowing my children needed to learn the value and privilege of prayer, I sought to pray with them often and teach them to watch for God to answer. My youngest daughter received a birthstone ring for her thirteenth birthday. She was pleased with it and showed it off to her friends, often. In her hurry, one afternoon she did not put it back on her finger, but rather, carelessly and unknowingly, dropped the ring . . . somewhere! Her heart was broken as she cried uncontrollably. After consoling her, I told her God knew exactly where that little ring was and we could ask Him to help us find it. Reluctantly she agreed, and we prayed. To our amazement the next day we pulled into a parking space we had been in the day before and as my daughter opened the back door and looked down, her ring lay on the pavement. Her joy was magnified and her faith strengthened. God cares about the smallest sparrow, and ring, that falls.

~TOMMY HENSCHEL (1947–) ELLERSLIE, GA

THE ANCIENT OF DAYS

After this I saw in the night visions.
DANIEL 7:7 KJV

In Daniel 7, we see the Ancient of Days seated on the throne of judgment; His garment was white as snow, and the hair of His head like the pure wool; His throne and His wheels were as burning fire, and a fiery stream issued and came forth from before Him. In Revelation 1 we see the Son of Man Himself clothed with a garment down to the foot, and His head and His hair were white as wool, white as snow; but the bride sees her Bridegroom in all the vigor of youth, with locks "bushy, and black as a raven." The eyes of the risen SAVIOR are described as "a flame of fire," but His bride sees them "like doves beside the water brooks." In Revelation, "His voice is as the voice of many waters . . . and out of His mouth proceeded a sharp two-edged sword." To the bride, His lips are as lilies, dropping liquid myrrh, and His mouth most sweet. The countenance of the risen SAVIOR was "as the sun shineth in his strength," and the effect of the vision on John—"when I saw Him, I fell at His feet as one dead"—was not unlike the effect of the vision given to Saul as he neared Damascus. But to His bride "His aspect is like Lebanon, excellent as the cedars." The LION of the tribe of Judah is to His own bride the KING of love; and, with full heart and beaming face, she so recounts His beauties that the daughters of Jerusalem are seized with strong desire to seek Him with her, that they also may behold His beauty.

~J. HUDSON TAYLOR (1832–1905)

THE CHOSEN PATH

RUN FOR HEAVEN

Your adversary the devil, as a roaring lion,
walketh about, seeking whom he may devour.

1 PETER 5:8 KJV

They that will have heaven must run for it; because the devil, the law, sin, death, and hell, follow them. There is never a poor soul that is going to heaven, but the devil, the law, sin, death, and hell, make after that soul. "Your adversary, the devil, as a roaring lion, walketh about, seeking whom he may devour" (1 Peter 5:8). And I will assure you, the devil is nimble, he can run apace, he is light of foot, he hath overtaken many, he hath turned up their heels, and hath given them an everlasting fall. Also the law, that can shoot a great way, have a care thou keep out of the reach of those great guns, the ten commandments. Hell also hath a wide mouth; it can stretch itself further than you are aware of. And as the angel said to Lot, Take heed, "look not behind thee, neither tarry thou in all the plain," that is, anywhere between this and heaven, "lest thou be consumed" (Genesis 19:17). So say I to thee, Take heed, tarry not, lest either the devil, hell, death, or the fearful curses of the law of God, do overtake thee, and throw thee down in the midst of thy sins, so as never to rise and recover again. If this were well considered, then thou, as well as I, wouldst say they that will have heaven must run for it.

~JOHN BUNYAN (1628–1688)

MIRACLES . . . THEN AND NOW
(PART 1)

FROM ACTS 12:1–11 NIV

"It was about this time that King Herod arrested some who belonged to the church, intending to persecute them. He had James, the brother of John, put to death with the sword. When he saw that this pleased the Jews, he proceeded to seize Peter also. After arresting him, he put him in prison, handing him over to be guarded by four squads of four soldiers each. Herod intended to bring him out for public trial after the Passover. The night before Herod was to bring him to trial, Peter was sleeping between two soldiers, bound with two chains, and sentries stood guard at the entrance. Suddenly an angel of the Lord appeared and a light shone in the cell. He struck Peter on the side and woke him up. "Quick, get up!" he said, and the chains fell off Peter's wrists. Then the angel said to him, "Put on your clothes and sandals." And Peter did so. "Wrap your cloak around you and follow me," the angel told him. Peter followed him out of the prison, but he had no idea that what the angel was doing was really happening; he thought he was seeing a vision. They passed the first and second guards and came to the iron gate leading to the city. It opened for them by itself, and they went through it. When they had walked the length of one street, suddenly the angel left him. Then Peter came to himself and said, "Now I know without a doubt that the Lord sent his angel and rescued me from Herod's clutches and from everything the Jewish people were anticipating." Peter's release from prison was certainly a miracle.

~**EARLENE RICHARDS STROTHER** (1933–) CLAYTON, GA

MIRACLES . . . THEN AND NOW
(PART 2)

The blind receive sight, the lame walk, those who have leprosy are cured, the deaf hear, the dead are raised, and the good news is preached to the poor.

MATTHEW 11:5 NIV

In the society in which we live, we do not expect to see miracles like the one Peter witnessed. We have heard stories of miracles from missionaries in countries where Christianity is costly. In some countries in the world, Christians are still imprisoned because of their faith and their witnessing. People do see visions and miracles do happen today. One is the remarkable true story of a Chinese Christian, Brother Yun, and sometimes called "The Heavenly Man." During the Cultural Revolution, in 1974, the Lord called Brother Yun to follow him. At age seventeen, he was arrested and imprisoned for four years for preaching the gospel. After being released he preached in home churches all over China. His second imprisonment was a three-year sentence for "seriously disturbing the social order." Brother Yun's miraculous escape, so like Peter's, was during his third imprisonment in the spring of 1997. Guards broke Yun's legs. In prison, he was unable to walk and suffered intense pain. Three fellow prisoners were given the task of carrying him between his cell, the torture room, and the toilet. One of these was Peter Xu, known as "the Billy Graham of China." Yun experienced a vision of his wife telling him to open the door. He later said that the Lord spoke to him, "This is the hour of your salvation." When Peter Xu came to take him to the toilet, he said, "Yun, you must escape!" In the morning of May 5, 1997, Yun's legs were miraculously healed and he could walk.

~EARLENE RICHARDS STROTHER (1933–) CLAYTON, GA

THE CHOSEN PATH

MIRACLES . . . THEN AND NOW
(PART 3)

He (Jesus) told them, "The harvest is plentiful,
but the workers are few. Ask the Lord of the harvest,
therefore, to send out workers into his harvest field.

LUKE 10:2 NIV

Yun walked through several doors that were usually guarded and locked. Guards were miraculously looking away and doors were unlocked. He picked up a broom, walked down stairs, and through a busy courtyard to the main gate, normally the securest of all. Neither of the usual guards was there and the gate was unlocked. Immediately, a taxi-van pulled up and the driver asked, "Where are you heading?" Other Christians protected Yun and helped him to get to Beijing and then on to Germany. After many more trials, his family was able to join him. Today, three leading house church figures, Brother Yun, Peter Xu, and Enoch Wang, are working with the "Back to Jerusalem" missionary effort to convert people to Christianity all along the Silk Road back to Jerusalem. Miracles happened then and miracles happen now.

~EARLENE RICHARDS STROTHER (1933–) CLAYTON, GA

THE LAST DEPOSIT

Be on the alert, stand firm in the faith, act like men, be strong.
1 CORINTHIANS 16:13 NASB

It's smart to leave every encounter on a positive note. For instance, when you're leaving the house in the morning, it's much nicer to ask your spouse to pick up the dry cleaning first and save the "I love you" for last. Think about it. If you said, "I love you," then said, "Please pick up the dry cleaning," your spouse might feel manipulated. And suppose you died in a car crash right after you left? Your spouse would always remember your last words were, "Please pick up the dry cleaning," instead of, "I love you." Yes, last impressions are important. I use this example because it is simple and clear. However, it is devastating to those who had had the misfortune of not being able to change their last words. This is true not just in regard to those you make the last impression on but also for when someone else or something else (radio, TV, newspaper) makes the last impression on you. If a person gave you that blah or down feeling, change the deposit by going to another person to get a quick fix. Call one of your friends or acquaintances who is an upbeat person and chat a couple of minutes. You might start by asking what is the most exciting thing or happening at the moment. The beauty of this approach is that both you and your friend will be better off as a result of the call. Remember, our minds dwell on that last deposit until the imagination builds it bigger and bigger, and it's much better to have a big positive than a big negative.

~ZIG ZIGLAR (1926–) ADDISON, TX

THE CHOSEN PATH

CHRISTIAN FORTITUDE

He that is slow to anger is better than the mighty;
and he that ruleth his spirit than he that taketh a city.

PROVERBS 16:32 KJV

The whole Christian life is compared to a warfare, and fitly so. And the most eminent Christians are the best soldiers, endued with the greatest degrees of Christian fortitude. And it is the duty of God's people to be steadfast and vigorous in their opposition to the designs and ways of such as are endeavoring to overthrow the kingdom of Christ, and the interest of religion. But yet many persons seem to be quite mistaken concerning the nature of Christian fortitude. It is an exceedingly diverse thing from a brutal fierceness, or the boldness of the beasts of prey. True Christian fortitude consists in strength of mind, through grace, exerted in two things; in ruling and suppressing the evil and unruly passions and affections of the mind; and in steadfastly and freely exerting, and following good affections and dispositions, without being hindered by sinful fear, or the opposition of enemies. But the passions that are restrained and kept under, in the exercise of this Christian strength and fortitude, are those very passions that are vigorously and violently exerted in a false boldness for Christ. And those affections that are vigorously exerted in true fortitude, are those Christian, holy affections that are directly contrary to them. Though Christian fortitude appears, in withstanding and counteracting the enemies that are without us; yet it much more appears, in resisting and suppressing the enemies that are within us; because they are our worst and strongest enemies, and have the greatest advantage against us.

~JONATHAN EDWARDS (1703–1758)

THE "I DON'T FEEL LIKE IT" BAPTIST CHURCH

Now therefore, says the LORD of hosts: "Consider your ways!"

HAGGAI 1:5 NKJV

Do you attend the "I Don't Feel Like It Baptist Church?" The Southern Baptist Convention reports that we have over 16 million members, but let's be honest: in most cases the FBI couldn't find half our members on a given Sunday! What's the problem? It is the same problem that the prophet Haggai was called to challenge in 520 B.C. (historical context in Ezra chapters 1–6). In 538 B.C., 50,000 people under the leadership of Zerubbabel and Joshua the High-Priest (cf. Ezra 3:2) retuned to Jerusalem. Two years later (536 B.C.), they began to rebuild the Temple. Almost immediately they began to receive opposition from their neighbors. Disappointment led to discouragement, and discouragement led to disinterest in rebuilding the Temple. God's people didn't feel like completing the job. Instead they focused on their own houses and let God's house lie in ruins. Haggai was sent by God into this situation. Haggai challenged the people with their lack of priority and purpose. They had allowed comforts, conveniences, and cravings take first place in their lives. The challenge "Consider your ways" is intended to draw people back to God. Haggai points out their lack of contentment and satisfaction in their lives is due to their misplaced priorities. That's the bad news. The good news is found when the Lord says, "I am with you" (1:13). God had given them a God-sized challenge. And thankfully, God gives no non-funded heavenly mandates. He promised that He would provide exactly what was needed to finish the task.

~KEVIN KING (1962–) STEAMBOAT SPRINGS, CO

THE CHOSEN PATH

JESUS CAN BE TRUSTED

You believe that God is one; you do well.
The demons also believe—and they shudder.

JAMES 2:19 HCSB

Jesus is what He is said to be, Jesus will do what He says He will do; therefore we must each one trust Him, saying, "He will be to me what He says He is, and He will do to me what He has promised to do; I leave myself in the hands of Him who is appointed to save, that He may save me. I rest upon His promise that He will do even as He has said." This is a saving faith, and he that hath it hath everlasting life. Whatever his dangers and difficulties, whatever his darkness and depression, whatever his infirmities and sins, he that believeth thus on Christ Jesus is not condemned, and shall never come into condemnation. Trust, and be at rest. The great matter is to believe on the Lord Jesus at once. Never mind distinctions and definitions. A hungry man eats though he does not understand the composition of his food, the anatomy of his mouth, or the process of digestion: he lives because he eats. Another far more clever person understands thoroughly the science of nutrition; but if he does not eat he will die, with all his knowledge. There are, no doubt, many at this hour in Hell who understood the doctrine of faith, but did not believe. On the other hand, not one who has trusted in the Lord Jesus has ever been cast out, though he may never have been able intelligently to define his faith. Oh dear reader, receive the Lord Jesus into your soul, and you shall live forever! "He that believeth in Him hath everlasting life."

~C. H. SPURGEON (1834–1892)

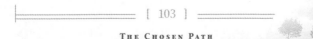

THE CHOSEN PATH

ADJUST THE AGE TO THE BIBLE

This book of the law shall not depart out of thy mouth; but thou shalt meditate therein day and night, that thou mayest observe to do according to all that is written therein: for then thou shalt make thy way prosperous, and then thou shalt have good success.

JOSHUA 1:8 KJV

If some men were sentenced to hear their own sermons, it would be a righteous judgment on them; but they would soon cry out with Cain, "My punishment is greater than I can bear." Try to get saturated with the gospel. I always find that I can preach best when I lie down in it and let it soak into me . . . become saturated with spices, and you will smell of them. There has been a growing pandering to sensationalism; and, as this wretched appetite increases in fury the more it is gratified, it is at last found to be impossible to meet its demands. I have frequently said of myself that I would not go across the street to hear myself preach. We shall not adjust our Bible to the age; but before we have done with it, by God's grace, we shall adjust the age to the Bible.

~C. H. SPURGEON (1834–1892)

HIDE AND SEEK

As the deer longs for streams of water, so I long for you, O God. I thirst
for God, the living God. When can I go and stand before him? Day
and night I have only tears for food, while my enemies continually taunt
me, saying, "Where is this God of yours?" Why am I discouraged?
Why is my heart so sad? I will put my hope in God! I will praise him again.

PSALM 42:1–3, 5 NLT

As I read this psalm I am reminded of one of my favorite childhood games, "Hide and Seek." I was always a good hider; I would find the most unusual places to hide that I could. My little sister would try to find me. Often she would get frustrated as she searched. At times she would be so close that I could have reached out and touched her. Sometimes I would give her little hints, make a noise or something to put her on the right path. Hide and seek is a fun game, but the goal is to be found. I really believe that God loves to play hide and seek with us. His goal is to be found too. David searched for God and found Him. During good times or bad, we should seek God. I believe it is during our times of deep distress that God will make a noise or stick his foot out just a little bit so that we can find him. Seek God; He wants you to find Him today.

~**TERRENCE ROBERTS** (1964–) **MERIDIAN, MS**

CHRISTIAN DEVOTION

He that hath ears to hear, let him hear.

MARK 4:9 KJV

If contempt of the world and heavenly affection is a necessary temper of Christians, it is necessary that this temper appear in the whole course of their lives, in their manner of using the world, because it can have no place anywhere else. If self-denial be a condition of salvation, all that would be saved must make it a part of their ordinary life. If humility be a Christian duty, then the common life of a Christian is to be a constant course of humility in all its kinds. If poverty of spirit be necessary, it must be the spirit and temper of every day of our lives. If we are to relieve the naked, the sick, and the prisoner, it must be the common charity of our lives, as far as we can render ourselves able to perform it. If we are to love our enemies, we must make our common life a visible exercise and demonstration of that love. If content and thankfulness, if the patient bearing of evil be duties to God, they are the duties of every day, and in every circumstance of our life. If we are to be wise and holy as the new-born sons of God, we can no otherwise be so, but by renouncing everything that is foolish and vain in every part of our common life. If we are to be in Christ new creatures, we must show that we are so, by having new ways of living in the world. If we are to follow Christ, it must be in our common way of spending every day.

~WILLIAM LAW (1686–1781)

CAN YOU TELL ME HOW TO FEEL FOR JESUS?

Listen! I stand at the door and knock. If anyone hears My voice and opens the door, I will come in to him and have dinner with him, and he with Me.

REVELATION 3:20 HCSB

Finding our advertisement in the local newspaper, Claudia called to ask if she could attend our English classes. When she arrived at school, it was evident that she had had a good English teacher in Germany. Her husband was in the army and had brought her to Alaska before securing housing on the military installation. They had very little money. Living in a one-room apartment with no means of getting additional funds was stressful. Our church was hosting a conference for Alaska Natives, and we needed assistance. Our weekday Bible studies and Sunday services needed childcare help. Claudia agreed to help and was able to earn money for food. She enjoyed being at our church. Even after her financial situation improved, she continued to work at the church but gave the money back to the church. Even when she wasn't needed, she would attend the worship services. She had attended church in Germany but had never heard about a personal relationship with Jesus. One day she asked me, "Will you come to my apartment and explain to me how to feel for Jesus?" I gladly agreed. Claudia's English was very good conversationally, but her ability to understand spiritual matters in English was limited. With careful explanation, she realized how a person could feel for Jesus. Claudia prayed to receive Christ. God is always knocking. I get busy doing good things and fail to realize how God uses small things. A newspaper advertisement brought a person into my life that I might be a witness.

~**DAVID BALDWIN (1943–) ANCHORAGE, AK**

RECYCLED

Therefore, if anyone is in Christ, he is a new creation.

2 CORINTHIANS 5:17 NIV

This is the age of the disposable. We have disposable pens, tableware, and diapers. New flashlights and lighters feature sealed-in batteries. When it no longer lights consistently, we proclaim it more trouble than it's worth and toss it in file thirteen. Most soft-drink manufacturers have changed from return-for-deposit bottles to no-deposit disposable bottles, crushable two-liter containers, and aluminum cans. But aluminum cans are not totally disposable. Although they still have value, they are thrown away along every highway, and occasionally, into trash cans. When an energetic person picks them up and sells them to a recycling firm, they begin the process of being made into useable cans again. Recycling the useless into the useful is a process that takes times and effort. God sent Jeremiah to the potter's house to learn a lesson about recycling (Jeremiah 18). The vessel that the potter was forming on the wheel became marred, evidently from some fault in the clay. But the potter didn't throw away the defective clay. Instead, he reworked it into a beautiful vessel. And Jeremiah learned that God is in the recycling business. God wants to make new creations out of all his marred vessels. Paul wrote that those who have accepted Christ have already been reworked and are then given the ministry of bringing others to Christ.

~VICKI HUFFMAN (1946–) MT. JULIET, TN

CHRIST THE WAY,
THE TRUTH, AND THE LIFE

Jesus saith unto him, I am the way, the truth,
and the life: no man cometh unto the Father, but by me.

JOHN 14:6 KJV

Christ says, "I am the way." Jesus pitied the poor sons of Adam vainly struggling to find out a way into the paradise of God, and He left the bosom of the Father, just that He might open up a way for us into the bosom of the Father. And how did He do it? Was it by escaping the vigilance of the flaming sword? No, for it turned every way. Was it by exerting His Divine authority, and commanding the glittering blade to withdraw? No, for that would have been to dishonor his Father's law instead of magnifying it. He therefore became a man in our stead—yea, became sin. God caused to meet on Him the iniquities of us all. He advanced in our stead to meet that fiery meteor. He fell beneath its piercing blade; for He remembered the word of the prophet, which is written: "Awake, O sword! Against my shepherd, and against the man that is my fellow, saith the Lord of hosts." And now, since the glittering blade is bathed in the side of the Redeemer, the guiltiest of sinners— whoever you be, whatever you be—may enter in over His bleeding body, may find access to the paradise of God, to eat of the tree of life, and live forever. Come quickly, doubt not; for He says, "I am the way."

~R. M. McCheyne (1813–1843)

THE CHOSEN PATH

GOD PREPARES THE WAY

Trust in the LORD with all your heart, and do not rely on your own
understanding; think about Him in all your ways,
and He will guide you on the right paths.

PROVERBS 3:5–6 HCSB

Attending our English as a Second Language (ESL) ministry was a Chilean lady whose husband had a Mexican heritage. He was in the military stationed in Alaska. One Tuesday night at class, the lady mentioned she was having a Bible study in her home. She wondered if there were different kinds of Bibles. The book the women were using sounded different. The women represented a non-Christian group. She asked that I come to her home and explain the Bible to her. We set a date. I prayed to seek God's guidance in what to say and searched the Scriptures for verses to counter the arguments of the women. As I drove into her parking lot, I noticed the husband, whom I had never met, was home. My heart sank. I thought, *I'll not be able to meet the wife alone and deal with her questions.* I discovered later that the wife scheduled the meeting when her husband would be home. I entered the home and after the social graces required in a Spanish home were complete, I brought up the questions the wife had asked in class. To my surprise, the husband stayed in the room and was the one who really had the questions. The Holy Spirit had already been at work. Both husband and wife prayed to receive Christ. God reminded me that the work of salvation is not the result of my planning, good arguments or defense of the faith. It is His work. My responsibility is to be a faithful witness.

~DAVID BALDWIN (1943–) ANCHORAGE, AK

THE CHOSEN PATH

BELIEVERS DELIGHT IN THE LAW OF GOD

After those days, saith the LORD, I will put My
law in their inward parts, and write it in their hearts;
and will be their God, and they shall be my people.

JEREMIAH 31:33 KJV

The spirit of God writes the law on the heart. Coming to Christ takes away your fear of the law; but it is the Holy Spirit coming into your heart that makes you love the law. The Holy Spirit is no more frightened away from that heart; He comes and softens it; He takes out the stony heart and puts in a heart of flesh; and there He writes the holy, holy, holy law of God. Then the law of God is sweet to that soul; he has an inward delight in it. "The law is holy, and the commandment holy, and just, and good." Now he unfeignedly desires every thought, word, and action to be according to that law. "Oh that my ways were directed to keep Thy statutes: great peace have they that love Thy law, and nothing shall offend them." The one hundred nineteenth Psalm becomes the breathing of that new heart. Now also he would fain see all the world submitting to that pure and holy law. "Rivers of waters run down mine eyes because they keep not Thy law." Oh that all the world but knew that holiness and happiness are one! Oh that all the world were one holy family, joyfully coming under the pure rules of the gospel! Do you remember when you hated the law of God? Do you love it now? Do you long for the time when you shall live fully under it—holy as God is holy, pure as Christ is pure?

~R. M. McCheyne (1813–1843)

RESCUED AND SAFE

He rescued me from my powerful enemy and from
those who hated me, for they were too strong for me.

PSALM 18:17 HCSB

Trees were a favorite place to play when I was a kid. Height didn't matter . . . the higher the better. Tree houses, wild cherries, scuppernong, and muscadine vines and other intriguing offerings awaited every adventure. One warm summer day, my friend Ronnie and I stood underneath one of our best climbing trees, hearing a faint "meow" from above. Thinking it was his new kitten, he said, "That's my cat up there!" So Ronnie set out on his rescue mission. Ronnie found himself in a dilemma. Holding a cat in a tree is not an easy task. That cat wanted to grip real tight to something. So he dug in, digging deeper and deeper, as Ronnie climbed down the tree. Stepping to the ground, with hands scratched and bleeding, he said, "THAT'S not my cat." That's how my family inherited a new cat. We named him Tiger, which seemed to be an appropriate name for him. We didn't necessarily want a new cat, but that's the way it goes sometimes. Tiger lived with us many years. He was a little on the wild side but that's understandable, considering how he came into our lives. He was one of my favorite cats. When God rescues us, it is never by accident. He knows us, where we are, and what the problems are. He is always aware of our every situation and what it will take to rescue us. It didn't matter that He had to "climb a tree," resulting in "bleeding hands," to give us a home. In fact, He planned it that way. And He calls you by name for a reason.

~RANDOLPH (RANDY) ALAN MCCOLLUM (1952–) BLOOMINGTON, IN

HONESTY IS THE BEST POLICY

Behold, thou desirest truth in the inward parts.

PSALM 51:6 KJV

A few years ago, a well-known public leader confessed, "I am a father to a daughter who was born outside of my marriage." Although it was a new revelation to many of us, it was no surprise to the one who confessed it, for he was simply revealing a "secret" that had been with him a long time. Almost everyone I know has secrets. Some of them, of course, are good secrets—the kind we "keep" when we are planning a surprise birthday party or the kind we hide underneath pretty Christmas wrapping, waiting to be opened at the appropriate time. But some secrets are bad for us. To carry them around weighs us down emotionally, spiritually, and even physically. When David tried to keep his elicit affair with Bathsheba a secret, he discovered that his bones wasted away and he felt dehydrated. But those consequences were small compared to what his secret did to his relationship with God and the people around him. When we have a heavy conscience over something we have done, we can't be real in front of others. We have to start living a lie because it seems too costly to admit we have made a mistake. Honesty comes from God, who IS truth. If I'm going to be right with Him—and right with the world He created, I have to live with the TRUTH. If I fail in some aspect of life, I have to be willing to admit it to myself, and then to God, and then to the people I have wronged. What's your secret? If it's good, you can keep it! But if it's bad, honesty is the best policy.

~JIM DOWNS (1950–) GREEN BAY, WI

CHRIST IN THE VESSEL

*And the same day, when the even was come, he saith unto them,
Let us pass over unto the other side. And when they had sent away
the multitude, they took him even as he was in the ship. And there were
also with him other little ships. And there arose a great storm of wind,
and the waves beat into the ship, so that it was now full. And he was in
the hinder part of the ship, asleep on a pillow: and they awake him,
and say unto him, Master, carest thou not that we perish? And he
arose, and rebuked the wind, and said unto the sea, Peace, be still.*

MARK 4:35–39 KJV

"Man's extremity is God's opportunity." This is a very familiar saying. It often passes among us; and no doubt, we fully believe it; but yet, when we find ourselves brought to our extremity, we are often very little prepared to count on God's opportunity. It is one thing to utter or hearken to a truth, and another thing to realize the power of that truth. It is one thing, when sailing over a calm sea, to speak of God's ability to keep us in the storm, and it is another thing altogether to prove that ability when the storm is actually raging around us. And yet God is ever the same. In the storm and in the calm, in sickness and in health, in pressure and in ease, in poverty and in abundance, "the same yesterday, and today, and forever"—the same grand reality for faith to land upon, cling to and draw upon, at all times for under all circumstances.

~C. H. MACINTOSH (1820–1896)

MARRIAGE THAT WORKS IS WORK

*"I have come that they may have life,
and that they may have it more abundantly."*

JOHN 10:10 NKJV

Marriage has been in trouble for many years and, some in the secular media have referred to America as the "divorce culture." Sadly, Evangelical Christians have a slightly higher divorce rate than the culture as a whole. When covenant marriage is practiced, there are significantly fewer divorce suits filed. Covenant marriage couples choose to covenant to stay together, rather than looking for a way out. Often, marriages fail because one partner has committed adultery or something of that magnitude, but approximately 60 percent of marriages break up as loneliness and boredom creep in, or small unresolved resentments coalesce into percolating volcanoes. All relationships begin with infatuation, but maturing past that first stage to real committed love is the only way a troubled marriage will not be the joy to some divorce attorney. Marriage can work because it is God ordained. It requires hard work, faith, and a trusting commitment to Christ and His ways. It requires honor for and value of your spouse, and both the man and woman to function together under the guidance and wisdom of Christ. The pain of divorce extends to all who know the couple. It is the way of grace in God's kingdom that marriages be healed and restored to better than ever before. The truths of a covenant marriage, where Christ is the head, can be realized no matter what adversity the couple faces, and the benefits are worth much more than any amount of effort it takes to make it succeed.

~JAMES RUDY GRAY (1953–) SENECA, SC

PRIORITIES

There's a bandit on earth, he is running about
Stealing my time, making me shout
When will I get all this stuff done?
Cooking and cleaning just not much fun
The kids are hollering, the dog needs fed
What will I do with this aching head?
Hubby is home, it's half past six
Don't have a clue what dinner I'll fix
The laundry is building, got nothing to wear
Then I will cry and pull out my hair
Then I'd be bald and oh how they'd stare
This very moment I really don't care
Priorities have not been a part of my day
Shopping and talking got in my way
By Your Spirit failed to be led
Yes that's why I'm hanging my head
Forgive me Lord, fill me up once more
Don't want to go back through that door
Direct my path, lead each step of the way
Yes this is how to have a good day.

~LINDA SMITH (1948–) SENECA, SC

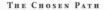

THE BRIDE

Let us rejoice and be glad and give him glory! For the wedding
of the Lamb has come, and his bride has made herself ready.

REVELATION 19:7 NIV

"I am the first to see her when she appears at the back of the church. But she snaps heads sidewards with every row she passes. She remains hidden from friends and relatives inside the church until the playing of the four-measure fanfare of Wagner's Wedding March. She steps out in view of all of us who face the congregation. Row by row, people turn to face the center aisle. They gasp, they cry, they laugh, they beam, they rejoice. That's the way it is for the bride" (Chuck Swindoll, *The Bride*, p. 9). January 3rd, 1997. I experienced those very same emotions as my Bride walked down the aisle. No one focused on me or even was concerned about me! All watched with such incredible joy as all that was pure and lovely personified in my Bride seemed to effortlessly float to the altar. Captivating! I remember looking into her eyes as they shone like fine crystal. I understood for the first time that "the Bride in all her glory and splendor is never more illuminating than on her wedding day." My Bride's preparation was very detailed, time consuming, and hard work, but the result was sheer perfection: the most beautiful bride of all! We (Jesus' Bride) are in the preparation stages for our fast approaching wedding day. As the Bride of Christ, we have almost forgotten who we are: Christ's Bride. Along with our forgetfulness, we seem to have forgotten about those visions and aspirations of a life-ETERNAL with our omnipotent Groom. How seriously are we preparing?

~**MILES ROHDE (1972–) MARSHALL, MN**

JOHN 1:1–16 KJV

In the beginning was the Word, and the Word was with God, and the Word was God. The same was in the beginning with God. All things were made by him; and without him was not any thing made that was made. In him was life; and the life was the light of men. And the light shineth in darkness; and the darkness comprehended it not. There was a man sent from God, whose name was John. The same came for a witness, to bear witness of the Light, that all men through him might believe. He was not that Light, but was sent to bear witness of that Light. That was the true Light, which lighteth every man that cometh into the world. He was in the world, and the world was made by him, and the world knew him not. He came unto his own, and his own received him not. But as many as received him, to them gave he power to become the sons of God, even to them that believe on his name: Which were born, not of blood, nor of the will of the flesh, nor of the will of man, but of God. And the Word was made flesh, and dwelt among us, (and we beheld his glory, the glory as of the only begotten of the Father,) full of grace and truth. John bare witness of him, and cried, saying, This was he of whom I spake, He that cometh after me is preferred before me: for he was before me. And of his fulness have all we received, and grace for grace.

~St. John

THE DISCIPLINE OF A GODLY CONVERSATION

But you, when you pray, go into your inner room, close your door and pray to your Father who is in secret.

MATTHEW 6:6 NASB

As humans, we have a deep need to communicate. We constantly desire to express our feelings and emotions. Think for a moment of the ways we have created to communicate with each other. Sometimes we use the spoken word. At other times we write, we e-mail, we call, we text-message, we use pagers and BlackBerries, cell phones, and the occasional letter. We use Post-it notes. Some are versed with sign language. Nonverbally, we wink, we nod, we smile, and we shake our heads. The world of nature continues the theme . . . dogs bark, cats meow, birds sing, crickets chirp, and pigs oink. No one on the planet can deny the importance of communication. In fact, apart from communication, no relationship can grow. How, then, can any of us expect our relationship with God to grow apart from the discipline of a godly conversation? When asked to teach about prayer, Jesus offered His disciples some very practical advice. He told them to find a quiet place and talk honestly with the Father. He told them to use carefully chosen words, not meaningless repetition. He told them to pray for the both the biggest and smallest needs of life. He wanted them to begin the habit of a daily conversation with God. Jesus knew the conversation would lead to a greater relationship. In the midst of a dozen conversations you will have this day, let me challenge you to take the time for the most important one . . . the one you need to have with your Father.

~JON R. ROEBUCK (1960–) FRANKLIN, TN

THE CHOSEN PATH

THE PERSON OF CHRIST

Splendor and majesty are before Him, Strength and joy are in His place.

1 CHRONICLES 16:27 NASB

All the attributes of divinity are ascribed to him, eternity of existence, self-existence, omnipotence, omnipresence, omniscience, presence in heaven and on earth, the contemplation of and unity with the Father, and co-working with him. These are declared of him and manifested by him while he stood in the form of man in the midst of his disciples and the multitude. It was while in the same form that he performed acts which none other than God can of himself do, declaring that these acts were done by his own power. He turned water into wine, not by the ordinary and slow process of nature, but instantly and without a word. He created bread and fish in the hands of his disciples. He controlled the winds and the waves. He forgave sin. He gave life to the dead. He made known events in distant places. He searched the hearts and revealed the secret thoughts of men. He laid down his own life and took it up again. The constant workings of his divine power and energy, by which he is essentially, as God, always working with the Father, were indeed concealed; but thus, at times, before the people at large, and more frequently before his disciples, the divinity shone through the veil which ordinarily concealed it, and testified that he was as truly God as he was also man.

~J. P. BOYCE (1827–1888)

UNITY

*And all those who had believed were together
and had all things in common.*

ACTS 2:44 NASB

The church today needs to take a lesson from that of the Acts church. We need to have all things in common! Seems like a daunting task with all the differences that scream out at us; do we sing choruses or hymns, or both? Do we use screens or hymnals, or print the words in the program? Do we stand or sit during the singing? Do we tailor our services to the seekers or to the believers? The problem is that we are asking the wrong person! What worked in the church at Acts still works in the modern-day church: the Holy Spirit! It's time that deacons, elders, congregations, and we the pastors fall on our faces before the Lord and ask Him what He wants! The plans and programs that man devise only bring human results. God is not so concerned about our methods but our heart. When our heart is toward God, and His desires are our desires, then we will be in unity and have all things in common. I love my wife's observation: babies coo, young children baby-talk, teenagers shout, and adults reason. We don't go to our cooing babies and demand that they talk on an adult level. In fact, as parents, we enjoy hearing our babies coo and discover new sounds. You know what? I enjoy hearing the coos and shouts of the young people of the church. They will learn to reason soon enough! More importantly, the heavenly Father loves to hear all his children praise Him and inhabits the praises of His people!

~ANDY DIETZ (1950–) BORGER, TX

THE CHOSEN PATH

"GO YE" NOT "SEND YE"

Go ye therefore, and teach all nations, baptizing them in the name
of the Father, and of the Son, and of the Holy Ghost.
MATTHEW 28:19 KJV

Oh, my friends, we are playing at things. We have not begun to take religion seriously, any of us. We profess to believe in the coming of Christ, and we profess to believe that the one reason why Christ has not come back yet is because His Church, His Body, is not yet complete. We believe that when His body is complete He will come back. And my friends, His "body" never, never, will be complete until the last of His elect people will be called out, and His elect people are called out under the preaching of the gospel by the power of the Holy Spirit, and if you are really anxious for Christ to come back soon, then you had better be more wide awake to your responsibility in connection with taking or sending the gospel to the heathen! Christ's word, and it is Christ's word to us, is "Go ye into all the world and preach the gospel." He does not say, "Send ye." He says, "Go ye," and you have to answer to Christ yet because you have not gone! Well, you say, do you mean by that that everyone of us here tonight ought to go out to the mission field? I have not said that, I am not any man's judge. Many of you here tonight have a good reason which will satisfy Christ why you have not gone. He gave you work to do here. He put you in a position here. He has given you responsibilities to discharge here, but every Christian who is free to go, and does not go, has got to answer to Christ for it yet.

~A. W. PINK (1886–1952)

EASTER

"The Son of Man must be betrayed into the hands of sinful men,
be crucified, and rise on the third day."

LUKE 24:7 HCSB

In a world not so different from ours, where terror stalked and tyrants raged, where peace was rare and where religion often seemed to be no more than another reason for humans to hate, in a world where pride and sin and death mocked the Living God, Easter happened. Betrayed, tortured, humiliated, and killed, the Son of God refused to stay put in His grave. The gentle man of sorrows proved to be mightier than all the armies of wickedness, mightier than the very laws of nature, for He was nature's God and humanity's Savior, and it was impossible for death to hold Him. Too long we have thought of the garden of the resurrection as a quiet, pastel place, with singing birds and the dew of spring, far removed from our sorrowful and desperate world. We forget that it was a little cemetery, in the shadows of the city wall and of the execution hill they called The Skull, where death was decisively defeated. We forget how the earth shook and the guards collapsed, how the angels came down, and how the broken followers of Jesus cried for joy as they knelt in the presence of the living Lord, not in some hazy, peaceful fantasy place, but right here, on this earth. And because we forget, we do not quite grasp the joy of the promise—the promise sealed by Easter, that because He lives, we who remain here, who trust Him, with all those who have loved Him, shall also live. This Easter, may you remember, and may you rejoice.

~DAVID F. RASMUSSEN (1952–) GREENCASTLE, PA

THE AGONY OF CHRIST

And being in an agony he prayed more earnestly: and his sweat was
as it were great drops of blood falling down to the ground.

LUKE 22:44 KJV

It was the corruption and wickedness of men that contrived and effected his death; it was the wickedness of men that agreed with Judas, it was the wickedness of men that betrayed him, and that apprehended him, and bound him, and led him away like a malefactor; it was by men's corruption and wickedness that he was arraigned, and falsely accused, and unjustly judged. It was by men's wickedness that he was reproached, mocked, buffeted, and spit upon. It was by men's wickedness that Barabbas was preferred before him. It was men's wickedness that laid the cross upon him to bear, and that nailed him to it, and put him to so cruel and ignominious a death. This tended to give Christ an extraordinary sense of the greatness and hatefulness of the depravity of mankind. Because hereby in the time of his sufferings he had that depravity set before him as it is, without disguise. When it killed Christ, it appeared in its proper colors. Here Christ saw it in its true nature, which is the utmost hatred and contempt of God; in its ultimate tendency and desire, which is to kill God; and in its greatest aggravation and highest act, which is killing a person that was God. But yet at the same time, so wonderful was the love of Christ to those who exhibited this hateful corruption, that he endured those very sufferings to deliver them from the punishment of that very corruption.

~JONATHAN EDWARDS (1703–1758)

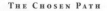

THE CHOSEN PATH

THE CRUCIFIED ONE

We have been planted together in the likeness of his death.

ROMANS 6:5 KJV

Many Christians are content to look upon the Cross, with Christ on it dying for their sins, who have little heart for fellowship with the Crucified One. They have no conception of what it is to be crucified with Christ, that bearing the cross means likeness to Christ in the principles which animated Him in His path of obedience. The entire surrender of all self-will, the complete denial to the flesh of its every desire and pleasure, the perfect separation from the world in all its ways of thinking and acting, the losing and hating of one's life, the giving up of self and its interests for the sake of others—this is the disposition which marks him who has taken up Christ's Cross, who seeks to say, "I am crucified with Christ; I abide in Christ, the Crucified One." The faith that believes in the blood that pardons, and the life that renews, can only reach its perfect growth as it abides beneath the Cross, and in living fellowship with Him seeks for perfect conformity with Jesus the Crucified. O Jesus, our crucified Redeemer, teach us not only to believe on Thee, but to abide in Thee, to take Thy Cross not only as the ground of our pardon, but also as the law of our life. O teach us to love it not only because on it Thou didst bear our curse, but because on it we enter into the closest fellowship with Thyself, and are crucified with Thee, as we yield ourselves wholly to be possessed of the Spirit in which Thou didst bear the Cross, we shall be made partakers of the power and the blessing to which the Cross alone gives access.

~**ANDREW MURRAY (1828–1917)**

ALAS! AND DID MY SAVIOR BLEED

Alas! And did my Savior bleed, and did my Sovereign die?

Would He devote that sacred head for such a worm as I?

Was it for crimes that I had done He groaned upon the tree?

Amazing pity, grace unknown, and love beyond degree!

Well might the sun in darkness hide and shut his glories in,

When God, the mighty Maker, died for man the creature's sin.

Thus might I hide my blushing face while His dear cross appears,

Dissolve my heart in thankfulness, and melt mine eyes to tears.

But drops of grief can ne'er repay the debt of love I owe;

Here, Lord, I give myself away, 'tis all that I can do.

~ISAAC WATTS (1674–1748)

CHRIST THE LORD IS RISEN TODAY; ALLELUIA!

Christ the Lord is risen today, Alleluia!
Christians, haste your vows to pay, Alleluia!
Offer ye your praises meet, Alleluia!
At the Paschal Victim's feet, Alleluia!
For the sheep the Lamb hath bled, Alleluia!
Sinless in the sinners' stead, Alleluia!
"Christ is risen," today we cry, Alleluia!
Now He lives no more to die, Alleluia!
Christ, the Victim undefiled, Alleluia!
God and man hath reconciled, Alleluia!
While in strange and awe-full strife, Alleluia!
Met together Death and Life, Alleluia!
Christians, on this happy day, Alleluia!
Haste with joy your vows to pay, Alleluia!
"Christ is risen," today we cry, Alleluia!
Now He lives no more to die, Alleluia!
Christ, who once for sinners bled, Alleluia!
Now the First-born from the dead, Alleluia!
Throned in endless might and power, Alleluia!
Lives and reigns forevermore, Alleluia!
Hail, eternal Hope on high, Alleluia!
Hail, Thou King of victory, Alleluia!
Hail, Thou Prince of Life adored, Alleluia!
Help and save us, gracious Lord, Alleluia!

~AUTHOR UNKNOWN (PROBABLY 11TH OR 12TH CENTURY)

HE IS KING

He humbled himself, and became obedient
unto death, even the death of the cross.

PHILIPPIANS 2:8 KJV

He is also King as the reward of his obedience unto death. Satan offered him sovereignty in return for one act of homage, and Christ refused, and descended the mountain to poverty and shame and death; but through these things he has won for himself a Kingdom which is yet in its infancy, but is destined to stand when all the kingdoms of this world have crumbled to dust. As Christ emerged from the cross and the grave, where he had purged our sins, it seemed as if words were addressed to him which David had caught ages before: "The LORD said unto my Lord, Sit on my right hand, until I make thine enemies thy footstool" (Psalm 90:1). The Lamb is in the midst of the Throne. Behold his majesty, and worship him with angels and archangels, and all the throng of the redeemed. Prostrate yourself at his feet, consecrating to him all you are and all you have. Comfort yourself also by remembering that he would not sit to rest from his labors in redemption, and in the purging away of sins, unless they were so completely finished that there was nothing more to do. It is all accomplished; and it is all very good. He has ceased from his works, because they are done; and therefore he is entered into his rest. And that word "until" is full of hope. God speaks it, and encourages us to expect the time when he shall have put down all rule and all authority and power; and when death itself, the last enemy, shall be destroyed.

~F. B. MEYER (1847–1929)

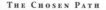

THE CHOSEN PATH

WHAT'S YOUR FAVORITE FRUIT?

I am the vine, ye are the branches: He that abideth in me, and I in him,
the same bringeth forth much fruit: for without me ye can do nothing.

JOHN 15:5 KJV

I am convinced that one of the devil's greatest ploys is to work at trying to make us bad people. He will often settle for making you busy. How many of us have a time and a place where we meet God every day? I often have people tell me, "I just don't have time to read my Bible or to pray every day. I can't even work in a short little devotion every day of the week." How many hours do you have in your day? God has given every person on this planet the same amount of time. I don't know about you, but I think God was right to stop at a twenty-four day. I personally don't want longer days to accomplish what I didn't finish in twenty-four hours! I must allow God to set my priorities in my days and I can't do that unless I give Him all of my time. After all, He gave it to me in the first place. I am a husband, father, teacher, preacher, music director, principal, and an administrator, and these positions require that I accomplish certain things every day. I must go to the Lord daily and tell Him, "I don't have time to not be with You every day." I need God to accomplish every task I undertake. I don't have the ability to accomplish anything without Him. Be careful; your life will reveal your heart. What kind of fruit are you bearing? Who is pruning? God or Satan? Don't be deceived! Produce God's Fruit!

~TIMOTHY RAY PITTMAN (1959–) SHIFFIELD, VA

THE CHOSEN PATH

SPIRITUAL GIANT

Not my will, but thine.
LUKE 22:42 KJV

There are times I have been a "spiritual giant," saying to this mountain and that mountain "be removed and cast into the sea" and calling those things that are not as though they are. I can still recall the happiness when those things did indeed come to pass, not in my power but His. Moving from faith to faith, I can also recall times that I couldn't hold a thought. Times when the only prayer I could pray was simply to say the name Jesus over and over and over. It was a time in my life when the top came down, the sides caved in, and the bottom had fallen out. Circumstances had taken their toll. It was like living the book of Job. The only thing I had left was Jesus. During this time, the most amazing thing happened. I learned through experience the more I decreased and allowed Jesus to increase, a whole new world of understanding opened up to me. He allows us to interact with people and the use of possessions for His good pleasure and for His purpose. I am a witness of God moving in extraordinary ways. I have seen Him bring things to pass through situations, circumstances, His people, and what must have been angels. Through every trial, temptation, and test, I can testify that God is well able. He is a way maker. His word is like a hammer that shatters a rock. He is a very present help in time of trouble. He is my deliverer, my strength, my high tower. He heals the broken hearted and He honors a contrite and humble spirit. His lovingkindness is everlasting. There is no better place to be than in His mighty right hand.

~**MICHAEL GOODS (1958–) NICHOLASVILLE, KY**

THE CHOSEN PATH

ON THE ATTRIBUTES OF GOD

Neither is there any creature that is not manifest in his sight: but all things are naked and opened unto the eyes of him with whom we have to do.
HEBREWS 4:13 KJV

The Attributes of God are those peculiarities which mark or define the mode of his existence, or which constitute his character. They are not separate nor separable from his essence or nature, and yet are not that essence, but simply have the ground or cause of their existence in it, and are at the same time the peculiarities which constitute the mode and character of his being. As they are not separable from his essence, so they are not to be regarded as so many different powers and peculiarities or faculties, which so belong to God that he is "composed of different elements." This would take away the simplicity of the divine nature and make it compound and therefore divisible and changeable. But, on the other hand, they are not simply our different conceptions of God. They have existence independently of his creatures. There is some true foundation in God himself for the distinctions between them, so that, when we speak of God as wise, we do not only say that we conceive of him differently than when we call him just, but we mean that there is that in God which makes it proper that we should conceive of him under the different aspects of wisdom and justice.

~J. P. BOYCE (1827–1888)

THE CHOSEN PATH

PRAYER AND DESIRE

Blessed are they which do hunger and thirst after
righteousness: for they shall be filled.
MATTHEW 5:6 KJV

Desire is not merely a simple wish; it is a deep seated craving; an intense longing, for attainment. In the realm of spiritual affairs, it is an important adjunct to prayer. So important is it, that one might say, almost, that desire is an absolute essential of prayer. Desire precedes prayer, accompanies it, is followed by it. Desire goes before prayer, and by it, created and intensified. Prayer is the oral expression of desire. If prayer is asking God for something, then prayer must be expressed. Prayer comes out into the open. Desire is silent. Prayer is heard; desire, unheard. The deeper the desire, the stronger the prayer. Without desire, prayer is a meaningless mumble of words. Such perfunctory, formal praying, with no heart, no feeling, no real desire accompanying it, is to be shunned like a pestilence. Its exercise is a waste of precious time, and from it, no real blessing accrues. And yet even if it be discovered that desire is honestly absent, we should pray, anyway. We ought to pray. The "ought" comes in, in order that both desire and expression be cultivated. God's Word commands it. Our judgment tells us we ought to pray—to pray whether we feel like it or not—and not to allow our feelings to determine our habits of prayer. Lack of spiritual desire should grieve us, and lead us to lament its absence, to seek earnestly for its bestowal, so that our praying, henceforth, should be an expression of "the soul's sincere desire."

~E. M. BOUNDS (1835–1913)

THE CHOSEN PATH

WHAT NOT TO WEAR

*Now you're dressed in a new wardrobe. Every item of your new
way of life is custom-made by the Creator, with his label on it.
All the old fashions are now obsolete.*

COLOSSIANS 3:10 MSG

There is a reality television show called *What Not to Wear*. The
hosts of the show provide help for fashion misfits. Most of these people
don't know they have a problem. It is the same way with some believers,
still dressed in unrighteousness, having worn these clothes for so long,
they don't know that they look terrible. Could you be wearing clothing
that doesn't fit your lifestyle as a child of God? I had an old green Izod
shirt my wife begged me to get rid of, but it was hard even though it
didn't fit my lifestyle. In my spiritual closet, I have a couple green shirts
that also needed to be thrown out. How about you, what's in your
closet? On the show, the person must trade in their old clothes for a
whole new wardrobe. Their old clothes are put in the trash. Likewise,
our worldly clothes must be destroyed. But we get a whole new
wardrobe created by the famous designer: Jesus Christ. Dressed in these
new clothes, we can't help but to feel better. Trade your old wardrobe
and upgrade to holy designer fashions. Don't worry about the cost.
Jesus paid for you new clothes the same time He paid for your sins on
Calvary.

~TERRENCE ROBERTS (1964–) MERIDIAN, MS

THE CHOSEN PATH

THE DISEASE OF HYPOCRISY

Those that be planted in the house of the LORD
shall flourish in the courts of our God.

PSALM 92:13 KJV

Hypocrisy is a disease in the vitals of religion, which will consume all at length; it is a leak in the ship, that will certainly sink it. Sincerity of grace will make it lasting, be it never so weak; as the smallest twig, that is sound at the heart, will draw nourishment from the stock and grow, while the greatest bough that is rotten can never recover, because it receives no nourishment. Labor to be steadfast in the truths and way of God. A rolling stone gathers no moss, and a wavering judgment makes a fruitless life. Though a tree be never so sound, yet how can it grow, or be fruitful, if you be still removing it out of one soil into another? Endeavor to cut off the suckers, as gardeners do, that their trees may thrive. These are unmortified lusts; therefore "mortify your members that are upon the earth" (Colossians 3:5). When the Israelites got meat to their lusts, they got leanness to their souls. She that has many hungry children about her hand, and must be still putting into their mouths, will have much ado to get a bit put into her own. They must refuse the cravings of inordinate affections, who would have their souls to prosper. Improve, for these ends, the ordinances of God. The waters of the sanctuary are the means appointed of God, to cause His people to grow as willows by the water courses. Therefore drink in with "desire, the sincere milk of the word, that ye may grow thereby" (1 Pet. 2:2).

~THOMAS BOSTON (1676–1732)

SOUL WINNING (PART 1)

*Even the righteousness of God which is by faith of Jesus Christ unto
all and upon all them that believe: for there is no difference.*

ROMANS 3:22 KJV

He who is successful in soul-winning, will prove to have been a wise
man in the judgment of those who see the end as well as the beginning.
Even if I were utterly selfish, and had no care for anything but my own
happiness, I would choose, if I might, under God, to be a soul-winner,
for never did I know perfect, overflowing, unutterable happiness of the
purest and most ennobling order, till I first heard of one who had
sought and found a Savior through my means. I recollect the thrill of
joy which went through me! No young mother ever rejoiced so much
over her first-born child—no warrior was so exultant over a hard-won
victory. Oh! The joy of knowing that a sinner once at enmity has been
reconciled to God, by the Holy Spirit, through the words spoken by our
feeble lips. Let afflictions come, let trials be multiplied as God wills, still
this joy preponderates above all others, the joy that we are unto God a
sweet savor of Christ in every place, and that as often as we preach the
Word, hearts are unlocked, bosoms heave with a new life, eyes weep for
sin, and their tears are wiped away as they see the great Substitute for
sin, and live. Beyond all controversy, it is a joy worth worlds to win
souls, and, thank God, it is a joy that does not cease with this mortal life.
Are you a soul winner?

~C. H. SPURGEON (1834–1892)

THE CHOSEN PATH

SOUL WINNING (PART 2)

For all have sinned, and come short of the glory of God.

ROMANS 3:23 KJV

It must be no small bliss to hear, as one wings his flight up to the eternal throne, the wings of others fluttering at one's side towards the same glory, and turning round and questioning them, to hear them say, "We are entering with you through the gates of pearl; you brought us to the Savior." To be welcomed to the skies by those who call us father in God—father in better bonds than those of earth, father through grace and sire for immortality, it will be bliss beyond compare, to meet in you eternal seats with those begotten of us in Christ Jesus, for whom we travailed in birth, till Christ was formed in them the hope of glory. This is to have many heavens—a heaven in every one won for Christ; according to the Master's promise, "they that turn many to right- eousness, shall shine as the stars for ever and ever." The soul-winner must be a master of the art of prayer. You cannot bring souls to God if you go not to God yourself. You must get your battle-axe, and your weapons of war, from the armory of sacred communion with Christ. If you are much alone with Jesus, you will catch his Spirit; you will be fired with the flame that burned in his breast, and consumed his life. You will weep with the tears that fell upon Jerusalem when he saw it perishing, and if you cannot speak so eloquently as he did, yet shall there be about what you say somewhat of the same power which in him thrilled the hearts and awoke the consciences of men.

~C. H. SPURGEON (1834–1892)

SOUL WINNING (PART 3)

*Being justified freely by his grace through the
redemption that is in Christ Jesus . . .*

ROMANS 3:24 KJV

There are some of you—I bless you, and I bless God at the remembrance of you—who are in season, and out of season, in earliest for winning souls, and you are the truly wise: but I fear there are others whose hands are slack, who are satisfied to let me preach, but do not preach themselves; who take these seats, and occupy these pews, and hope the cause goes well, but that is all they do. Oh, do let me see you all in earnest! A great host of four thousand members—for that is now as nearly as possible the accurate counting of our numbers—what ought we not to do if we are all alive, and all in earnest! But such a host, without the spirit of enthusiasm, becomes a mere mob, an unwieldy mass, out of which mischief grows, and no good results arise. If you were all firebrands for Christ, you might set the nation on a blaze. If you were all wells of living water, how many thirsty souls might drink and be refreshed! "Are you saved?" for you can answer, "Ay, that I am, for it is written, 'He that believeth in him is not condemned.'" Trust him, then, trust him now, and then God help you to be a soul-winner, and you shall be wise, and God shall be glorified.

~C. H. SPURGEON (1834–1892)

THROUGH THE DARK TUNNEL

The water I shall give him will become in him a fountain
of water springing up into everlasting life.

JOHN 4:14 NKJV

When my father became a Christian at age forty-eight, he drank from the Living Water and jumped into the Lord's work with both feet. The professors who helped to shape my life became his mentors. I never dreamed my father would serve for twenty-five years in full-time ministry, write four books, and develop a ministry in Romania. The one thing my father feared most when I went to CIU was that I might become something gosh-awful like a missionary. Little did he know that he would be the missionary. Traveling with my dad to Romania to be a part of his ministry in 1998, the Lord impressed upon my heart that things were going to change. I did not know that those changes would be through a disease called Alzheimer's, which quickly diminished his brilliant mind and left him confused. For his family, especially my mother, the journey with this disease has been like going through a dark tunnel. You desperately want to see light at the end, but it's only another freight train coming. Although in the last few years, my father has not always known who we were, or who he was, he always lights up when he hears Christian music or hears the Lord's name. Although faint, the Living Water he first tasted remains. We yearn for the day when he is transformed to a new body and a renewed mind—on the other side. Drink freely from the Living Water while the day is young and spring to life everlasting. You will never thirst again.

~GINNY DENT BRANT (1955–) SENECA, SC

THE UNITY OF THE FAMILY (PART 1)

Likewise, ye husbands, dwell with them according to knowledge,
giving honour unto the wife, as unto the weaker vessel, and as being
heirs together of the grace of life; that your prayers be not hindered.

1 PETER 3:7 KJV

I'd like to take our thoughts back to something that is of an extreme importance: THE UNIT OF THE FAMILY. You don't ignore that today there are a lot of different elements against the family and its integrity. Shortening its dimensions, every day loosening its stability, more and more abdicating its functions and institutionalizing it, to watch the woman's emancipation as more important than her maternal job in favor of her ostensive presence in the society, having the media to absorb precious time that should be dedicated to the communication and dialog, the family is been disintegrated, disunited, weak on the accomplishment of its functions. Jesus Christ said about this: "Wherefore they are no more twain, but one flesh. What therefore God hath joined together let not man put asunder," which is according with the institution of the family, of the marital society, when God spoke: "and they shall be one flesh." The spiritual and moral fellowship, with the similarities of the sexes and its complimentaries, but each one exercising different functions. You and I need to be perceptive of the Will of God about our families. More love, more time to the communication between husband and wife, parents and kids, even if you have to turn off the TV or radio for some hours; the prayer in family, the recreation in family, the study of the necessities of the family, all of this will definitely contribute to make our family united and happy. Where is your family tonight?

~WILLIAN WOJCICKI (1957–) SÃO PAULO, BRAZIL

THE UNITY OF THE FAMILY (PART 2)

Likewise, ye husbands, dwell with them according to knowledge,
giving honour unto the wife, as unto the weaker vessel, and as being
heirs together of the grace of life; that your prayers be not hindered.

1 PETER 3:7 KJV

United and adjusted, the family will accomplish the procreated function, educational, economical, and spiritual, forming men and women of good will, for the construction of a better world, because we know that the world will be happier, when "Yea, though I walk through the valley of the shadow of death, I will fear no evil: for thou art with me; thy rod and thy staff they comfort me" (Psalm 23:4 KJV). The families that live here are more united and more happy. Whatever kind of family that you have, big or small, rich or poor, whatever are the problems that you are having right now, please know that God wants your family to be united. Renounce, forgive, understand, help, be patient, be an important factor in the fellowship of your family. Martin Luther said, "You can not put your faith in your pockets." The same way, the family can not be hiding, because it reflects the Light of Christ.

~**WILLIAN WOJCICKI (1957–) SÃO PAULO, BRAZIL**

COME, YOUR HEART AND VOICES RAISING

Come, your hearts and voices raising,
Christ the Lord with gladness praising;
Loudly sing His love amazing,
Worthy folk of Christendom.
Sin and death may well be groaning,
Satan now may well be moaning;
We, our full salvation owning, cast our every care away.
See how God, for us providing, gave His Son and life abiding;
He our weary steps is guiding from earth's woe to heavenly joy.
Christ, from heaven to us descending
And in love our race befriending,
In our need His help extending, saved us from the wily Foe.
Jacob's Star in all its splendor beams with comfort sweet and tender,
Forcing Satan to surrender, breaking all the powers of hell.
From the bondage that oppressed us,
From sin's fetters that possessed us,
From the grief that sore distressed us, we, the captives, now are free.
Oh, the joy beyond expressing when by faith we grasp this blessing
And to Thee we come confessing,
That our freedom thou hast wrought!
Gracious Child, we pray Thee, hear us,
From Thy lowly manger cheer us,
Gently lead us and be near us
Till we join the angelic choir.

~PAUL GERHARDT (1607–1676)

DISCOVERING THE TRUTH

*Let your light shine before men, that they may see
your good deeds and praise your Father in heaven.*

MATTHEW 5:16 NIV

My Internet church can be very frustrating. Like all pastors, I feel the inspired need to deliver the good news of Jesus Christ. Unlike land-based pastors, however, I have little contact with my parishioners. Except for prayer requests and spiritual counsel, I rarely hear from those who come to visit or worship at www.godfocus.net. We offer all the basic services: worship services with music, prayer and good sermons; an intercessory prayer list; various informational pages; and religious education. But I get very few pats on the back or anyone coming to me after the service saying, "That was a good service pastor." On the surface, it appears that my Internet church is a combination of service and important lessons in humility. My job is to keep the church filled with ministry, which is then used as needed by those who visit. One day I was particularly down and feeling unappreciated. Then it all came together and I saw the truth in a very clear light. I knew that my Internet church was inspired by God as an answer to my prayers because chronic illness prevented me from doing little else. Yet, there was something deeper and richer that embraced me. You see, pastoring this Internet church was a personal gift from God to me. Rather than letting me feel useless, worthless, and negative, He gave me something that would give my life meaning. And it has. I thought it was just a way for me to minister. But I found out it was really God ministering to me.

DAVID SCHOLTON (1951–) SANFORD, NC

TRUE AND FALSE REPENTANCE

*For godly sorrow worketh repentance to salvation not to be
repented of: but the sorrow of the world worketh death.*

2 CORINTHIANS 7:10 KJV

A person may see sin to be hurtful and abominable, while yet his
heart loves it, and desires it, and clings to it. But when he truly repents,
he most heartily abhors and renounces it. In relation to God, he feels
towards sin as it really is. And here is the source of those gushings of
sorrow in which Christians sometimes break out, when contemplating
sin. The Christian views it as to its nature, and simply feels abhorrence.
But when he views it in relation to God, then he weeps; the fountains of
his sorrow gush forth, and he wants to get right down on his face and
pour out a flood of tears over his sins. Then as to the tendencies of sin,
the individual who truly repents feels it as it is. When he views sin in its
tendencies, it awakens a vehement desire to stop it, and to save people
from their sins, and roll back the tide of death. It sets his heart on fire,
and he goes to praying, and laboring, and pulling sinners out of the fire
with all his might, to save them from the awful tendencies of sin. When
the Christian sets his mind on this, he will bestir himself to make
people give up their sins. And when he thinks of such a sinner being
saved, he feels a sense of gratitude that he never knew anything of till
he was a Christian.

~CHARLES FINNEY (1792–1875)

RESTING IN THE ARMS OF JESUS

Take my yoke upon you.
MATTHEW 11:29 KJV

Life sometimes gives us reasons to ask God why. Standing with my best friend and his family as his first-born child took her last breath, tears streaming down our cheeks, I assured him she is resting in the arms of Jesus. He responded, "I know. I am too." To have the assurance that Jesus loves us so much that He helps us in our most difficult times is a concept that nonbelievers find hard to embrace. But He does. My friend said, "I know, pastor, but it is hard. But I know that He will help me through this." When things are too hard for us is when Jesus wants us to come to Him. He said, "I will give you rest." The arms of Jesus are not only open to us in death, but they are open right now to help us through all times. Believers have a unique opportunity to be testimonies to onlookers who have not accepted Christ as Savior and Lord. We can demonstrate that as we face life. Jesus cares. The question should not be, "God, why?" but rather, "God, why not?" What better place can one be than in the arms of Jesus? To find rest is to know security. We can be confident that He is in control of all that is going on around us. Jesus said learn of Me for My yoke is easy and My burdens are light. He is more than the world against us. When you find yourself facing a situation that is too much to bear, take it to Jesus in prayer. He will help you and give you rest for your soul.

~D. D. ALEXANDER (1945–) INGLEWOOD, CA

HOLINESS

The benefit you reap leads to holiness, and the result is eternal life.

ROMANS 6:22 NIV

Set free! What does that mean? When someone releases a helium balloon, what happens? The balloon goes up. It tosses and turns with the directions of the wind. Sometimes whipping to the left, sometimes floating to the right, but it is free to be directed in any direction it is pushed. We, too, have that freedom in Christ when we are set free. Some choose paths that hide their freedom. Some become servants to unhealthy things. But some become slaves to God. That is the difference between people and a balloon. We choose. We decide what we will allow to push us in the direction we go. Now that we have been freed from sin, we chose to become slaves. This seems like the opposite of what we would want to do, but Jesus said in Matthew, "Anyone who does not take his cross and follow me is not worthy of me." Choosing to become a slave to God reaps holiness. Holiness defined is belonging to God and consecrated to His service. Personal holiness is a work of gradual development. It is carried on under many obstacles, which is why we are frequently told to be watchful, to pray, and to endure. How do we pursue holiness? We pursue in three ways. The first is inwardly. We do this by choosing what we are putting into our heart and mind. Next we pursue outwardly by what we allow to come out. Lastly we focus upwardly in how much we are giving back to the Lord. As you live your day today, evaluate how you are pursuing holiness in these three ways.

~TODD FUEHRER (1967–) BISMARCK, ND

THE CHOSEN PATH

NO NEED TO FEAR (PART 1)

"Peace I leave with you."
JOHN 14:27 HCSB

It was about 125 miles from my home to my grandparent's house in Opelika, AL. In the '50s, we drove several times a year to visit them. We would leave the mountains of North, AL, and travel to the flatter, southern part of the state. Certain landmarks still stand out in my mind today. One-of-a-kind independently owned motels were scattered along the way. Little towns, with their unique characteristics, grabbed my attention and I would look at the residents and wonder what they were doing as they moved about. Kudzu, not yet so common in my part of the state and still fairly new to the South, was establishing itself to become "part" of the South. It added to the mystery this part of the state offered me. My grandparents lived in a small, four-room house located on a busy highway in Opelika. At night, when the flow of traffic became irregular, I would lay in the bed, staring into the dark, and listen for the next automobile to come by. I would hear the faint sound of the engine in the distance accompanied by the airy *swish* sound as it cut through the air. The cement highway caused a *thump-thump, thump-thump* sound as the tires rolled along their path. The sounds grew louder and louder as it approached, then would fade just as quickly into the darkness. Have you ever experienced sounds while in the dark that only Christ could make sense of? He promised to never leave nor forsake us. He was with me that night.

~RANDOLPH (RANDY) ALAN MCCOLLUM (1952–) BLOOMINGTON, IN

NO NEED TO FEAR (PART 2)

"Peace I leave with you."
JOHN 14:27 HCSB

Do you find the mysteries of life threatening you? Have you looked more into the darkness of the future of circumstance rather than the bright way of God's future? Proverbs 3:6 teaches us that when we remember to acknowledge God in all the ways of our lives, He will make our paths straight. Jesus knew of the threat the world offer His disciples after when He was taken from them. He told them, "Peace I leave with you. My peace I give to you. I do not give to you as the world gives. Your heart must not be troubled or fearful" (John 14:27 HCSB). His peace is sufficient for all circumstances in life. It is sufficient throughout the ages, regardless of the problem we face. It's a matter of our willingness to trust in Him.

~RANDOLPH (RANDY) ALAN MCCOLLUM (1952–) BLOOMINGTON, IN

WHY CHRISTIANS PERSEVERE

God is faithful, by whom ye were called unto the
fellowship of his Son Jesus Christ our Lord.

1 CORINTHIANS 1:9 KJV

In what the Lord has done, we see strong reasons for our preservation and future glory, because the Lord has called us into the fellowship of His Son, Jesus Christ. It means into partnership with Jesus Christ, and I would have you carefully consider what this means. If you are indeed called by divine grace, you have come into fellowship with the Lord Jesus Christ, so as to be joint-owner with Him in all things. Henceforth, you are one with Him in the sight of the Most High. The Lord Jesus bore your sins in His own body on the tree, being made a curse for you; and at the same time, He has become your righteousness, so that you are justified in Him. You are Christ's and Christ is yours. As Adam stood for his descendants, so does Jesus stand for all who are in Him. More than this, believers are members of the Body of Christ, and so are one with Him by a loving, living, lasting union. God has called us into this union, this fellowship, this partnership, and by this very fact He has given us the token and pledge of our being confirmed to the end. If we were considered apart from Christ, we should be poor perishable units, soon dissolved and borne away to destruction; but as one with Jesus, we are made partakers of His nature, and are endowed with His immortal life. Our destiny is linked with that of our Lord, and until He can be destroyed, it is not possible that we should perish.

~C. H. SPURGEON (1834–1892)

THE CHOSEN PATH

JESUS ASSUMED WE WOULD GO

FROM MATTHEW 28:16–20 NKJV

Of all the commissioning passages in the four Gospels and the book of Acts, this is perhaps the best known and often referred to as the Great Commission. In this passage, the Lord Jesus Christ is standing on the Mount of Ascension, about to return to His Father in heaven. While many worshiped, some still doubted that Jesus was indeed the Christ, the Son of the living God. When Jesus commissioned His followers, He sent them with His authority and promised them His abiding presence. His commission was very specific, and often seems to be somewhat misunderstood. First, Jesus did not command His followers to go. He said to them, "As you go . . ." Jesus assumed His followers would go with the good news of salvation. If you count yourself as one of His followers, are you "going" with the good news? Second, Jesus did not instruct His followers to get anyone to "make a decision for Christ." Rather, He commanded them to "make disciples," that is, students who would make their life's calling loving Jesus Christ and being made like Him. Third, Jesus described the course of a disciple. A disciple is to be baptized into the name of God the Father, Jesus Christ the Son and the Holy Spirit. Have you confessed faith in Jesus Christ and submitted to believers' baptism? Then Jesus commands that all who will be His followers will submit themselves with a teachable spirit to the serious study of "all things" that Jesus has commanded. Does that describe you? Are you a serious student of the Scriptures? Do you longingly desire to be like Jesus Christ? Are you spending your life for Him? Can you honestly say that you are His disciple?

~BILL ASCOL (1952–) SHREVEPORT, LA

ARE YOU TRULY COME UNTO CHRIST?

Come unto me, all ye that labour and
are heavy laden, and I will give you rest.

MATTHEW 11:28 KJV

Matthew 11:28 contains a gracious invitation, made by the compassionate Savior to a particular class of sinners. The "all" is at once qualified, clearly and definitely, by the words which immediately follow it. The character of those to whom this loving word belongs is clearly defined: It is those who "labor" and are "heavy laden." Most clearly then it applies not to the vast majority of our light-headed, gay-hearted, pleasure-seeking fellows who have no regard for God's glory and no concern about their eternal welfare. No, the word for such poor creatures is rather, "Rejoice, O young man, in thy youth, and let thy heart cheer thee in the days of thy youth, and walk in the ways of thine heart, and in the sight of thine eyes; but know thou, that for all these things God will bring thee to judgment" (Eccl. 11:9). But to those who have "labored" hard to keep the law and please God, who are "heavy laden" with a felt sense of their utter inability to meet His requirements, and who long to be delivered from the power and pollution of sin, Christ says, "Come unto Me, and I will give you rest."

~A. W. PINK (1886–1952)

KEYS FOR SUCCESSFUL FAMILIES

FROM PSALM 127

God must be a participant in the family building process, but we must work at it also. We are laborers together with God. Watching out for our family members is part of the process. We need to know that when our family goes its several ways each day, and when we sleep each night, God is watching, sometimes called Jehovah-roi, the God who sees me. You will not find what you're looking for until you seek to live a life that pleases God. He gives rest to those who are in a love relationship with him! Each of us has the responsibility to try to leave the world a better place than it was when we entered it. Each of us has something unique to offer. There is no waiting for such a task and there is no retirement from such a task. Look beyond the time-oriented surface to glimpse the eternal truth. What can we learn about Arrows & Warriors that we can use? The warrior cares for the arrows. He keeps them sharp, clean, ready, and available. The warrior sends the arrows at an appointed time, in a definite direction and toward a definite goal. Every member of the family must be encouraged to define their dreams, determine their destiny, herald their hopes and grasp their goals. There is a Family where you can find faithful brothers and encouraging sisters everywhere you go. There is a Father who is patient and loving, who will always work to get the best out of you and who will never let you struggle alone. I'm talking about the Family of God. Why not go to Church this Sunday!

~MARK A. CROSTON, SR. (1959–) SUFFOLK, VA

PSALM 127

The Blessing of the Lord

Unless the LORD builds a house,
its builders labor over it in vain;
unless the LORD watches over a city,
the watchman stays alert in vain.

In vain you get up early and stay up late,
working hard to have enough food—
He gives sleep to the one He loves.
Yes, Sons are indeed a heritage
from the LORD, children, a reward.

Like arrows in the hand of a warrior
are the sons born in one's youth.

Happy is the man who has filled his quiver with them.

Such men will never be put to shame when
they speak with their enemies at the city gate.

HCSB

HUNGERING AND THIRSTING

"Blessed are those who hunger and thirst for
righteousness, for they will be filled."

Matthew 5:6 niv

Let's look at hunger and thirst. They are the most sensitive physical appetites. Sometimes we can be so thirsty that we feel hungry. When you are hungry and thirsty, you are not contented, happy or comfortable. Your stomach growls, you get headaches, some people get very grouchy. When looking at hungering and thirsting for righteousness, ONLY righteousness will satisfy. We are so busy in our lives that sometimes we neglect to feed ourselves righteousness. If you think you are feeding yourself righteousness, what is your lunch schedule like? Do you take the time to sit down and eat lunch? Do you even eat lunch? If you are not feeding your physical body properly, how can you say that you are feeding your spirit enough righteousness? How does a hungry and thirsty person act? They are alertly looking for food and drink. They are not indifferent. They are focused on their need. As believers, we hunger and thirst for God and the things of God. We do this in His Word, in prayer, and in regular fellowship. Hungry people are not finicky about what they eat. This needs to be the desire for our soul. We need to devour everything from the Word of God. They are not concerned about the condition of the eating establishment. You never see a truly hungry or thirsty person complain about the serving pieces or the restaurant. Hunger always seeks the object of worship, not the means. Are you hungry and thirsty for righteousness?

~Todd Fuehrer (1967–) Bismarck, ND

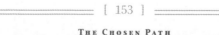

LORD . . . ?

"Lord, save us: we perish."
MATTHEW 8:25 KJV

The wind, as boisterous and blustering as it sometimes is, was more obedient to the command of God than the prophet. He says to one wind, "Go," and it goes; and to another, "Come," and it cometh. He makes use of them to various ends and purposes. Sometimes in a way of mercy, as when he made a wind to pass over the earth, and the waters of the flood were assuaged; when there went forth a wind from the Lord, and brought quails from the sea, and let them fall by the camp of the Israelites for their food and refreshment; when the wind brought up a great rain, after the land of Israel had been without one for three years and a half; when the Lord caused the sea to go back, by a strong east wind all night, and made the sea a dry land, and the waters were divided, so that the Israelites could pass through as on dry land. And sometimes he uses them in a way of judgment; as when he did blow with his wind, the sea covered them, the Egyptians; they sunk as lead in the mighty water. But, whether it be in one way or another, he makes use of them, the stormy wind is fulfilling his word, either of promise or command; for it is always at his beck. However, certain it is, God has the sole power of raising and laying the wind.

~JOHN GILL (1697–1771)

LORD, TEACH US

Lord, teach us to pray.

LUKE 11:1 KJV

Fellow Christians, let us awake! The devil is blinding our eyes. He is endeavoring to prevent us from facing this question of prayer. Do we realize that there is nothing the devil dreads so much as prayer? His great concern is to keep us from praying. He loves to see us "up to our eyes" in work, provided we do not pray. He does not fear because we are eager and earnest Bible students, provided we are little in prayer. Someone has wisely said, "Satan laughs at our toiling, mocks at our wisdom, but trembles when we pray." All this is so familiar to us, but do we really pray? If not, then failure must dog our footsteps, whatever signs of apparent success there may be. Let us never forget that the greatest thing we can do for God or for man is to pray. For we can accomplish far more by our prayers than by our work. Prayer is omnipotent; it can do anything that God can do! When we pray God works. All fruitfulness in service is the outcome of prayer, of the worker's prayers, or of those who are holding up holy hands on his behalf. We all know how to pray, but perhaps many of us need to cry as the disciples did of old, "Lord, teach us to pray."

~UNKNOWN CHRISTIAN

CALL THE DESIGNER

In the beginning was the Word, and the Word
was with God, and the Word was God.

JOHN 1:1 NIV

John makes no qualms about it: Jesus is God. Genesis begins, "In the beginning God created the heavens and the earth." John begins, "In the beginning was the Word; and the Word was with God, and the Word was God. He was with God in the beginning. All things were created through Him, and apart from Him not one thing was created that has been created" (HCSB). The similarities are not by chance. John goes to great length in this gospel account to teach the readers that Jesus is God. He is the God of creation, the God of nature, the God over sickness, death, and disease, the God of life—He is the God of salvation. A friend had trouble with a Ford Mustang. He brought it in for service and it never ran the same. Though it was "souped up" from the factory and had a turbo-charger, it was now sluggish and lacked power. After weeks of maintenance at the dealership with no success, Ford finally sent a representative (a designer of the turbo-charger installed) all the way to Meridian, Mississippi, to look at it. As soon as he lifted the hood, he saw it, "That's not my hose," he said. A vacuum hose was accidentally replaced during service on the turbo-charger. It looked similar but it did not allow the proper flow for optimum performance. The mechanic changed it and "viola," all was well. Jesus is our designer and creator. He created us for good works (Ephesians 2:10)—optimum performance. Whatever your trouble, look to your designer first.

~JOE JONES (1964–) GOODYEAR, AZ

LETTING GO AND HOLDING ON

I thank my God upon every remembrance of you.
PHILIPPIANS 1:3 KJV

There they were on our front street: two wooden crates, each one four feet wide, seven feet long, and seven feet high, planted firmly on the bed of the Mayflower Moving and Storage truck, their mouths wide and gaping with great appetite, eager to be stuffed and crammed with the worldly possessions that we, as newly appointed missionaries, would be taking to France. And there we were, my wife and I, like two wooden statues, our mouths wide and gaping with no appetite, unbelieving . . . the crates looked so small. They were. And as we stood there, bewildered, wondering how it could all possibly fit, the veteran Mover and Crater put his hand on my shoulder and said, "Now don't you worry about how all of this stuff will fit in the crates. No need to worry, 'cause THERE AIN'T NO WAY ALL THIS STUFF IS GONNA FIT! So just eliminate some of it. But don't worry. It's just stuff." His advice seemed almost scriptural. So we eliminated about one-third of those "bare necessities." It took a bit of time and tears, but we let go, and we went to France. But isn't it wonderful that in the "letting go" periods of our lives, we never have to let go of people, only things . . . stuff. Because distance and even death may physically separate us from those we love, but the Spirit of Christ keeps us together in a bond of love that transcends time and space. And then we can truly say with Paul, "I thank my God upon every remembrance of you."

~ROY MILLER (1935–) WHEAT RIDGE, CO

THE CHOSEN PATH

SUPPER

And the servant said, Lord, it is done as thou hast commanded,
and yet there is room. And the lord said unto the servant,
Go out into the highways and hedges, and compel them to come in,
that my house may be filled. For I say unto you, That none of
those men which were bidden shall taste of my supper.

LUKE 14:22–24 KJV

"Come," repent and believe the gospel. Nothing is required on man's part, but to come, or accept of the gospel offer. It is not according to the old covenant, "Do and live," but only "come, believe, and thou shalt be saved." All things are ready. Nothing is wanting on God's part. "All things are now ready." There seems to be a particular emphasis to be put upon now, implying, this was an especial season of grace, and God was now exerting his last efforts, to save lost man. Well then, if the great God be at so great an expense, to make so great a supper, for perishing creatures, and sends so great a person as his own Son, in the form of a servant, to invite them to come to it; one would imagine, that all who heard these glad tidings, should readily say, "Lord, lo we come." The parable therefore speaks to saints as well as sinners. Come ye to the marriage-feast, you are as welcome now as ever. And may God set your souls a longing for that time when we shall sit down and eat bread in the kingdom of heaven! There we shall have full draughts of divine love, and enjoy the glorious Emanuel for ever more. Even so, Lord Jesus, Amen.

~GEORGE WHITEFIELD (1714–1770)

THE CHOSEN PATH

GUIDED TO SAFE PLACES

You will be secure, because there is hope;
you will look about you and take your rest in safety.

JOB 11:18 NIV

I was about thirteen with many tree climbing years under my belt. The number of trees I had climbed in my vast experience was beyond calculation. Seldom had I made a mistake. But this time, I had slipped up. I was hanging by my arms, out on a limb about thirty feet from the ground. Carelessness had put me there. Many attempts to get back to safety had not helped. With energy quickly draining, I was about to give up hope. Looking down I thought, *That's not so far. I could probably drop right to the ground.* Then, out of nowhere I heard a strong voice. "You better not jump from there." Again it spoke, "You better not jump from there." Hearing it renewed my strength and determination. Again I began to swing back and forth trying to pull myself to safety. Finally making it, I stood up on the limb with a smile. Looking across the way, I saw my neighbor, Mr. Barger. It was his voice I had heard. It had probably been a long time since he had climbed a tree. Seeing my dilemma, he stepped up at the right time to warn me of the danger. God is like that. He lets us grow by making decisions. When we make bad decisions, He warns us. Through His Son, He has experienced the temptations of life. He understands our weaknesses. He offers His wisdom and His strength to guide us. He sends His messengers just at the right time. If we are willing to listen, it will renew my strength and determination, guiding us to safety.

~RANDOLPH (RANDY) ALAN McCOLLUM (1952–) BLOOMINGTON, IN

IT IS THE WILL OF THE FATHER THAT MATTERS

It is not of him that willeth, nor of him that
runneth, but of God that sheweth mercy.

ROMANS 9:16 KJV

Is it the Christian's strength in the Lord, not in himself? Surely then the Christless person must needs be a poor impotent creature, void of all strength and ability of doing anything of itself towards its own salvation. If the ship launched, rigged, and with her sails spread cannot stir, till the wind come fair and fill them, much less the timber that lies in the carpenter's yard hew and frame itself into a ship. If the living tree cannot grow except the root communicate its sap, much less can a dead rotten stake in the hedge, which hath no root, live of its own accord. In a word, if a Christian, that hath his spiritual life of grace, cannot exercise this life without strength from above, then surely one void of this new life, dead in sins and trespasses, can never be able to beget this in himself, or concur to the production of it. The state of unregeneracy is a state of impotency. And as Christ found the lump of mankind covered with the ruins of their lapsed estate (no more able to raise themselves from under the weight of God's wrath which lay upon them, than one buried under the rubbish of a fallen house is to free himself of that weight without help), so the Spirit finds sinners in as helpless a condition, as unable to repent, or believe on Christ for salvation, as they were of themselves to purchase it. If any man would have strength to believe, let them become weak, and die to their own, for, "by strength shall no man prevail," 1 Samuel 2:9.

~**WILLIAM GURNALL (1617–1679)**

HOLD YOUR TONGUE

Remind them to be subject to rulers and authorities, to obey,
to be ready for every good work, to speak evil of no one,
to be peaceable, gentle, showing all humility to all men.

TITUS 3:1–2 NKJV

Paul had a lot to say about everyday things in this letter to Titus. He gave Titus good advice about relationships, homes, families, and employment. But one message that seems to be constant throughout this letter is "hold your tongue." He speaks of idle talk (1:10), slander (2:3, 3:2), talking back (2:9), and foolish debates (3:9). Our tongues play an important part in our lives! Any relationship can be strained or fractured by our words. The old adage "sticks and stones may break my bones, but words will never hurt me" is not really true. The truth is—words hurt! As Christians, we must exercise caution with our tongues. Technology has made it increasingly easy to practice slander. If you have e-mail, surely you have received wild claims about someone. This is especially true during election seasons. More often than not, the claims are untrue. And when we click "forward to all" without checking the facts, we become slanderers ourselves. Slander is communicating false or misrepresented charges that hurt or defame another. It is not limited to the spoken word. Paul also warns against "talking back." This applies to us being good employees. We are not to be the difficult employee, but rather the employee that works as unto the Lord. Nor are we to be a person who is simply impossible to get along with. Commit today that you will not participate in slander, idle talk, or any sort of foolishness involving your tongue, but rather praise others on any occasion that arises.

~JOE JONES (1964–) GOODYEAR, AZ

ARE YOU READY?

. . . kept by the power of God through faith unto salvation
ready to be revealed in the last time.

1 PETER 1:5 KJV

We are thankful for a free gospel and an open Bible. But we cannot shut our eyes to the fact that there is a fearful amount of laxity, unsubduedness, and self-indulgence going hand-in-hand with the evangelical profession of the day. We notice with the deepest anxiety, many young professors who have, or seem to have, a very clear insight, so far as the intellect goes, into the truth of the sinner's title, who, if we are to judge from their style, deportment, and habits, are not "ready" in their moral condition—in the real state of their hearts. We are at times, we must confess, sadly cast down when we see our young friends decking their persons in the vain fashions of a vain and sinful world; feeding upon the vile literature that issues in such frightful profusion from the press; and actually singing vain songs and engaging in light and frivolous conversation. It is impossible to reconcile such with "Be ye also ready."

~R. M. McCheyne (1813–1843)

WHOSE RULES?

The Law and the Prophets were proclaimed until John.
Since that time, the good news of the kingdom of God
is being preached, and everyone is forcing his way into it.

LUKE 16:16 NIV

People like to "write their own rules." Have you ever seen two children playing? They make up rules as they go, changing them to suit the situation. We are not very different from children! We may say it in differently, but it adds up to the same thing. Some may say, "If it feels right, do it," or "What is true for you might not be true for me." Basically, we are changing the rules to suit ourselves. Jesus states that the law had been preached up until John's time—and the law was still true. Many people today try to say that the Bible was written thousands of years ago, and that it does not apply to us today. Jesus made His point, though, with a subject that is still in question today—marriage. Jesus pointed out that divorce was sin. The scripture does make allowance for remarriage in the cases of adultery, abandonment by a non-believing spouse, or death of a spouse. But the Jewish society had come to the place where frivolous divorce was very common and Jesus used it as an example. The same is true today. No matter what the U.S. Supreme courts, Congress, or the president himself says, marriage is defined by God and dictated by His unchanging law. But Jesus was not just referring to God's law in relationship to marriage, but to the whole law. It is God's law, not our morals that must dictate our actions. Our morals are far too unreliable, but God's law will never fail.

~JOE JONES (1964–) GOODYEAR, AZ

BELIEVERS WILL GROW LIKE WILLOWS

Those that be planted in the house of the
LORD shall flourish in the courts of our God.

PSALM 92:13 KJV

There is nothing more distressing in our day than the lack of growth among the children of God. They do not seem to press forward. They do not seem to be running a race. How different in the New Testament when the Spirit is poured out! They shall be like willows. You have seen the willow, how it grows, ceases not day or night, ever growing, ever shooting out new branches. Cut it down, it springs again. So you would you be, dear Christians, if there were a flood time of the Spirit, a day of Pentecost. What would change you if this flood time came? There would be less care about your business and your workshop, more prayer and praises. There would be more change in your heart, victory over the world, the devil, and the flesh. There is no greater joy than for a believing soul to give himself all to God. This has always been the way in times of refreshing. It was so at Pentecost. I can claim no right to myself, in this understanding, this will, these affections. Neither have I right to this body, or any of its members, no right to this tongue, these hands, these feet, these eyes, these ears. I have given myself clean away. Oh! would that you knew the joy of giving yourself away. You cannot keep yourself. This day try and give all to Him. Lie in His hand, little children! I wish that you would become like him who said, "I am God's boy altogether, mother!" Write on your hand: "I am the Lord's."

~R. M. McCheyne (1813–1843)

MY PROTECTOR

So the great dragon was cast out, that serpent of old,
called the Devil and Satan, who deceives the whole world.

REVELATION 12:9 NKJV

One lovely spring morning as I sat on our deck having my quiet time, a tiny baby bird jumped out of the tree and fell three feet in front of me. He seemed so confident and happy to be out of his nest and on a new journey. Chirping was heard from "Dad and Mom" as they called to their little one. While I watched absolutely still and quiet, the little bird hopped from the deck toward the chirping. All of a sudden the chirping became louder and more intense as the little bird continued his hopping toward the beckoning calls. I no longer saw the little bird that was engulfed by the azaleas. Here and there the parent birds flew in panic trying to tell their little one something very important. Not knowing bird language, I couldn't imagine what they were trying to say. I whispered to myself, "You better go see if you can help that little bird." While I parted the azaleas to see where the little bird was, my fear instinct caused me to stop. There, curled up with his new meal in his mouth was a huge black snake. Running back to the safety of the deck I kept watching the poor "Mom" and "Dad" birds fruitlessly trying to "fight" the determined predator—then silence. How sad! That poor little bird had no idea of the danger he encountered. Thank You, Lord, for overcoming that ancient serpent, and daily protecting Your children.

~JOYCE CARPENTER (1931–) SENECA, SC

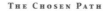

WHAT ARE YOU DOING
FOR HEAVEN'S SAKE?

FROM ACTS 1:6–11 NKJV

All of us to want to know the future. When faced with major life decisions, we want to know how everything will turn out before we make our choices. The same is true about the Second Coming of Jesus Christ. Just before ascending, Jesus told His disciples there were some things about the future that were not for them to know. He went on to tell them two things that they did need to know. First, they needed to know the Holy Spirit would be powerfully given to them. When this happened (Acts 2), the same timid people who had been praying in the Upper Room came out and spoke with boldness. In the same way, we must trust the Lord, Who gave us His Holy Spirit when He saved us, to fill us and empower us to witness for Him. Second, they needed to know that they would be His witnesses "in Jerusalem, and in all Judea and Samaria, and to the end of the earth." He did not say that they might be His witnesses. He said, "You shall be witnesses to Me." The book of Acts tells us that they did not act immediately or even voluntarily on this fact. Rather, they mostly stayed in Jerusalem (where they were faithful in their gospel witness) and it was not until the church came under great persecution (Acts 8:4) that those who were scattered by the persecution went everywhere preaching the gospel. Have you ever wondered what God will have to do to get us looking outside ourselves (or "beyond our own noses") to see the multiplied millions of people around the world dying apart from Jesus Christ?

~BILL ASCOL (1952–) SHREVEPORT, LA

PRESSING ON

(PHILIPPIANS 3)

I'm pressing on to the upward call
I'm pressing on He's my all and all
I'm pressing on to higher ground
I'm pressing on, I'm pressing on, I'm pressing on

Just let my mind be of Christ alone
To humble myself, yield to Him always
Let me exalt Him, let me bow my knee
I'm pressing on, I'm pressing on, I'm pressing on

I want my light to twinkle bright for Him
In this old world sick and full of sin
Holding high the word of truth and life
I'm pressing on, I'm pressing on, I'm pressing on

That I may know Him makes my heart rejoice
Resurrection power is my strength and source
Standing fast in one spirit and mind
I'm pressing on, I'm pressing on, I'm pressing on

I've got a goal to become like Him
I'll run this race right to the very end
Doing all through Christ who strengthens me
I'm pressing on, I'm pressing on, I'm pressing on

Have not laid hold of everything just yet
One thing I know I must forget
The past and press toward the upward call
I'm pressing on, praise be to God, I'm pressing on

~LINDA SMITH (1948–) SENECA, SC

THE CHOSEN PATH

THE SIMPLICITY OF GOD

These things have I written unto you that believe on the name of
the Son of God; that ye may know that ye have eternal life,
and that ye may believe on the name of the Son of God.

1 JOHN 5:13 KJV

The nature of God, comprising his essence and his attributes, is simple or uncompounded pure spirit. It means more than his unity, for the latter expresses only the fact that there is but one being, that is, God. Were God both matter arid spirit, or compounded in any other way, His unity would not be affected. Were there but one man in the world, we should ascribe to him unity, and if there could be but one, we should ascribe essential unity. It means more than the spirituality of God, for that includes only that He must be spiritual, and, also, as we have seen, that He should be purely spiritual. But there is nothing contradictory in the idea, that created spirits might have a composite spiritual nature, composed, for example, of mind, soul and spirit, as three distinct essences, or that a spiritual nature should have a spiritual body, as well as a spiritual soul. But in God there can be no composition, and therefore His spiritual nature must be uncompounded. Even His attributes and His nature must be in such a manner one, that His attributes essentially inhere in that nature and are not capable of separation from it, which really makes them one with that nature.

~J. P. BOYCE (1827–1888)

THE CHOSEN PATH

WE ARE IN CHRIST, BUT ABIDING?

He is the source of your life in Christ Jesus, whom God made our wisdom,
our righteousness and sanctification and redemption.

1 CORINTHIANS 1:30 RSV

Would you know how Christ can become our righteousness, and our sanctification, and redemption? It is just as bringing, and revealing, and communicating these that He is made unto us wisdom from God. There are a thousand questions that at times come up, and the attempt to answer them becomes a weariness and a burden. It is because you have forgotten you are in Christ, whom God has made to be your wisdom. Let it be your first care to abide in Him in undivided fervent devotion of heart; when the heart and the life are right, rooted in Christ, knowledge will come in such measure as Christ's own wisdom sees meet. And without such abiding in Christ, the knowledge does not really profit, but is often most hurtful. The soul satisfies itself with thoughts which are but the forms and images of truth, without receiving the truth itself in its power. God's way is ever first to give us, even though it be but as a seed, the thing itself, the life and the power, and then the knowledge. Man seeks the knowledge first, and often, alas, never gets beyond it. God gives us Christ, and in Him hid the treasures of wisdom and knowledge. O let us be content to possess Christ, to dwell in Him, to make Him our life, and only in a deeper searching into Him, to search and find the knowledge we desire. Such knowledge is life indeed.

~ANDREW MURRAY (1828–1917)

REMEMBER LOT'S WIFE

Remember Lot's wife.

LUKE 17:32 KJV

I ask the children of religious parents to mark well what I am saying. It is the highest privilege to be the child of a godly father and mother, and to be brought up in the midst of many prayers. It is a blessed thing indeed to be taught the gospel from our earliest infancy, and to hear of sin, and Jesus, and the Holy Spirit, and holiness, and heaven, from the first moment we can remember anything. But, O, take heed that you do not remain barren and unfruitful in the sunshine of all these privileges: beware lest your hearts remain hard, impenitent, and worldly, not withstanding the many advantages you enjoy. You cannot enter the kingdom of God on the credit of your parents' religion. You must eat the bread of life for yourself, and have the witness of the Spirit in your own heart. You must have repentance of your own, faith of your own, and sanctification of your own. If not, you are no better than Lot's wife. I pray to God that all professing Christians in these days may lay these things to heart. May we never forget that privileges alone cannot save us. Light and knowledge, and faithful preaching, and abundant means of grace, and the company of holy people are all great blessings and advantages. Happy are they that have them! But after all, there is one thing without which privileges are useless: that one thing is the grace of the Holy Ghost. Lot's wife had many privileges; but Lot's wife had not grace.

~J. C. RYLE (1816–1900)

FAITH, HOPE, AND TRUST

Consider it pure joy, my brothers, whenever you face trials of many kinds, because you know that the testing of your faith develops perseverance.

JAMES 1:2–3 NIV

I've been sick for ten years with cancer, viral illnesses, and chronic fatigue. For a long time, I was depressed and felt hopeless. I couldn't do what I used to do and sometimes I couldn't do anything. Every day was something to be gotten through rather than a gift from God. One cannot escape these feelings. But the Lord tells us through James that there is a better way to view adversity. This not only gave me hope but also made me stronger. It also helped me realize that I could improve and possibly overcome my difficulties. Most importantly, it showed me the kind of person Jesus wanted me to be. I realized that experiencing adversity and using God's solutions would enable me to help others from my own experiences. So I began concentrating on helping others rather than myself as much as I could. I delved into scripture and found motivation and solace in how Paul went on to become the most prolific of all the apostles despite his thorn (2 Corinthians 12:7–10). The Lord told Paul that His grace was sufficient and that power is perfected in weakness. Paul began to understand that relying on the Lord would allow Christ to dwell in him and that through weakness, he could find his true strength. This is a learning process, the goal being to align my actions with God's will. By persevering in the Lord, I have been rewarded with increased endurance and spiritual stamina that I can apply to all situations. And God has expanded my faith and given me peace because I've moved closer to him.

DAVID SCHOLTON (1951–) SANFORD, NC

THE CHOSEN PATH

TO BELIEVE IS TO RECEIVE

Believe on the Lord Jesus Christ, and thou shalt be saved.
ACTS 16:31 KJV

To believe in the Lord Jesus Christ, is to receive him as he is revealed in the Gospel. Christ is God's first gift, with, or for the sake of whom, he bestows all others; and believing in him corresponds with it. If God first gives Christ, and with him all things freely, we must first receive Christ, and with him all things freely. Hence it is said, "He that hath not the Son of God, hath not life." We must receive him as that for which he was given, which was to be a sacrifice, or propitiation for sin, that God might be just in justifying poor ungodly sinners who believe in him. We must trust in him as the sole ground of hope, and plead for pardon only in his name. Receiving Christ as by a marriage-covenant, we become one with him, and so are interested in all that he hath done and suffered on earth, and in all that he is now doing at the right hand of God. But though believing in Christ has a special respect to him as the way of acceptance with God, yet, when you receive him as your atoning Priest, you will also receive him as your King. In your journey to the heavenly world, you will have much to do, much to oppose, and it may be, much to suffer; but by a life of faith on him in whom you first believed, you will find strength equal to your day.

~ANDREW FULLER (1754–1806)

THE CHOSEN PATH

IT IS A FIGHT TO KNOW JESUS

For the sinful nature desires what is contrary to the Spirit,
and the Spirit what is contrary to the sinful nature. They are in
conflict with each other, so that you do not do what you want.

GALATIANS 5:17 NIV

For some odd reason, there is a distorted theory within Christianity that teaches all is well once a commitment to follow Jesus is made. It teaches that we will automatically wake up at 5 a.m. to spend a couple of hours praying for the nations and memorizing the Old Testament. One day we are lost sinners and the next day we are dropping everything to become the next great Bible scholar or theologian. Most of us, if we are honest, know that this is not the case at all. Pursuing a love relationship with Jesus Christ is a fight. There is no way of getting around it. It is a fight against our schedules when we attempt to spend time with God. It is a fight against our hobbies and interests when they come into conflict with His desires for us. All of this can be summed up by saying it is a fight against our flesh. There is a constant battle within the Christian between the flesh (the things our sin wants to do) and the things of the Spirit (who leads us to the things of God). This fight against the flesh is a daily choice to pursue Jesus or rely upon our own strength and desires. Each choice in which we are faced is an opportunity to choose the Spirit over the flesh and give Christ the victory. This does not have as much to do with the validity of our salvation as it does the lordship of our lives.

~**CHRIS JAMES** (1978–) **LOWELL, MA**

A DEBTOR (PART 1)
I Have a Debt

I am debtor both to the Greeks, and to the Barbarians;
both to the wise, and to the unwise.

ROMANS 1:14 KJV

Paul said, "I have a debt that drives me to witness." Have you ever noticed that debt is an insistent thing? Through an oversight, I once neglected to pay Australian government import duties on a box of tapes and CDs from the United States. Some months later, I was shocked and surprised to be rung up by a debt collection agency. Now they weren't actually promising to break both legs if I didn't pay up immediately. But the burden became insistent until I had sorted the matter out. Have you noticed that you are not a hero because you pay your debts? It's simply your obligation, your duty, and your responsibility. When I paid up on the government duties, the Australian government didn't send me a letter thanking me. They ignored me. I was no longer on their radar screens. Robert Murray McCheyne died when he was just thirty years old. He was a young Scottish preacher in the 1830s. But he left an indelible impression upon the world through his godly ministry. He wrote the words to a beautiful hymn:

Chosen not for good in me, Wakened up from wrath to flee,
Hidden in the Savior's side, By the Spirit sanctified,
Teach me, Lord, on earth to show, By my love, how much I owe.

You have a debt to share the good news of salvation with those who are lost simply because you are told by the Lord to tell others. Will you pay your debt to the Lord?

~STEVEN GROSE (1959–) NEW CASTLE, NEW SOUTH WALES

A DEBTOR (PART 2)
My Debt to the Lost

I am debtor both to the Greeks, and to the Barbarians;
both to the wise, and to the unwise.

ROMANS 1:14 KJV

We are debtors to those who need us. To the person who is broken, to the one in pain, to the one with a tortured body or a tortured mind, you and I owe the debt of the unfathomable, unsearchable riches of the mercy of God in Jesus Christ. God made it that way. We are in their debt. Sometimes I wonder that my heart can be so cold that I do not see the lostness of the lost around me. Sometimes I am disturbed that I do not cry out more in prayer with tears for those who do not know our Lord Jesus Christ, who do not have this marvelous gift of eternal life. As a young university student, I assisted in house-to-house visitation in a notorious part of Sydney. The government-supplied housing had interesting residents. Many were needy. Some drove Mercedes Benzes. One wondered how they were acquired. One of the more "prosperous" housing residents, a man who stood well over six feet tall, his tanned, tattooed, scarred body clad in shorts and singlet, indicated the source of his wealth. He had neatly fenced off a newly planted front lawn with string and sticks. Mindful of his lostness, I stepped across the string, across his newly planted lawn, walked up to him, offered him a tract, and invited him to the new church. I realized what I had done and quickly walked away. The elderly pastor of the church was standing nearby. "The only thing that saved you was that he was so stunned at your zeal he stood there speechless." How much do you care?

~**STEVEN GROSE (1959–)** NEW CASTLE, NEW SOUTH WALES

THE CHOSEN PATH

A DEBTOR (PART 3)
My Debt to the Locals

I am debtor both to the Greeks, and to the Barbarians;
both to the wise, and to the unwise.

ROMANS 1:14 KJV

It may seem strange that Paul speaks of Greeks when he is writing to Romans. At this time, the word *Greek* had lost its racial sense altogether. It did not mean primarily a native of the country of Greece. The conquests of Alexander the Great had taken the Greek language and Greek thought all over the world. And a Greek was no longer only one who was a Greek by race and birth; he was one who knew the culture and the mind of Greece. A barbarian is literally a man who says bar-bar, that is, a man who speaks an ugly and rough tongue rather than the beautiful, flexible Greek language. Most in the community are not university educated. So are they to be left to perish? Aidan was the apostle to the Saxons. Away back in A.D. 630 the Saxon king had sent to Iona a request that a missionary be sent to his kingdom to preach the gospel. The missionary came back talking of the "stubborn and barbarous disposition of the English." "The English have no manners," he said, "they behave like savages." He reported that the task was hopeless, and then Aidan spoke. "I think, brother," he said, "that you may have been too severe for such ignorant hearers, and that you should have led them on gently, giving them first the milk of religion before the meat." So Aidan was sent to Northumbria, and his gentleness won for Christ that very people whom the critical severity of his brother monk had repelled. Are you fulfilling your debt to the cultured and uncultured locals?

~STEVEN GROSE (1959–) NEW CASTLE, NEW SOUTH WALES

A DEBTOR (PART 4)
My Debt to the Lost

I am debtor both to the Greeks, and to the Barbarians;
both to the wise, and to the unwise.
ROMANS 1:14 KJV

You are a debtor to the lost. Have you noticed some of the lost are wise and some unwise? Today we may say, some are Sunday school taught and some are completely ignorant of Christian things or a Christian world-view. Some have heard the gospel before, in Sunday school or bible class. Some have never heard the gospel before. We tend to stick with those who know something. Sometimes we think it is just too hard to reach those who have never heard the gospel. You've all heard of the town of "Nowhere"? It's a little town in the country, the outback of Australia. Well, this was twenty-five miles out back of that. The teeming crowds were gathering—all seventeen of them. I preached with all of the fervor and passion of my heart. When I got through, this tall farmer came up and said, "You were wrong!" "Well," I said, "I've been wrong often. Tell me where I am wrong." He said, "In your sermon you said you can lead a horse to water, but you can't make him drink. And that ain't true, 'cause you can feed him salt." You may be thinking that you can't lead your neighbor to Christ, because he is too ignorant of the gospel, but you can feed him salt until he listens to you. You can talk to him about Christmas or Easter. You can pray with him when he hits a life crisis of illness or stress. Are you fulfilling your debt to the locals? Are you ultivating their friendships so you can gain a hearing for the Lord?

~STEVEN GROSE (1959–) NEW CASTLE, NEW SOUTH WALES

THE CHOSEN PATH

DRAWN TO JESUS
(EPHESIANS 1)

Clothes on my back, got plenty to wear, highlights of blond put in my hair

Red fiery nails had them just done, wondering why not having much fun

Hungry oh no, have plenty to eat; never feel full, so much defeat

A soda here, a candy bar there, with all these goodies why so much despair?

Career chosen, gone right to the top, lonely, afraid, feel like a flop

Empty inside, feeling so sad, to the enemy I listened, yes I've been had

A drawing I feel from heaven above, showers of love flow down like a dove

Reaching for Him, He poured out His grace, set me on course, I'm in a new race

The race I run is to reach the lost. Eternity without Jesus, too great a cost,

They're hungry, naked and empty inside, from You sweet Jesus let them not hide

Open their eyes, teach them Your word, bring in Your sheep; take them out of his herd

Dead in trespasses, You give them new life, peace and joy enters, put away strife

Spiritual blessings in Christ alone, now we can worship and bow at His throne

A new life to live by His Spirit within, victory in Jesus, deliverance from sin.

~LINDA K. SMITH (1948–) SENECA, SC

INGRAFTED INTO CHRIST (PART 1)

His seed remaineth in him.

1 JOHN 3:9 KJV

There is a great difference between the Christian's growing simply, and his growing at all times. All true Christians do grow, but I do not say that they grow at all times. A tree that has life and nourishment grows to its perfection, yet it is not always growing; it grows not in the winter. Christians also have their winters, wherein the influences of grace, necessary for their growth, cease, "I sleep." It is by faith the believer derives gracious influences from Jesus Christ, as each lamp in the candlestick received oil from the bowl, by the pipe going between them. Now, if that pipe be stopped, if the saint's faith lie dormant and inactive, then all the rest of the graces will become dim, and seem ready to be extinguished. In consequence whereof, depraved nature will gather strength and become active. What then will become of the soul? Why, there is still one sure ground of hope. The saint's faith is not as the hypocrite's, like a pipe laid short of the fountain, whereby there can be no conveyance: it still remains a bond of union between Christ and the soul; and therefore, because Christ lives, the believer shall live also (John 14–19).

~THOMAS WATSON (1620–1686)

INGRAFTED INTO CHRIST (PART 2)

His seed remaineth in him.

1 JOHN 3:9 KJV

Mud thrown into a pool may lie there at ease; but if it be cast into a fountain, the spring will at length work it out, and run as clear as formerly. Secondly, Christians may mistake their growth, and that two ways. By judging of their case according to their present feeling they observe themselves, and cannot perceive themselves to be growing; but there is no reason thence to conclude they are not growing (Mark 4:27). "The seed springs and grows up, he knoweth not how." Were a person to fix his eye never so steadfastly on a growing tree, he would not see it growing; but if he compare the tree as it now is, with what it was some years ago, he will certainly perceive that it has grown. In like manner, may the Christian know whether he be in a growing or declining state, by comparing his present with his former condition. Christians may mistake their case, by measuring their growth by the advances of the top only, not of the root. Though a man be not growing taller, he may be growing stronger.

~THOMAS WATSON (1620–1686)

THE MINISTRY OF INTERCESSION

. . . an holy priesthood, to offer up spiritual sacrifices,
acceptable to God by Jesus Christ.

1 PETER 2:5 KJV

"The Spirit of the Lord God is upon me: because the Lord hath anointed me." These are the words of Jesus in Isaiah. As the fruit of His work, all redeemed ones are priests, fellow-partakers with Him of His anointing with the Spirit as High Priest. As every son of Aaron, so every member of Jesus' body has a right to the priesthood. But not every one exercises it: many are still entirely ignorant of it. And yet it is the highest privilege of a child of God, the mark of greatest nearness and likeness to Him, 'who ever liveth to pray.' Do you doubt if this really be so? Think of what constitutes priesthood. There is, first, the work of the priesthood. This has two sides, one Godward, the other manward. On the one hand, the priest had the power to draw nigh to God, to dwell with Him in His house, and to present before Him the blood of the sacrifice or the burning incense. This work he did not do, however, on his own behalf, but for the sake of the people whose representative he was. He received from the people their sacrifices, presented them before God, and then came out to bless in His Name, to give the assurance of His favor and to teach them His law.

~ANDREW MURRAY (1828–1917)

SATAN HAS A GOSPEL TOO!

*I marvel that ye are so soon removed from him that called you
into the grace of Christ unto another gospel: which is not another;
but there be some that trouble you, and would pervert the gospel of Christ.*

GALATIANS 1:6–7 KJV

In the seventh chapter of Matthew, there are two scriptures which give us approximate results of Christ's Gospel and Satan's counterfeit. First, in verse 13 and 14, "Enter ye in at the strait gate: for wide is the gate and broad is the way that leadeth to destruction, and many there be which go in thereat. Because strait is the gate, and narrow is the way, which leadeth unto life, and few there be that find it." Second, in verse 22 and 23, "Many will say to Me in that day, Lord, Lord, have we not prophesied (preached) in Thy name? And in Thy name cast out demons, and in thy name done many wonderful works? And they will I profess unto them, I never knew you; depart from Me, ye that work iniquity." Yes, my reader, it is possible to work in the name of Christ, and even to preach in His name, and thought the world knows us, and the Church knows us, yet to be unknown to the Lord! How necessary it is then to find out where we really are; to examine ourselves and see whether we be in the faith; to measure ourselves by the Word of God and see if we are being deceived by our subtle Enemy; to find out whether it is erected on the Rock which is Christ Jesus.

~A. W. PINK (1886–1952)

CRITICIZING OTHERS

Judge not, that ye be not judged.
MATTHEW 7:1 KJV

Jesus' instructions with regard to judging others is very simply put; He says, "Don't." The average Christian is the most piercingly critical individual known. Criticism is one of the ordinary activities of people, but in the spiritual realm nothing is accomplished by it. The effect of criticism is the dividing up of the strengths of the one being criticized. The Holy Spirit is the only one in the proper position to criticize, and He alone is able to show what is wrong without hurting and wounding. It is impossible to enter into fellowship with God when you are in a critical mood. Criticism serves to make you harsh, vindictive, and cruel, and leaves you with the soothing and flattering idea that you are somehow superior to others. Jesus says that as His disciple you should cultivate a temperament that is never critical. This will not happen quickly but must be developed over a span of time. You must constantly beware of anything that causes you to think of yourself as a superior person. There is no escaping the penetrating search of my life by Jesus. Every wrong thing that I see in you, God finds in me. Every time I judge, I condemn myself (Romans 2:17–24). Stop having a measuring stick for other people. There is always at least one more fact, which we know nothing about, in every person's situation.

~OSWALD CHAMBERS (1874–1917)

FROM A MIGHTY MAN OF GOD

Some people are like wheelbarrows; useful only when pushed, and very easily upset.

God uses broken things. It takes broken soil to produce a crop, broken clouds to give rain, broken grain to give bread, broken bread to give strength. It is the broken alabaster box that gives forth perfume. It is Peter, weeping bitterly, who returns to greater power than ever.

Sometimes your medicine bottle has on it, "shake well before using." That is what God has to do with some of His people. He has to shake them well before they are ever usable.

Too many are not willing to give the Gospel a fair trial. They are too ignorant to speak wisely but not wise enough to speak ignorantly. A man is not a sinner because he is a skeptic; he is a skeptic because he is a sinner.

We are sometimes repentant because of the harm we have done ourselves and others in our transgressions but there is little repentance toward God. We may regret what our sins do to our testimony and the evil effect on others but we are little concerned because the fellowship with God is broken. This makes for shallow and inadequate confession because we have not touched the heart of the trouble.

~VANCE HAVNER (1901–1986)

HE WITH US; WE WITH HIM

The fear of the LORD prolongeth days:
but the years of the wicked shall be shortened.

PROVERBS 10:27 KJV

There is no doubt about it. The fear of the Lord leads to virtuous habits, and these prevent that waste of life which comes of sin and vice. The holy rest which springs out of faith in the Lord Jesus also greatly helps a man when he is ill. Every physician rejoices to have a patient whose mind is fully at ease. Worry kills, but confidence in God is like healing medicine. We have therefore all the arrangements for long life, and if it be really for our good, we shall see a good old age and come to our graves as shocks of corn in their season. Let us not be overcome with sudden expectation of death the moment we have a finger ache, but let us rather expect that we may have to work on through a considerable length of days. And what if we should soon be called to the higher sphere? Certainly there would be nothing to deplore in such a summons but everything to rejoice in. Living or dying, we are the Lord's. If we live, Jesus will be with us; if we die, we shall be with Jesus.

~C. H. SPURGEON (1834–1892)

LION AND LAMB

. . . Behold, the Lion . . .

REVELATION 5:5 KJV

He is called a Lion. Behold, the Lion of the tribe of Judah. He seems to be called the Lion of the tribe of Judah, in allusion to what Jacob said in his blessing of the tribe on his death-bed; who, when he came to bless Judah, compares him to a lion (Genesis 9:9). It is much on account of the valiant acts of David that the tribe of Judah, of which David was, is in Jacob's prophetical blessing compared to a lion; but more especially with an eye to Jesus Christ, who also was of that tribe, and was descended of David, and is in our text called "the Root of David;" and therefore Christ is here called "the Lion of the tribe of Judah." He is called a Lamb. John was told of a Lion that had prevailed to open the book, and probably expected to see a lion in his vision; but while he is expecting, behold a Lamb appears to open the book, an exceedingly diverse kind of creature from a lion. A lion is a devourer, one that is wont to make terrible slaughter of others; and no creature more easily falls a prey to him than a lamb. And Christ is here represented not only as a Lamb, a creature very liable to be slain, but a "Lamb as it had been slain," that is, with the marks of its deadly wounds appearing on it.

~JONATHAN EDWARDS (1703–1758)

THE CHOSEN PATH

WHOSE PLAN ARE YOU LIVING BY?

Many plans are in a man's heart, but the LORD's decree will prevail.
PROVERBS 19:21 HCSB

One of the worst things we can do in life is miss out on God's best for us. We often get caught up in our own plans that seem right at the time and end up making foolish decisions. In order to please God, we must live by His plan and seek His will for our lives. Have you ever heard anyone say, "I sure am glad I missed out on God's plan for my life"? Of course you will not hear anyone say that. Nobody likes being out of His will because when we are, things don't go so well. Some people make it a regular habit and live miserable lives as a result of it. Man's most serious and well-thought-out plans are only devices. The word *plans* found here in the scripture denotes the idea of schemes that are full of uncertainty. Man's plans are many; God's plan is one. Man's plans are often full of worry and end up fruitless. God's plans are secure and will stand forever. God's plans are firm and full of purpose. We desperately need God's wisdom and direction in this life. Our wisdom is limited, not trustworthy, and subjects us to making numerous mistakes. We need to be enlightened by God's Word and led by the Holy Spirit. We need to pray for His wisdom to guide us in this life and into eternity. Creator, redeemer, sustainer God stands ready to grant you all the wisdom you need to make good decisions and handle life with surety and stability. Ask Him for it today!

~**SETH POLK (1971–) POKA, WV**

THE CHOSEN PATH

CHRIST'S PEACE AND POWER

FROM JOHN 20:19–23 NKJV

The disciples had shut the doors (to keep out those who wanted to harm them), but that did not prevent Jesus Christ from coming among them. Some today talk about countries that are "closed" to the gospel. One student of world missions has correctly observed that there are no closed countries, only countries where the advance the gospel will come at great sacrifice. No human or satanic authority can keep Jesus out of any place He desires to enter. Jesus blessed them when He appeared to them. "Peace" is the essence of the new relationship that every Christian has with God. The Prince of Peace has reconciled men to God by His death on the cross. We can live with the settled confidence that nothing can happen to us outside God's divine plan for us. We need not fear what man can do to us. "We are immortal until God is finished with us." Jesus told them that He was sending them just as the Father had sent Him. But how did God the Father "send" Jesus? He sent Him to serve (Mark 10:45) and to suffer (Romans 8:16–18). Do you serve others in Jesus' name? What are some ways you could serve others for the sake of the gospel? Have you suffered because you bear the name of Jesus as one of His disciples? Are you willing to suffer for the sake of the gospel?

~BILL ASCOL (1952–) SHREVEPORT, LA

MY RESCUER

Spider, spider in my sight
Saying you won't win the fight
Stumbling, crumbling there you go
In the web that I did sew
Laughing, laughing hard at me
Poking at my sensitivity
Round and round and round you spin
This battle you intend to win
A voice from heaven calls to me
Don't worry love I'll set you free
A deeper healing soon will be
To help you love and honor Me
I see your heart, I hear your prayer
Deeper, deeper take me there
To places you so long to be
Feeding off My love for thee
It's quiet now you have no fear
I'll hold you close you are so dear
I came for you so long ago
I'll never, never let you go

~LINDA K SMITH (1948–) SENECA, SC

THE CHOSEN PATH

AMAZED AND GLORIFYING GOD

And they were all amazed, and they glorified God, and were
filled with fear, saying, We have seen strange things to day.
LUKE 5:26 KJV

We live in an hour when the foundations of civilization are crumbling, the night of apostasy is deepening, lawlessness runs wild to its awful climax, the powers of Anti-Christ increase and abound, and wars and rumors of wars belt the globe. Yet the Church of God, with the only hope and cure for mankind's sin and misery, rests, for the most part, at ease in Zion, and we who claim that Name above every name make mud pies and daisy chains and twiddle our thumbs while a world sweeps over the brink of disaster. We preach a Gospel that is God's dynamite and we live firecracker lives. We sing of showers of blessing and the old-time power and faith, the victory and higher ground, and then we leave it all in the hymn books and go home. We read that when our Lord held a service the congregation went home amazed and glorifying God and filled with fear and saying, "We have seen strange things today" (Luke 5:26). How many, do you think, go from our meetings today in such a frame of mind?

~VANCE HAVNER (1901–1986)

A TYPE OF CHRIST

Now these be the last words of David. . . . The Spirit of
the LORD spake by me, and his word was in my tongue.

2 SAMUEL 23:1–2 KJV

Christ, the antitypical David, is not only beloved of God, but also by his people. They know not how better to describe him, than as him whom their souls love. They love him in his whole person as God-Man: they love him as held forth in all his offices, in all his relations. They love him as he appears in all his truths and ordinances. They love the truths relating to him, that set forth the glory of his person and the riches of his grace. They love him in all his ordinances: they esteem his precepts concerning all things to be right, and hate every false way. And they love Christ superlatively above all others, angels, or men; they say, Whom have I in heaven but thee? and there is none on earth that I desire beside thee. They love him above all natural relations, friends, and acquaintance, be they ever so near and dear to them. They love him with all their hearts and with all their souls, with sincerity and uprightness of heart, and can appeal to him as the searcher of hearts, and trier of the reins of the children of men, that as he knows all things, he knows they do love him. Thus our Lord Jesus Christ answers to the name David, which signifies beloved; he is beloved of his Father, and beloved of his people.

~THOMAS WATSON (1620–1686)

THE CHOSEN PATH

A LITTLE OF MARTHA—
A LOT OF MARY

As Jesus and his disciples were on their way, he came to a village where a
woman named Martha opened her home to him. She had a sister called
Mary, who sat at the Lord's feet listening to what he said. But Martha was
distracted by all the preparations that had to be made. She came to him
and asked, "Lord, don't you care that my sister has left me to do the work by
myself? Tell her to help me!" "Martha, Martha," the Lord answered, "you
are worried and upset about many things, but only one thing is needed.
Mary has chosen what is better, and it will not be taken away from her."

LUKE 10:38–42 NIV

Here we have two sisters, Mary and Martha. Mary sat at Jesus' feet.
She gave her undivided attention. She was receiving the Word into her
heart. Martha was distracted by all the preparations. She was divided
between many things—entertaining in her house. The conflict from
this passage occurs when Martha accuses her sister, Mary, of
abandoning her to do all the work. She asks Jesus to make Mary help.
The lesson comes from the Lord's reply, "You are worried and upset
about many things." Often we get too many irons in the fire. This causes
us to lose focus on the only thing that matters, being with Jesus. How
can we avoid this conflict? We can slow down. Does your to-do list
reflect eternal value? We can also calm down. We feel that we must live
up to everyone's demands on our time. We need to sit down. We do not
know how to just be quiet and listen. Sit at the feet of Jesus daily. Be still
and know that He is God.

~TODD FUEHRER (1967–) BISMARCK, ND

PERSISTENCE

I press on toward the goal to win the prize for which
God has called me heavenward in Christ Jesus.

PHILIPPIANS 3:14 NIV

A hunter bought two pedigree setters, trained them to be fine bird dogs, and kept them in a fenced backyard, which faced an alley. One morning, a little bulldog came down the alley, saw the dogs in the fence, and squeezed under it. Watching through the window, the owner thought he should lock up the setters so they wouldn't hurt the little dog. But then he decided it was their territory, and they had a right to defend it against intruders. He figured they would teach the bulldog a lesson he wouldn't soon forget. As soon as the stump-tailed little bulldog got in the fence, the fur started to fly, and it was all bulldog fur. The little dog finally called it quits and went back home to lick his wounds. For three successive days the bulldog crawled under the fence growling and ready to take on the tag-team of setters. He came out a few minutes later quite the worse for wear and ran home. When the owner returned home from a lengthy business trip, his wife gave him an update. "At the same time every day the bulldog came to the backyard and fought with our setters and now when our setters hear him snorting down the ally, they start to whine and run to the basement. The little bulldog struts around our backyard as if he owns it." Christians can learn persistence and determination from the little bulldog. Paul, beset by enemies and hindrances, was determined to do what God called him to do. Are you?

~VICKI HUFFMAN (1946–) MT. JULIET, TN

PAY DAY!

For they have sown the wind, and they shall reap the whirlwind.

HOSEA 8:7 KJV

To the home that has no room for Christ, death and grave clothes are certain. . . . "Ichabod" will be written about the church that soft-pedals on unpleasant truth or that stands not unwaveringly for "the faith once delivered"—and it will acknowledge its retribution in that it will become "a drifting sepulcher manned by a frozen crew." "The Lord will not hold him guiltless that taketh his name in vain" (Exodus 20:7). A man can, if he will, follow the way of some wicked woman; but God leaves him not without warning as to the pay-day . . . many strong men have been slain by her. Her house is the way to hell, going down to the chambers of death (Proverbs 7). The certainty of "Pay Day, Someday" for all who regard not God or man is set forth in the words of an unknown poet: You'll pay. The knowledge of your acts will weigh heavier on your mind each day.

> The more you climb, the more you gain,
> The more you'll feel the nagging strain.
> Success will cower at the threat of retribution. Fear will fret
> Your peace and bleed you for the debt;
> Conscience collects from every crook
> More than the worth of what he took,
> You only thought you got away
> But in the night you'll pay and pay.

~ DR. R. G. LEE (1886–1978)

THE CHOSEN PATH

FROM C. T. STUDD

Too long have we been waiting for one another to begin! The time of waiting is past! The hour of God has struck! War is declared! In God's Holy Name let us arise and build! "The God of Heaven, He will fight for us," as we for Him. We will not build on the sand, but on the bedrock of the sayings of Christ, and the gates and minions of hell shall not prevail against us. Should such men as we fear? Before the world, aye, before the sleepy, lukewarm, faithless, namby-pamby Christian world, we will dare to trust our God, we will venture our all for Him, we will live and we will die for Him, and we will do it with His joy unspeakable singing aloud in our hearts. We will a thousand times sooner die trusting only our God, than live trusting in man. And when we come to this position the battle is already won, and the end of the glorious campaign in sight. We will have the real Holiness of God, not the sickly stuff of talk and dainty words and pretty thoughts; we will have a Masculine Holiness, one of daring faith and works for Jesus Christ.

~C. T. STUDD (1860–1931)

A VOICE FOR THE VOICELESS

If you do nothing in a difficult time, your strength is limited.
Rescue those being taken off to death, and save those stumbling toward
slaughter. If you say, "But we didn't know about this," won't He who
weighs hearts consider it? Won't He who protects your life know?
Won't He repay a person according to his work?

PROVERBS 24:10–12 HCSB

An unidentified German man has shared a vivid childhood memory of the Nazi holocaust that killed six million Jews. He said that his church was located right near a railroad track and the congregation regularly heard the piercing screams of Jews being transported to concentration camps. The Jews saw the church and cried out for help. Even though the church members were tormented by the screams of these suffering people each week, they felt helpless and decided that the only way to drown out the awful sound was to sing hymns when the train passed by. If the screams were still heard, they would just sing louder. This man still hears the screams in his mind and prays for God to forgive the Christians in Germany who were silent. Is this same scenario being replayed today? Could it be that there are helpless people heading toward the slaughter while Christians just sing louder? Read the following examples. Since 1973, over 44 million unborn babies have been killed in the womb in the United States. The increase of orphaned children throughout the world now numbers in the millions. Reports of Christians being imprisoned and martyred in countries hostile to the gospel of Jesus Christ continue to rise. The trains of today may be on different tracks, but the suffering continues. What can you do, with God's help, to be a voice for the voiceless?

~RYAN BOWMAN (1972–) LEE'S SUMMIT, MO

THE SERMON ON THE MOUNT

FROM MATTHEW 5:3–12

Blessed are the poor in spirit,
because the kingdom of heaven is theirs.

Blessed are those who mourn, because they will be comforted.

Blessed are the gentle, because they will inherit the earth.

Blessed are those who hunger and thirst for righteousness,
because they will be filled.

Blessed are the merciful, because they will be shown mercy.

Blessed are the pure in heart, because they will see God.

Blessed are the peacemakers,
because they will be called sons of God.

Blessed are those who are persecuted for righteousness,
because the kingdom of heaven is theirs.

Blessed are you when they insult you and persecute you and
falsely say every kind of evil against you because of Me.

Be glad and rejoice, because your reward is great in heaven.
For that is how they persecuted the prophets who were before you.

THE CALL OF GOD

FROM 1 SAMUEL 3:1-10

God calls all of us as believers to be ministers in Jesus' name. In our Baptist history, we have numerous examples of God's clear call to service. A Virginia teacher by the name of Harriett Baker felt God's call to China. She became the first single female missionary appointed by the Foreign Mission Board of the Southern Baptist Convention. In February 1849, she wrote to J. B. Taylor, corresponding secretary of the board, and expressed her desire to be a missionary. She wrote, "M. B. Shepard placed in my hands a number of the Commission in which I saw stated the great need of female missionaries and in which I saw that the Board had determined to send one or two single females to China so I concluded to write you immediately about the matter. Brother Taylor, if there be but one sent out let me be that one." Miss Baker arrived in China in 1850 and established a girls' school in Shanghai, but was forced by illness to return home in 1853. She never returned to China. Some twenty years later, another single female Virginia teacher, by the name of Lottie Moon, felt God's urgent call and followed Baker's steps to China. How important it is that we listen to Christ about where we are to serve and are willing to walk that chosen path.

~BILL SUMNERS (1950–) FRANKLIN, TN

THE CHOSEN PATH

DO IT NOW!

"Agree with your adversary quickly."
MATTHEW 5:25 NKJV

Wanting to make sure that my adversary gives me all my rights is a natural thing. But Jesus says that it is a matter of inescapable and eternal importance to me that I pay my adversary what I owe him. From our Lord's standpoint, it doesn't matter whether I am cheated or not, but what does matter is that I don't cheat someone else. Am I insisting on having my own rights, or am I paying what I owe from Jesus Christ's standpoint? Do it quickly—bring yourself to judgment now. In moral and spiritual matters, you must act immediately. If you don't, the inevitable, relentless process will begin to work. God is determined to have His child as pure, clean, and white as driven snow, and as long as there is disobedience in any point of His teaching, He will allow His Spirit to use whatever process it may take to bring us to obedience. The fact that we insist on proving that we are right is almost always a clear indication that we have some point of disobedience. No wonder the Spirit of God so strongly urges us to stay steadfastly in the light!

~OSWALD CHAMBERS (1874–1917)

THE GOAL OF THE GOSPEL

And being in Bethany in the house of Simon the leper, as he sat
at meat, there came a woman having an alabaster box of ointment
of spikenard very precious; and she brake the box, and poured it on
his head. Jesus said, . . . Verily I say unto you, Wheresoever the gospel
shall be preached throughout the whole world, this also that she
hath done shall be spoken of for a memorial of her.

MARK 14:3, 6, 9 KJV

The Lord ordained that the story of Mary anointing Him with that costly ointment should always accompany the story of the Gospel; that what Mary has done should always be coupled with what the Lord has done. That is His own statement. What does He intend that we should understand by it? I think we all know the story of Mary's action well. From the details given in (John 12), where the incident follows not long after her brother's restoration to life, we may gather that the family was not a specially wealthy one. No doubt every penny mattered to them. Yet one of those sisters, Mary, having among her treasures an alabaster cruse containing "three hundred pence" worth of ointment, expended the whole thing on the Lord. Human reasoning said this was really too much; it was giving the Lord more than His due. That is why Judas took the lead, and the other disciples supported him, in voicing a general complaint that Mary's action was a wasteful one.

~WATCHMAN NEE (1903–1972)

THE CHOSEN PATH

WAY TO GO!

*Jesus said to him, "I am the way, the truth, and the life.
No one comes to the Father except through Me."*

JOHN 14:6 NKJV

Any traffic-tensed traveler veering his vehicle through the villes of France learns very quickly that you can steer more sedately over the twisting, spaghetti streets if you know your final destination. And if you get lost, then all you have to do is look for the arrowed signs that say, *Toutes Directions* (All Directions) or *Autres Directions* (Other Directions) Almost every town has these signs. They will lead you to a street corner that shows directional arrows to many villages in the near vicinity as well as to major cities far away. But since these arrows give you multiple choices of places to go, you really must know where you want to go, your destination out of all these *Autres Directions*. Because if you don't, it's easy to get lost and go in *Toutes Directions*. Life is like the system of road signs. We have a lot of choices of ways to go, but when we follow Jesus, making heaven our final destination, we don't have to worry about being lost or about going in *Toutes Directions*. Because Jesus said, "I am the Way, the Truth, and the Life . . ." There are no *Autres Directions* to heaven.

~**ROY MILLER (1935–) WHEAT RIDGE, CO**

PARENTS' HOMEWORK

Lo, children are an heritage of the LORD:
and the fruit of the womb is his reward.

PSALM 127:3 KJV

Every person who has ever attended school understands the importance of doing one's homework. During my sophomore year in college I took a calculus course. The professor lectured every class and gave us ten problems to do for homework. However, he never checked the homework. After completing two assignments and seeing that the teacher was not checking the work, I stopped doing my homework. During the first test, the professor announced that we had to turn in all of our assignments since they would make up 50 percent of the test grade. Of course, I failed my first calculus test. The lesson I learned was this: I am responsible to do every assignment given to me because someday it will have to be turned in for a grade. The verse above states that children are a heritage from the Lord. This verse takes on greater significance when one realizes that this phrase can be paraphrased this way. Children are God's homework assignment to parents. Have you ever thought of your children in this way? It is important that we, as parents, see our children as our homework assignments from God. Then we must search the Bible and make sure that we follow His instructions on how we must complete these assignments. If we are faithful in doing our homework God's way, He will bless us and we will see our children walk in truth.

~Dr. Glen Schultz (1947–) Hendersonville, TN

SPEAK WHAT HE TEACHES

Now therefore go, and I will be with thy mouth,
and teach thee what thou shalt say.

EXODUS 4:12 KJV

Many a true servant of the Lord is slow of speech, and when called upon to plead for his Lord, he is in great confusion lest he should spoil a good cause by his bad advocacy. In such a case, it is well to remember that the Lord made the tongue which is so slow, and we must take care that we do not blame our maker. It may be that a slow tongue is not so great an evil as a fast one, and fewness of words may be more of a blessing than floods of verbiage. It is also quite certain that real saving power does not lie in human rhetoric, with its tropes, and pretty phrases, and grand displays. Lack of fluency is not so great a lack as it looks. If God be with our mouth, and with our mind, we shall have something better than the sounding brass of eloquence or the tinkling cymbal of persuasion. God's teaching is wisdom; His presence is power. Pharaoh had more reason to be afraid of stammering Moses than of the most fluent talker in Egypt; for what he said had power in it; he spoke plagues and deaths. If the Lord be with us in our natural weakness we shall be girt with supernatural power. Therefore, let us speak for Jesus boldly, as we ought to speak.

~C. H. SPURGEON (1834–1892)

THE CHOSEN PATH

ATTUNED TO A TURTLE

Death and life are in the power of the tongue.

PROVERBS 18:21 KJV

One morning my wife and I were riding bikes when I noticed something moving up the hill to my right. As I focused on this something, I quickly realized that it was a turtle. Persistent in his plight, initially he ignored me as I approached. His movements seemed to suggest that he would get as far away from me as he could before stopping to protect himself from intruders. "What kind of turtle is it?" my wife asked. Hoping not to be obviously evasive and since I had no clue, I said, "This one is different from the one we found in our yard . . . a terrapin." I wanted to reassure God's tiny creature that no harm would befall him while I was there. Knowing only God was listening (and I made a quick look around to confirm that fact), I moved gingerly around and spoke softly so as not to frighten the turtle. Emboldened I found myself talking to the little creature. When the turtle stuck out his neck, it was clear that he was not afraid and actually seemed to trust me. Our heavenly Father is constantly speaking works of affirmation to His children. As we learn to trust Him we are assured that we have His armor to protect us, for He is always with His children.

~MIKE GOODE (1958–) NICHOLASVILLE, KY

LOTTI MOON,
A VOICE FROM THE PAST
(LOTTIE MOON'S CHRISTMAS OFFERING)

"Simple justice demands that women should have equal rights with men in mission meetings and in the conduct of their work."

"What women want who come out to China is free opportunity to do the largest possible work . . . what women have a right to demand is perfect equality."

"Can we wonder at the mortal weariness and disgust, the sense of wasted powers and the conviction that her life is a failure, that comes over a woman when, instead of the ever broadening activities that she had planned, she finds herself tied down to the petty work of teaching a few girls?"

~**LOTTIE MOON (1840–1912)**

FAITH THAT TAKES

Therefore I say unto you, What things soever ye desire,
when ye pray, believe that ye receive them, and ye shall have them.

MARK 11:24 KJV

What a promise! So large, so Divine, that our little hearts cannot take it in, and in every possible way seek to limit it to what we think safe or probable; instead of allowing it, in its quickening power and energy, just as He gave it, to enter in, and to enlarge our hearts to the measure of what His love and power are really ready to do for us. Faith is very far from being a mere conviction of the truth of God's word, or a conclusion drawn from certain premises. It is the ear which has heard God say what He will do, the eye which has seen Him doing it, and, therefore, where there is true faith, it is impossible but the answer must come. If we only see to it that we do the one thing that He asks of us as we pray: Believe that ye have received; He will see to it that He does the thing He has promised: "Ye shall have them." The key-note of Solomon's prayer in 2 Chronicles 6:4, "Blessed be the Lord God of Israel, who hath with His hands fulfilled that which He spake with His mouth to my father David," is the key-note of all true prayer: the joyful adoration of a God whose hand always secures the fulfillment of what His mouth hath spoken.

~ANDREW MURRAY (1828–1917)

GOD IS ABLE

(EPHESIANS 3:20–4:2)

God is able, He is able
He is absolutely, positively able
To perform and to deliver
All that He has promised to

He's exceedingly and abundantly
And generously able to do
Far above all we ask or think
It's His power that works within

He has everything that is needed
The only problem comes from us
Our thoughts and prayers are oh so small
That they mock His will and word

He calls us higher oh so much higher
We must keep our eyes on Him
He's El Shaddai—Almighty God
Do no waver just trust in Him

I beseech you my dear brothers
To walk worthy of the call
With all lowliness and with gentleness
Bearing one another in love

To Him be glory, to Him be honor
In the church of Jesus Christ
To all people and generations
Forever and ever
~Amen

THE CHOSEN PATH

STANDING ALONE

What, could ye not watch with me one hour?
MATTHEW 26:40 KJV

You will spend much time alone with God, and the greatest struggles and the greatest battles of your life will take place when you are alone. There will be meetings and there will be messages, but you must have something that will take you through alone. Until you have something that will defy the devil and defeat all hell and drive back the powers of darkness when you are alone, you will never have much victory. It is good to have someone to pray with, that is the right thing, but there is nothing that will give you courage and build up your character so much as being alone with God in the great battles of your life. We are apt to depend on people, and we are apt to listen to them. Jesus was left by the multitude and left by His followers, that is the thing; left by His followers, those who had been with Him and knew Him best. They were tired and weary, and they had no conception of what was going on; they saw it not. It is good to be with our friends and to hear their encouraging words, but, beloved, you will get more alone with God in prayer, in communion and in struggle than you will ever get in any other way. This is the point where a great many fail they are not prepared to go through alone with nobody around. Remember you will have to die alone, and God wants you to get the victory alone.

~CHARLES STALKER (1848–1927)

TAKE A SHOT

As for me and my house, we will serve the LORD.
JOSHUA 24:15 KJV

I have a cartoon in my office that has had a profound influence on how I live my life. In the first frame, Sally asks Norbert the question, "What is life?" Norbert answers, "Life is a basketball." In the final frame he says, "You can take a shot or dribble it away." Life is full of fancy dribblers. We find them throughout the Bible. Some examples are King Saul, the Scribes, and the Pharisees. These people tried to impress others with their talk but were not willing to step up and take a shot by trusting God completely. However, Joshua had the courage to take a shot for God. He told everyone that he and his house would serve the Lord. David was another person in Scripture who took a shot for God. Of course, the One who had the greatest amount of boldness in taking a shot in life was Jesus Himself. He went to the cross and took a shot at death and hell and won the game. Because of this shot, any person can experience victory over death and the grave by simply trusting Christ as his or her Lord and Savior. Even though Christ has won the game and Satan has lost, many people still choose to play on Satan's team. Christ has one, yet He doesn't force us to play for Him. It is each person's choice. Who are you playing for? It is important that you don't dribble life away. Have courage and take a shot for Christ.

~DR. GLEN SHULTZ (1947–) NASHVILLE, TN

THE CHOSEN PATH

DRAW NEAR TO GOD

But it is good for me to draw near to God.

PSALM 73:28 KJV

If we would draw near to God, let us study our own needs. Let us consider in what need we stand for God and that we cannot be happy without him. The prodigal never drew near to his father, until he "began to be in need." A proud sinner, who was never convinced of his need, minds not to come near God; he has a stock of his own to live upon, "We are Lords; we will come no more unto you." A full stomach despises the honey-comb. It is the sense of need which brings us near to God. Why did so many lame and paralytical resort to Christ but because they needed a cure? Why does the thirsty man draw near to a fountain but because he needs water? Why does a condemned man draw near his prince but because he needs a pardon? When a poor soul reviews its needs; I need grace; I need the favor of God, I am damned without Christ; this makes him draw near to God, and be an earnest supplicant for mercy. If we would draw near to God, let us be careful to clear our interest in God, "Let us draw near with a true heart in full assurance of faith." When we know him to be our God, then we draw near to him. If God be the treasure delighted in, our hearts will be drawn to him. Servile fear makes the soul fly from God; sacred love makes it fly to him.

~THOMAS WATSON (1620–1686)

I AM THE DOOR

(JOHN 10)

I am the door, I open the gate

Come in precious sheep, before it's too late

All those before Me, only robbers and thieves

Kill, steal and destroying, a life of defeat

I've come to give life, so rich and so free

Yes, life everlasting, life abundantly

My sheep hear My voice, I know them by name

They never shall perish, to them I lay claim

I lay down My life, no one takes it from Me

To rescue My sheep, bringing them back to Me

I have a dear Shepherd, He watches over me.

I hear His tender voice, He's always with me.

~LINDA K. SMITH (1948–) SENECA, SC

THE CHOSEN PATH

TROUBLES THAT TEACH

For our light and momentary troubles are achieving
for us an eternal glory that far outweighs them all.

2 CORINTHIANS 4:17 NIV

Through the forty days of purpose campaign our church studied, we have learned once again God has a purpose behind every problem! God uses circumstances to develop our character. In fact, He depends more on circumstances to make us like Jesus than He depends on your reading the Bible. The reason is obvious: you face circumstances twenty-four hours a day. Your most profound and intimate experiences of worship will likely be in our darkest days "when your heart is broken, when you feel abandoned, when you're out of options, when the pain is great" and you turn to God alone. This is so true because everything that happens to you has spiritual significance. Everything! Romans 8:28–29 (NLT) explains why: "We know that God causes everything to work together for the good of those who love God and are called according to his purpose for them. For God knew his people in advance, and he chose them to become like his Son." You see, every problem is a character-building opportunity, and the more difficult it is, the greater the potential for building spiritual muscle and moral fiber. Paul said, "We know that these troubles produce patience. And patience produces character" Romans 5:3–4 (NCV). What happens outwardly in your life is not as important as what happens inside you. Your circumstances are temporary, but your character will last forever.

~DOUG MILLAR (1957–) CANCUN, MEXICO

WEEPING

They that sow in tears shall reap in joy.

PSALMS 126:5 KJV

A godly man sometimes weeps out of the sense of God's love. A godly person weeps because the sins he commits are in some sense worse than the sins of other men. The sin of a justified person is very odious. The sin of a justified person is odious, because it is a sin of unkindness (1 Kings 11:9). Peter's denying of Christ was a sin against love. Christ had enrolled him among the apostles. He had taken him up into the Mount of Transfiguration and shown him the glory of heaven in a vision. Yet after all this mercy, it was base ingratitude that he should deny Christ. This made him go out and "weep bitterly" (Matthew 26:75). He baptized himself, as it were, in his own tears. The sins of the godly go nearest to God's Heart. The sins of others anger the Lord; the godly man's sins grieve Him. The sins of the wicked pierce Christ's side, the sins of the godly wound his heart. The unkindness of a spouse goes nearest to the heart of her husband. Repenting tears are precious. God puts them in His bottle (Psalm 56:8).

~THOMAS WATSON (1620–1686)

THE CHOSEN PATH

THE PATH OF LOVE

"You must love the LORD your God with all your heart,
all your soul, all your mind, and all your strength."

MARK 12:30 NLT

Love. Without some form of it, our race would have been destroyed long ago. Love. The first Christians were known by their love—for one another. A new standard of love entered the world made possible by the Truest Love that split the universe—Jesus, the Great Love, who came to die in order to teach us how to love, and how to live. Following Him requires us to love. Now, that sounds easy but the actual living of it is another matter. Something within us rises up, putting ourselves in the way of Love. We want to be loved and we want to love, but how? Somewhere deep inside we know that a plate of cookies for our neighbors at Christmas and a turkey for the poor and needy is not what He had in mind. Unfortunately, often we create strong cocoons of relationships that we call love and maybe they are. However, in the deepest moments of our Christian experience, when we at last put our hearts before Him in spite of the structures we have created to substitute for Him, we hear Him speak to the Bride about loving as He loved. Can it be that He wants a Bride that loves like He did? Or at least tries to love as He did. Brothers and sisters, the Word is plain. He said there were two great commandments—love God with all your heart and soul and, love your neighbor as yourself.

~JACQUELYN SHEPPARD (1943–) GREENWOOD, MO

LOVE CONTINUES

*Dear children, let us stop just saying we love
each other; let us really show it by our actions.*

1 JOHN 3:18 NLT

Could it be that He was really serious about our loving one another and loving the people of this world? What if we were asked upon reaching heaven, how well did you love one another? Could it be that being "right" about doctrine and practices are not as critical to our Christian lives as being "right" about how we love? What would happen if our platitudes and attitudes toward love were stripped away and our actions were evident as well as our words? Can the world recognize Christians now by our love? I don't know about you, but I want to love like He commanded. And that means actually doing something about loving God and loving people. It means a new level of sacrifice in how I respond to AIDS in Africa and the homeless man in the most prosperous nation in the world. It means something about how I respond to my brothers and sisters in the faith when we don't agree. It means that my heart has to change, not theirs. If I know anything about Calvary's love, my heart and life has to take on new and deeper revelations about love. And, frankly, it's time for us who call ourselves the Bride and the Body of Christ to change the way we are loving—not just the bruised and broken world of hurting people, but also how we love one another. Let us love not only with our words but also with our deeds.

~JACQUELYN SHEPPARD (1943–) GREENWOOD, MO

THE CHOSEN PATH

CHRISTIAN KNOWLEDGE

Ye have need that one teach you again which
be the first principles of the oracles of God.

HEBREWS 5:12 KJV

Christians are enabled to understand those things in divinity which are more abstruse and difficult to be understood, and which require great skill in things of this nature. This is more fully expressed in the two next verses: "For every one that useth milk is unskillful in the word of righteousness; for he is a babe. But strong meat belongeth to them that are of full age, even those who, by reason of use, have their senses exercised to discern both good and evil." It is such knowledge, that proficiency in it shall carry persons beyond the first principles of religion. For the time, they ought to have been teachers. As they were Christians, their business was to learn and gain Christian knowledge. They were scholars in the school of Christ; and if they had improved their time in learning, as they ought to have done, they might, by the time when the apostle wrote, have been fit to be teachers in this school. To whatever business any one is devoted, it may be expected that his perfection in it shall be answerable to the time he has had to learn and perfect himself. Christians should not always remain babes, but should grow in Christian knowledge; and leaving the food of babes, they should learn to digest strong meat.

~JONATHAN EDWARDS (1703–1758)

FAITHING IT

When everything was hopeless, Abraham believed anyway, deciding to live not on the basis of what he saw he couldn't do but on what God said he would do. And so he was made father of a multitude of peoples. God himself said to him, "You're going to have a big family, Abraham!"

ROMANS 4:18 MSG

Abraham is known as the father of faith. Not because he pretended to believe God, but because he believed God "anyway." Let me explain. Just because we attend church on Sunday, dress nice, speak well, pray the proper prayers, it doesn't mean we really believe God. It just means we know church. The church needs less people faking it, and more people "faithing it." The Scriptures teach us to walk by faith and not by sight. We fake it when we try to please other people, or God, pretending to live super holy on the outside, but are really without faith on the inside. Faith causes us to please God by acting like the person we are going to be through Him. Abraham was a man who was not perfect by anyone's standards. But Abraham was willing to trust God. What has God told you He was going to do for you? What promised inheritance has He placed in your spirit. Regardless of your circumstances right now, have faith that God does not lie. He speaks what He knows, because He sees it. When God told Abram that he would be the father of many, God wasn't making a prediction; He was looking into the future and telling Abram what He saw. God is telling you what He sees for you. Only God can speak into existence those things that do not exist.

~TERRENCE ROBERTS (1964–) MERIDIAN, MS

FIERY DARTS

(EPHESIANS 6)

A fiery dart of discouragement hit my heart today
Listened to another voice, it took my joy away
The Lord had called me to a work, to share of His great grace
But only seconds later, the enemy showed his face
How quickly it amazes me, my excitement turned to doubt
Put the helmet on your head a voice inside did shout
Putting on the armor of God, I spoke His word right out
Faith is the victory My child that overcomes all doubt
He is the faithful One I know, I've seen His work first hand
So resting in His perfect will, I know He'll work His Plan

~LINDA K. SMITH (1948~) SENECA, SC

SURETY OF THE COVENANT

By so much was Jesus made a surety of a better testament.
HEBREWS 7:22 KJV

Christ was made surety of a better testament. Aaron and his sons passed away; of Christ it is witnessed that He liveth. He is priest in the power of an endless life. Because He continueth ever, He hath an unchangeable priesthood. And because He ever liveth to make intercession, He can save to the uttermost, He can save completely. It is because Christ is the Ever-living One that His suretyship of the covenant is so effectual. He liveth ever to make intercession, and can therefore save completely. Every moment there rise up from His holy presence to the Father, the unceasing pleadings which secure to His people the powers and the blessings of the heavenly life. And every moment there go out from Him downward to His people, the mighty influences of His unceasing intercession, conveying to them uninter-ruptedly the power of the heavenly life. As surety with us for the Father's favor, He never ceases to pray and present us before Him; as surety with the Father for us, He never ceases to work, and reveal the Father within us.

~ANDREW MURRAY (1828–1917)

MAKE IT YOUR AIM!

*Study to shew thyself approved unto God, a workman that
needeth not to be ashamed, rightly dividing the word of truth.*

2 TIMOTHY 2:15 KJV

It does not take much TV watching or listening to the radio to understand that there is much "wrongly" dividing of the Word taking place. So, as a Christian then, it is necessary that we study the Bible for our own understanding, and so we might teach correctly. God has given us His Word, but He expects us to read it, study it, and even commit it to memory. He, then, through the Holy Spirit, will bring to our memories portions of Scripture that would apply to a given situation. But how do we go about studying in the first place? The first and most important thing is prayer. Ask for wisdom and understanding from our heavenly Father, and the Holy Spirit will come to your aid. After you pick a book to begin your studies, made it a point to be consistent and regular. Do not study on and off, but set aside a time or times every day to study. As you begin reading, pay close attention to what is actually being said. Look at the verses before and after. Determine whom the passage is talking to or about. Look at every word. As Paul told Timothy to study the Word to be able to rightly divide it, you and I need that same encouragement. So, let's study the Word on a regular basis. It will pay great dividends!

~JACK R. ELLIOTT (1941–) TOBACCOVILLE, NC

MOMENT BY MOMENT

In that day sing ye unto her, A vineyard of red wine. I the LORD do keep it;
I will water it every moment: lest any hurt it, I will keep it night and day.

ISAIAH 27:2–3 KJV

The vineyard was the symbol of the people of Israel, in whose midst the True Vine was to stand. The branch is the symbol of the individual believer, who stands in the Vine. The song of the vineyard is also the song of the Vine and its every branch. The command still goes forth to the watchers of the vineyard—would that they obeyed it, and sang till every feeble-hearted believer had learned and joined the joyful strain—"Sing ye unto her: I, JEHOVAH, DO KEEP IT; I will water it every moment: lest any hurt it, I WILL KEEP it night and day." What an answer from the mouth of God Himself to the question so often asked: Is it possible for the believer always to abide in Jesus? Is a life of unbroken fellowship with the Son of God indeed attainable here in this earthly life? Truly not, if the abiding is our work, to be done in our strength. But the things that are impossible with men are possible with God. If the Lord Himself will keep the soul night and day, yea, will watch and water it every moment, then surely the uninterrupted communion with Jesus becomes a blessed possibility to those who can trust God to mean and to do what He says. Then surely the abiding of the branch of the vine day and night, summer and winter, in a never-ceasing life-fellowship, is nothing less than the simple but certain promise of your abiding in your Lord.

~ANDREW MURRAY (1828–1917)

THE CHOSEN PATH

THE MOST IMPORTANT RELAY RACE IN LIFE

*For he established a testimony . . . they should make them known
to their children . . . that the generation to come might know them.*

PSALM 78:5–6 KJV

Four runners take their positions around the track. The first
runner takes the baton firmly in his hand, sets himself in the blocks,
and readies himself in the starting position. At the sound of the
starter's gun, he explodes out of the blocks toward the team's next
runner. As he nears the next runner, his teammate begins to run away
from him. The first runner must quickly pass the baton to the next
runner. He stretches and strains to put the baton firmly in the next
runner's hand, making sure that it is not dropped. The first runner now
watches as each teammate passes the baton to the next runner. Every
Christian parent is involved in an eternal relay race. This race
determines whether or not our children attain an eternal prize. The
baton is our faith in Christ. The goal is to pass this baton from our
hearts to our child's heart. As a child's birth draws close, parents must
set themselves in the starting blocks, readying themselves for the
starter's pistol. With their spiritual lives coiled for action, they must
explode out of the blocks when birth takes place. This is critical because
as soon as a child is born, he starts running away from us—it's called
growing up. Parents must expend their energy to accomplish one
goal—the passing on of their faith to their child. They must get the
baton firmly in their child's heart before the child gets too far down the
racetrack of life. Parents must run to win this important race.

~DR. GLEN SCHULTZ (1947–) HENDERSONVILLE, TN

THE CHOSEN PATH

BECAUSE OF WHOSE WE ARE

But if we walk in the Light as He Himself is in the Light, . . .
the blood of Jesus His Son cleanses us from all sin.

1 JOHN 1:7 NASB

Three years ago, my wife and I found out that three of our four children were getting married within fifteen months of each other. On a pastor's salary, paying for three weddings in fifteen months would take a miracle. Of course, Becky and I prayed about this matter and we trusted God to provide. We knew that just as we, as parents, wanted to give good gifts to our children, God also wanted to give good gifts to His children. That is how we prayed: "God, please give the gift of weddings to our children." A morning or two after our request to God, a friend telephoned my wife. The friend said, "Becky, what is God's perfect number?" Becky replied, "Seven!" "That's right, seven," the friend responded. "My husband and I want to give you and Andy seven thousand dollars to use for your children's weddings." We were speechless, and humbled. The late Ron Dunn told a story about taking his son and two friends to an amusement park. He bought several tickets and as the boys would line up for a ride, Ron would hand out the tickets. Later in the day, Ron was handing out the usual three tickets when he noticed a fourth hand extended. Ron responded to the boy, saying, "Son, I don't think I know you." Ron's son said, "Dad, it's okay. He's with me." It's not who we are that gets a response from God, it's because of who's we are. When we pray, Jesus responds, "It's okay, Dad. They're with me."

~**ANDY DIETZ (1950–) BORGER, TX**

THE CHOSEN PATH

WONDERFUL

His name shall be called Wonderful.

Isaiah 9:6 kjv

There are two hundred and fifty-six names given in the Bible for the Lord Jesus Christ, and I suppose this was because He was infinitely beyond all that any one name could express. Of the many names given to Christ, it is my purpose at this time to briefly consider this one: "His name shall be called Wonderful." Let us look into it somewhat and see whether He was true to the name given Him in a prophecy eight hundred years before He was born. Does the name fit Him? Is it such a name as He ought to have? Wonderful means something that is transcendently beyond the common; something that is away beyond the ordinary. It means something that is altogether unlike anything else, . . . He is true to His name, and that is—He is a wonderful Savior because He saved me. There is nothing that can be so convincing to a man as his own experience. I do not know that I am the son of my mother any more certainly than I know that I am a child of God, and I do not know that I have been born in a natural way any more convincingly than I know that I have been born of the Spirit. And now let me ask you this: Has this wonderful Savior saved you? Do you know Him as your Savior? Have you ever given Him your case? When the proof is so overwhelming that He does save, and has been saving for centuries, and that none have ever been saved or ever can be saved except through Him, is it not wonderful that any one can be indifferent to the claims of Jesus Christ?

~Billy Sunday (1862–1935)

THREE LITTLE LADIES
IN THEIR EIGHTIES

Open thou mine eyes, that I may behold wondrous things out of thy law.

PSALM 119:18 KJV

As the teenager entered the church, he was greeted by three ladies, all with glowing smiles and hugs for everyone. They immediately asked for his name and then emphatically stated, "We will be praying for you." They then turned and went to the alter and prayed. The teen was shocked. He had never seen people so committed. Every week they stated, "We are praying for you." Every week they went to the alter. He was so moved by their witness that he was convicted of his own life and began to question, "Why are they praying for me?" He even felt convicted just seeing these ladies out in town as they often would say to him, "We are praying for you." It didn't matter where he was, even in the grocery line. Those words would follow him every time he saw them. He could almost hear his name being called out to God by ladies he didn't really know. One evening at the end of a service, he could hold on no longer. He went to the alter and there he asked Christ to save him. He stood and turned around, and right behind him were the three little ladies. Their response was great; they smiled, gave hugs, and said, "We will be praying for you!" God used three little ladies in their eighties to touch the heart of a teenage boy. Their example of weeping and prayer opened the spiritual eyes of a boy who was lost. Their example of God's love brought the pages of God's Word to life. How many of us are praying for lost teens? For any lost soul?

~TIMOTHY RAY PITTMAN (1959–) SHIFFIELD, VA

A HIGH STANDARD

I will love thee, O LORD, my strength. The LORD is my rock, and my fortress,
and my deliverer; my God, my strength, in whom I will trust;
my buckler, and the horn of my salvation, and my high tower.

PSALM 18:1–2 KJV

Even if we have no constitutional temptation to fickleness, we must feel our own weakness if we are really quickened of God. Dear reader, do you not find enough in any one single day to make you stumble? You that desire to walk in perfect holiness, as I trust you do; you that have set before you a high standard of what a Christian should be—do you not find that before the breakfast things are cleared away from the table, you have displayed enough folly to make you ashamed of yourselves? If we were to shut ourselves up in the lone cell of a hermit, temptation would follow us; for as long as we cannot escape from ourselves we cannot escape from incitements to sin. There is that within our hearts which should make us watchful and humble before God. If He does not confirm us, we are so weak that we shall stumble and fall; not overturned by an enemy, but by our own carelessness. Lord, be Thou our strength. We are weakness itself.

~C. H. SPURGEON (1834–1892)

THIS MAKES SENSE!

A man's heart plans his way, but the LORD directs his steps.
PROVERBS 16:9 NKJV

Despite the obvious fact that as human beings, we have certain limitations, there is a persistent belief that if you can conceive an idea and believe you can accomplish it, your chances for accomplishing it go up dramatically. Unfortunately, there are many bankruptcies filed every year by people who conceived "marvelous" ideas and believed with all their hearts they could achieve them. They poured their hearts and souls into their endeavors and still ended in bankruptcy. Perhaps the idea was not sound, or they did not have the skills, ability, or training necessary to make the idea work. It could be that circumstances beyond their control prevented them from bringing their idea to a successful conclusion. Our jails and prisons are filled with people who conceived what they believed to be marvelous ideas, visions, or dreams. They believed with all their hearts they could reach them, worked extremely hard, and ended up behind the eight ball, compromised their integrity, and landed in prison. We were given minds so that we can gather information, mix it with common sense, and ultimately make sound judgments about what we can and want to do. Then we can plan accordingly. According to God's will for our lives.

~ZIG ZIGLAR (1926–) ADDISON, TX

THE CHOSEN PATH

QUENCHING THE SPIRIT

Quench not the Spirit.

1 THESSALONIANS 5:19 KJV

The Bible informs us that the Spirit influences the human mind by means of truth. The Spirit persuades men to act in view of truth, as we ourselves influence our fellow-men by truth presented to their minds. I do not mean that God presents truth to the mind in the same manner as we do. Of course, His mode of doing it must differ from ours. We use the pen, the lips, the gesture; we use the language of words and the language of nature. God does not employ these means now; yet still He reaches the mind with truth. Sometimes His providence suggests it; and then His Spirit gives it efficiency, setting it home upon the heart with great power. Sometimes the Lord makes use of preaching; indeed, His ways are various. But, whatever the mode, the object is always the same namely, to produce voluntary action in conformity to His law. Now, if the Bible were entirely silent on this subject, we should still know from the nature of mind, and from the nature of those influences which only can move the human mind, that the Spirit must exert not physical, but moral influences on the mind. Yet we are not now left to a merely metaphysical inference; we have the plain testimony of the Bible to the fact that the Spirit employs truth in converting and sanctifying men.

~CHARLES FINNEY (1792–1875)

BE STILL

Be still and know that I am God.

PSALM 46:10 KJV

December 22, 1998, was to be my last day in the office before Christmas. Driving into the parking lot after my lunch break, I caught sight of a fire truck parked in front of the entrance, lights flashing. Six months before, my mostly secretarial position description was restructured to include oversight of the use and maintenance of our 37,000-square-foot ministry center. When my boss discussed with me this rearrangement of responsibility, I confessed that my only experience in building maintenance was maintaining my very small first home. Actually my "expertise" was limited to reading the phone book and calling a repair person. We had only occupied the building for about eighteen months. Temperatures had dipped below 25 degrees Fahrenheit for several days and the overhead fire sprinkler pipes had frozen solid. As the sun warmed the attic space housing those pipes, the ice within the pipes melted, expanding them to the point of breakage . . . very loud breakage at that! The first of six "explosions" over a period of three days occurred in the kitchen area of the building with staff members on a lunch break nearby. The ceiling fell; water ran everywhere. Fortunately, no one was injured. Because no building contractors were available, all we could do was respond when the next piece of ceiling fell, moving debris and protecting furnishings as best we could. There were moments of internal distress during that time, as there have been many other times in my life; however, God is our refuge and continues to reveal Himself through daily experiences that might not always go as planned.

~MARSHA GRAY (1953–) VANCOUVER, WA

THE CHOSEN PATH

JOYFUL WORSHIP AND THE GREAT COMMISSION

FROM LUKE 24:44–53 NKJV

In this post resurrection encounter, Jesus appeared in the midst of a room where the two disciples who had encountered the Lord on the road to Emmaus were telling their story. He opened their understanding so that they were able to comprehend the Scriptures. Things that had been hazy and confusing to them now began to take on pointed meaning and powerful purpose. He showed them that His death and resurrection were foretold in the Old Testament. He taught them that a vital part of the gospel message was the preaching of the need to repent of sin and the promise of forgiveness to the repenting. He taught them that this gospel is to be preached in His name— declaring Him in His precious sinless life, His amazing atoning death, and His powerful resurrection. He identified the field of labor as "all nations." The word for nations is used differently than we tend to think of it. It is the word *ethnos* from which we get our term *ethnic groups*. Jesus instructed them to preach the gospel in His name to all people groups. He assured them that He would send "the Promise of My Father" (the Holy Spirit) and instructed them to wait in Jerusalem until they received power from on high to carry out the mission He had given to them. What about you? Have the eyes of your understanding been opened so that you understand the Scripture when you read it or hear it preached and taught? Is your life marked by a continual willingness to repent of your sin and forgive those who sin against you?

~BILL ASCOL (1952–) SHREVEPORT, LA

HE IS ALIVE!

*The God of our fathers raised up Jesus, whom ye slew and hanged on
a tree. Him hath God exalted with his right hand to be a Prince and
a Saviour, for to give repentance to Israel, and forgiveness of sins.*

ACTS 5:30–31 KJV

You are not asked to trust in a dead Jesus, but in One who, though
He died for our sins, has risen again for our justification. You may go to
Jesus at once as to a living and present friend. He is not a mere memory,
but a continually existent Person who will hear your prayers and answer
them. He lives on purpose to carry on the work for which He once laid
down His life. He is interceding for sinners at the right hand of the
Father, and for this reason He is able to save them to the uttermost who
come unto God by Him. Come and try this living Savior, if you have
never done so before. This living Jesus is also raised to an eminence of
glory and power. He does not now sorrow as "a humble man before his
foes," nor labor as "the carpenter's son;" but He is exalted far above
principalities and power and every name that is named. The Father has
given Him all power in Heaven and in earth, and he exercises this high
endowment in carrying out His work of grace. Hear what Peter and the
other apostles testified concerning Him before the high priest and the
council: The God of our fathers raised up Jesus, whom ye slew and
hanged on a tree. Him hath God exalted with His right hand to be a
Prince and a Savior, for to give repentance to Israel, and forgiveness of
sins (Acts 5:30–31).

~C. H. SPURGEON (1834–1892)

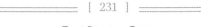

THE CHOSEN PATH

A PARENT'S GREATEST JOY

*I have no greater joy than this: to hear that
my children are walking in truth.*

3 JOHN V. 4 HCSB

Each day throughout America, parents cheer on the sidelines of athletic fields or gather in recital halls to proudly watch their children compete and perform to the best of their abilities. Many dollars and many hours are spent in an effort to help the children of our land excel in sports and the fine arts. In addition to these, parents long for their children to advance as far as possible academically with the hope of future vocational success that a good education promises. It is commendable for parents to provide these opportunities for personal development, but let us remember to not allow these "good things" to crowd out the "best things." When our children see these other events taking precedence over the spiritual life of a family, they receive a mixed signal about our family priorities. So, in the midst of baseball practices, piano recitals, and science fairs, let's not neglect the spiritual formation of our children. In all the days that occur between their first day of school and their wedding day, there are many important days for which our children must be prepared. But have we considered how we are preparing them for their final and most important day, Judgment Day, the day in which they will stand before the Lord and give account for their lives? Have we adequately prepared them to live faithfully for the Lord, in light of this approaching Day? Remember the words of the apostle John quoted above, and apply them to your family. On this very day, consider what you are doing to provide a lasting spiritual heritage that leads your children to walk with the Lord.

~RYAN BOWMAN (1972–) LEE'S SUMMIT, MO

THE CHOSEN PATH

NOT TOLERATION, BUT RIGHT

*Stand fast therefore in the liberty wherewith Christ hath made
us free, and be not entangled again with the yoke of bondage.*

GALATIANS 5:1 KJV

Baptists have one consistent record concerning liberty throughout all their long and eventful history. They have never been a party to oppression of conscience. They have forever been the unwavering champions of liberty, both religious and civil. Their contention now, is, and has been, and, please God, must ever be, that it is the natural and fundamental and indefeasible right of every human being to worship God or not, according to the dictates of his conscience, and, as long as he does not infringe upon the rights of others, he is to be held accountable alone to God for all religious beliefs and practices. Our contention is not for mere toleration, but for absolute liberty. There is a wide difference between toleration and liberty. Toleration implies that somebody falsely claims the right to tolerate. Toleration is a concession, while liberty is a right. Toleration is a matter of expediency, while liberty is a matter of principle. Toleration is a gift from God. It is the consistent and insistent contention of our Baptist people, always and everywhere, that religion must be forever voluntary and uncoerced, and that it is not the prerogative of any power, whether civil or ecclesiastical, to compel men to conform to any religious creed or form of worship, or to pay taxes for the support of a religious organization to which they do not believe. God wants free worshipers and no other kind.

~G. W. TRUETT (1867–1944)

BIBLICAL PATHS

PROVERBS 3:13–18

Happy is a man who finds wisdom
and who acquires understanding,
for she is more profitable than silver,
and her revenue is better than gold.
She is more precious than jewels;
nothing you desire compares with her.
Long life is in her right hand; in her left, riches and honor.
Her ways are pleasant, and all her paths, peaceful.
She is a tree of life to those who embrace her,
and those who hold on to her are happy.

PROVERBS 4:20–27

My son, pay attention to my words; listen closely to my sayings.
Don't lose sight of them; keep them within your heart.
For they are life to those who find them,
and health to one's whole body.
Guard your heart above all else, for it is the source of life.
Don't let your mouth speak dishonestly,
and don't let your lips talk deviously.
Let your eyes look forward; fix your gaze straight ahead.
Carefully consider the path
Or for your feet, and all your ways will be established.
Don't turn to the right or to the left; keep your feet away from evil.

HCSB

THE CHOSEN PATH

IT AIN'T OVER TILL IT'S OVER

It ain't over till it's over! Job was a man who had it all, then calamity struck and he lost it all: his children, his possessions, his health. The final straw was when his wife gave him some real sound advice . . . "Just curse God and die." This was his wife talking! She was supposed to be his right hand, his helper, his support and comforter. What a blow it must have been to Job for her to mock him in his lowest moment. Just for asking's sake, what would you have said in response? Knowing my temperament, it would not have been recordable in the Bible, but Job bit his tongue and only mildly scolded her for expecting only good things from God. When hard times come into many peoples lives their first reaction is to question God's goodness. Why? Why? In that moment of suffering it seems inappropriate to ask the question, "Why not?" What makes any of us immune to suffering and pain? We are ready to quote, "For all things work together for good to them that love the Lord and are called to His purpose" as it applies to someone else, but forget that it is equally true for me, even when it hurts. God rewarded Job with more than he had before his trial, but don't count on it happening to you. Our Father has different ways of rewarding us in this life. The Bible says, "Blessed is the man who endures temptation, for when he has been approved, he will receive the crown of life which the Lord has promised to those who love Him."

~G. W. STROTHER (1933–) CLAYTON, GA

SAFETY, FULLNESS, AND SWEET REFRESHMENT IN CHRIST

And a man shall be as an hiding-place from the wind,
and a covert from the tempest.

ISAIAH 32:2 KJV

We are told here that "a man shall be a hiding-place from the wind." There is an emphasis in the words, that "a man" should be this. If these things had been said of God, it would not be strange under the Old Testament; for God is frequently called a hiding-place for his people, a refuge in time of trouble, a strong rock, and a high tower. But what is so remarkable is, that they are said of "a man." But this is a prophecy of the Son of God incarnate. The things here foretold of him, and the commendations given him. "He shall be a hiding-place from the wind, and a covert from the tempest:" that is, he shall be the safety and defense of his people, to which they shall flee for protection in the time of their danger and trouble. Now when a man finds Jesus Christ, he is like one that has been traveling in those deserts till he is almost consumed with thirst, and who at last finds a river of cool and clear water. And Christ was typified by the river of water that issued out of the rock for the children of Israel in this desert: he is compared to a river, because there is such a plenty and fullness in him. He is the "shadow of a great rock in a weary land."

~JONATHAN EDWARDS (1703–1758)

DISCOVERING GOD'S WISDOM

"For my thoughts are not your thoughts," . . . *says the LORD.*
ISAIAH 55:8 NKJV

Tiny children are so funny as one observes them bragging about their dads. We have all probably heard them making such comparisons as: "My pop's smarter than your pop," or "My dad's better than your dad." Children love to admire and trust their dads. They think their earthly fathers can do anything. And how do we, as Christians, think of our heavenly Father? Well, when we are troubled, if we could think clearly about how smart our heavenly Father is, many of our misgivings about life would take different perspectives. How often do you think about how intelligent and wise God is? He is the wisest Father a person can have and He wants to listen to us through our prayers and advise us through the Bible's wisdom. (Cf. James 3:13–18.)

~JANET MILLER (1943–) WHEAT RIDGE, CO

THE CHOSEN PATH

SPIRITS OF LOVE

God is love.

1 JOHN 4:16 KJV

Does the Holy Spirit love us? There can be but one answer to this question. Yes! He does. As truly as the Father loveth us, as truly as the Son loveth us, so truly does the Spirit love us. The grace or free love which a sinner needs, and which has been revealed and sealed to us through the seed of the woman, the "Word made flesh," belongs equally to Father, Son, and Spirit. That love which we believe to be in God must be the same in each Person of the Godhead, else the Godhead would be divided; one Person at variance with the others, or, at least, less loving than the others: which is impossible. Twice over it is written, God is love (1 John 4:8, 16) and this applies to each Person of the Godhead. The Father is love; the Son is love; the Spirit is love. The Trinity is a Trinity of Love. When it is said, "God is a Spirit" (John 4:24), the words refer to each Person. If we lose sight of the love of one, we shall lose sight of the love of all. That which is the glory of Jehovah, is the glory of each of the three Persons. Let us beware of misrepresenting the Trinity by believing in unequal love, a love that is not equally large and free in each.

~HORATIUS BONAR (1808–1889)

GOD IS THE SPIRIT OF PEACE

*Let us therefore follow after the things which make for peace,
and things wherewith one may edify another.*

ROMANS 14:19 KJV

We must think right thoughts of God if we would worship Him as He desires to be worshipped; if we would live the life He wishes us to live, and enjoy the peace which He has provided for us. The want of stable peace, of which so many complain, may arise from imperfect views of the Spirit's love. True, our peace comes from the work of the Substitute upon the cross, from the blood of the one sacrifice, from the sin bearing of Him who has made peace by the blood of the cross. But it is the Holy Spirit who glorifies Christ to us, and takes the scales from our eyes. If then we doubt His love, can we expect Him to reveal the Son in our hearts? Are we not thrusting Him away, and hindering that view of the peacemaking which He only can give? Trust His love, and He will make known the Peacemaker to you. Trust His love, and He will show the precious blood by which the guiltiest conscience is purged, and the peace which passes all understanding is imparted. He is the Spirit of peace, and His work is the work of peace. His office is to make known to us the Prince of Peace. Can there be peace without the recognition of the Holy Spirit's love? Can there fail to be peace when this is recognized and acted on? Doubts as to the love of the Spirit must inevitably intercept the peace which the peacemaking cross presents to us.

~HORATIUS BONAR (1808–1889)

THE CHOSEN PATH

UNCHANGEABLE ALMIGHTY LORD

UNCHANGEABLE almighty Lord, our souls upon thy truth we stay; Accomplish now thy faithful word, and give, O give us all one way! O let us all join hand in hand who seek redemption in thy blood, Fast in one mind and spirit stand, and build the temple of our God! Thou only canst our wills control, our wild unruly passions bind, Tame the old Adam in our soul, and make us of one heart and mind. Speak but the reconciling word, the winds shall cease, the waves subside, We all shall praise our common Lord, our Jesus, and him crucified. Giver of peace and unity, send down thy mild, pacific Dove; We all shall then in one agree, and breathe the spirit of thy love. We all shall think and speak the same, delightful lesson of thy grace! One undivided Christ proclaim, and jointly glory in thy praise. O let us take a softer mould, blended and gathered into thee; Under one Shepherd make one fold, where all is love and harmony! Regard thine own eternal prayer, and send a peaceful answer down; To us thy Father's name declare; unite and perfect us in one! So shall the world believe and know that God hath sent thee from above, When thou art seen in us below, and every soul displays thy love.

~CHARLES WESLEY (1707–1788)

A MOTHER'S WITNESS

Humble yourselves therefore under the mighty hand of God,
that He may exalt you in due time.

1 PETER 5:6 KJV

Witnessing is not just something you say; sometimes it's something you don't say! A young man was sitting on the side of his prison bed when a chaplain came by and asked him about Christ. "Son, do you know Jesus?" The young man replied a simple, but rather emphatic, "No!" "Would you like to know about Jesus?" and again the same response. This chaplain was all too familiar with that type of response and did not allow it to deter his attempt to share Christ. The next day he asked the young man, "Whom do you know that has walked and talked their faith? Has anyone ever lived before you the testimony that they told you?" Without a moment of hesitation, the young man said simply, "My mother never swore!" The chaplain seized the opportunity and asked about the boy about his mother. The young man began, "I gave her every reason to curse, to hate me, to just turn away from me, but she never did." He went on and on about how his mother had lived. He painted such a picture that the chaplain felt he knew her himself. He watched a bitter young man melt at the thought of his mother, and he saw a new beginning in the lad's tear-stained eyes. That young man was able to believe in the same Jesus his mother loved and served. Lives can be changed and mothers who have prayed for years may not find out on this side of eternity that the child they prayed for did, in fact, commit their lives to the Lord. Humble yourselves. "Due Time" is near! Keep looking up.

~TIMOTHY RAY PITTMAN (1959–) SHIFFIELD, VA

PRAYER AND OBEDIENCE

O that there were such an heart in them, that they would fear me,
and keep all my commandments always.

DEUTERONOMY 5:29 KJV

Unquestionably obedience is a high virtue, a soldier quality. To obey belongs, preeminently, to the soldier. It is his first and last lesson, and he must learn how to practice it all the time, without question, uncomplainingly. Obedience, moreover, is faith in action, and is the outflow as it is the very test of love. What a marvelous statement of the relationship created and maintained by obedience! The Son of God is held in the bosom of the Father's love, by virtue of His obedience! And the factor which enables the Son of God to ever abide in His Father's love is revealed in His own statement, "For I do, always, those things that please Him." Furthermore: obedience is the conserver and the life of love. "If ye keep My commandments," says Jesus, "ye shall abide in My love, even as I have kept My Father's commandments and abide in His love." The gift of the Holy Spirit in full measure and in richer experience, depends upon loving obedience: "If ye love Me, keep My commandments," is the Master's word. "And I will pray the Father, and He shall give you another Comforter, that He may abide with you for ever." Obedience to God is a condition of spiritual thrift, inward satisfaction, stability of heart. "If ye be willing and obedient, ye shall eat the fruit of the land." Obedience opens the gates of the Holy City, and gives access to the tree of life. "Blessed are they that do His commandments, that they may have right to the tree of life, and may enter in through the gates, into the city."

~E. M. BOUNDS (1835–1913)

GOD IS FAITHFUL

God is faithful, by whom ye were called unto the
fellowship of his Son Jesus Christ our Lord.
1 CORINTHIANS 1:9 KJV

As I look at each of my sons, I am reminded that God is good and how richly He has chosen to bless me. Our two youngest remind me that "God is faithful" in all areas of our lives. He has been with us during the good times and the bad. Dustin (12) and Levi (9) were born with Hereditary Spherocitosis. Dustin was diagnosed at age three months. It began a roller-coaster ride of emotions for my wife and me, but we held to these few words, "God is faithful." He would see us through the physical, emotional, and financial needs that would arise. He helped us to grow spiritually in ways we could not have imagined. All we could do was trust Him. I learned, and believe completely, that He would never leave us nor forsake us. Others have failed me, and I have failed them, but God will never fail us. Praise and thanksgiving are constantly on my lips. All three of my sons love, and actively serve, the Lord. They are quick-witted and keep me on my toes. Recently in our youth Sunday school class we were discussing evolution versus creation. I asked my son Dustin, "Do you believe that you came from a monkey?" His answer: "No, I came from two monkeys." Whether it's through the fire or the flood, God is faithful. So when everything is going down hill. Look up! God is faithful.

~ALMER (ANDY) ANDERSON (1964–) BELLE FOURCHE, SD

MY FATHER CAN FIX IT

Even though I walk through the valley of the shadow of death, I will
fear no evil, for you are with me; your rod and your staff, they comfort me.

PSALM 23:4 NIV

On one occasion in my home, a fuse blew and left my entire family motionless and silent. Our four-year-old daughter with fear in her voice said, "Daddy, the lights are out and it's dark." Hearing the fear in her voice, I said, "It's going to be all right." I grabbed the flashlight, went to the breaker box, and turned back on the lights. Sometimes the breaker trips in our lives and we are cast into darkness. It's during the dark periods of our lives that we become afraid, filled with doubt, and we lose all hope that things are ever going to improve. I have come to realize that the dark periods of life are merely opportunities for me to depend on my Father. The psalmist reminds us, "Even though I walk through the valley of the shadow of death, I will fear no evil, for you are with me; your rod and your staff, they comfort me" (Psalm 23:4). It is comforting to know that our Father is present and He is able to turn the lights back on in our lives. Whenever the lights go out, remember, just depend on your heavenly Father and He will turn the lights back on in your life.

~WILLIAM M. BLACKFORD, IV (1969–) LOUISVILLE, KY

THE CHOSEN PATH

HOW TO WALK ON WATER

The boat was already a considerable distance from land.

MATTHEW 14:24 NIV

During the fourth watch of the night, Jesus went out to them, walking on the lake. When the disciples saw him walking on the lake, they were terrified. "It's a ghost," they said, and cried out in fear. But Jesus immediately said to them: "Take courage! It is I. Don't be afraid." "Lord, if it's you," Peter replied, "tell me to come to you on the water." "Come," he said. Then Peter got down out of the boat, walked on the water, and came toward Jesus. But when he saw the wind, he was afraid and, beginning to sink, cried out, "Lord, save me!" Immediately Jesus reached out his hand and caught him. "You of little faith," he said. "Why did you doubt?" How do we walk on water? Get out of the boat. It takes real faith to even step out of the boat. It means getting uncomfortable. It is only when we are uncomfortable that we need God. Don't lose focus on Jesus. Even a little faith, when focused on Jesus, quiets our doubts. The well-known poem entitled "Footprints" tells of a man looking over the path of his life seen as footprints along a beach. The path has two sets of prints: one his, the other Jesus'. At certain difficult times in his life there is only one set of prints in the sand. The man asked Jesus why he abandoned him at the low points of his life. Jesus said that it was then that he carried the man. The only way we can complete the tasks God has planned for us is to allow Jesus to carry us.

~TODD FUEHRER (1967–) BISMARCK, ND

THE BRIDEGROOM WAITS

That my joy might remain in you, and that your joy might be full.

JOHN 15:11 KJV

The Bridegroom is waiting for thee all the time; the conditions that debar His approach are all of thine own making. He will be most ready, most glad, to "Satisfy thy deepest longings, to meet, supply thine every need." What should we think of a betrothed one whose conceit and self-will prevented not only the consummation of her own joy, but of his who had given her his heart? Though never at rest in his absence, she cannot trust him fully; and she does not care to give up her own name, her own rights and possessions, her own will to him who has become necessary for her happiness. She would fain claim him fully, without giving herself fully to him; but it can never be: while she retains her own name, she can never claim his. She may not promise to love and honor if she will not also promise to obey, and till her love reaches that point of surrender, she must remain an unsatisfied lover—she cannot, as a satisfied bride, find rest in the home of her husband. What would be the feelings of an earthly bridegroom if he discovered that his bride-elect was dreading to marry him? Yet how many of the Lord's redeemed ones treat Him just so? True love cannot be stationary; it must either decline or grow. Divine love is destined to conquer.

~J. HUDSON TAYLOR (1832–1905)

OUR GOD, OUR HELP IN AGES PAST

Our God, our Help in ages past, our Hope for years to come,

Our Shelter from the stormy blast, and our eternal Home!

Under the shadow of Thy throne Thy saints have dwelt secure;

Sufficient is Thine arm alone, and our defense is sure.

Before the hills in order stood or earth received her frame,

From everlasting Thou art God, to endless years the same.

A thousand ages in Thy sight are like an evening gone,

Short as the watch that ends the night before the rising sun.

Thy word commands our flesh to dust: "Return ye sons of men!"

All nations rose from earth at first and turn to earth again.

Time, like an ever-rolling stream, bears all its sons away;

They fly forgotten as a dream dies at the opening day.

Like flowery fields the nations stand, pleased with the morning light;

The flowers beneath the mower's hand lie withering ere 'tis night.

Our God, our Help in ages past, our Hope for years to come,

Be Thou our Guard while troubles last and our eternal Home!

~ISAAC WATTS (1674–1748)

MOURNING

Blessed are the dead which die in the Lord.

REVELATION 14:13 KJV

When godly friends die, they are in a better condition; they are taken away "from the evil to come" (Isaiah 57:1). They are out of the storm and have gone to the haven: The godly have a portion promised them upon their marriage to Christ, but the portion is not paid till the day of their death. The saints are promoted at death to communion with God; they have what they so long hoped for, and prayed for. Why, then, should we be impatient at our friends' promotion? You who are a saint have a friend in heaven whom you cannot lose. Are you mourning somebody close to you? Look up to heaven and draw comfort from there; your best kindred are above. God will be with you in the hour of death: "though I walk through the valley of the shadow of death, thou art with me" (Psalm 23:4). Other friends you cannot keep. God is a friend you cannot lose. He will be your guide in life; your hope in death; your reward after death. A godly relation is parted with, but not lost. Religious friends have only gone a little ahead of us. A time will shortly come when there shall be a meeting without parting. Oh, what glorious applause there will be, when old relations meet together in heaven, and are in each other's embraces! What music in the choir of angels! How heaven will ring with their praises! And that which is the crown of all, those who were joined in the flesh here shall be joined nearer than ever in the mystic body, and shall lie together in Christ's bosom, that bed of perfume.

~THOMAS WATSON (1620–1686)

BE STILL AND KNOW

"Be still, and know that I am God."

PSALM 46:10 NIV

I was given a wonderful opportunity one summer to experience the stillness that I believe the psalmist wrote about in Psalm 46:10. In a beautiful cabin in the Northwoods of Minnesota, just feet from a wonderful lake, I practiced stillness. That was not the original purpose, but it was God's purpose. I had to stop and dwell on the fact that as a follower of the Savior, Jesus Christ, He is coming one day for me. Does that thought satisfy your heart? Or does the busyness of life overwhelm and cloud your heart and mind? We all struggle with the busy lives. We have families and the relationships they bring; some have jobs that are uninspiring, some lack employment; some right now deal with the reality of health problems and the uncertainty of it all; and some are living with the fact that finances consumes their life. This is what many call "real life"! The problem is not so much with the things that bring about a busy life, but with the fact that we seldom see God and the authority of His Word intertwined in the midst of our "real life." The fog of life easily dissipates our awareness of God, thereby leaving us consumed, feeling like we can't handle things in our life. All the while forgetting that the One who created you can most assuredly handle you! Take the time, even now, to be still and know that He is God and allow Him to be Lord over your life . . . your "real life."

~MILES ROHDE (1972–) MARSHALL, MN

THE CHOSEN PATH

TIME TO MAKE A CHOICE

*Therefore we must pay the closer attention to what
we have heard, lest we drift away from it.*

HEBREWS 2:1 RSV

Ah, how often the enemy succeeds, by one device or another, in tempting the believer away from that position of entire consecration to Christ in which alone the fullness of His power and of His love can be experienced. We say the fullness of His power and of His love; for he may not have ceased to love his Lord. In the passage before us, the bride still loves Him truly, though not wholly; there is still a power in His Word which is not unfelt, though she no longer renders instant obedience. She little realizes how she is wronging her Lord, and how real is the wall of separation between them. To her, worldliness seems as but a little thing; she has not realized the solemn truth of many passages in the Word of God that speak in no measured terms of the folly, the danger, the sin of friendship with the world. "Love not the world, neither the things that are in the world. If any man love the world, the love of the Father is not in him." We have to take our choice: we cannot enjoy both the world and Christ.

~HUDSON TAYLOR (1832–1905)

GOOD SLEEP CAN HELP
YOU LIVE A BETTER LIFE

When you lie down, you will not be afraid;
When you lie down, your sleep will be sweet.

PROVERBS 3:24 NASB

Even though many of us live very busy and active lives, the one constant that we cannot do without is adequate sleep. It seems more and more people are sleeping less and less, and paying the price for sleep deprivation. Insomnia is basically the inability to sleep or sleeplessness. In this disturbed or abnormal pattern of sleep, four distressing paths are commonly observed: resistance to falling asleep; difficulty in staying asleep; poor quality sleep; waking up too early. Loss of sleep affects us in different ways. Some of the typical signs of sleep deprivation include fatigue, irritability, inability to concentrate, short-term memory problems, drowsiness, abuse of stimulants, a strong-willed personality, and nightmares. The most common cause of sleeplessness is stress. In Esther 6:1, the king could not sleep. This was providential because God wanted the king to preserve Mordecai's life and his sleepless night was part of the plan. Most of our sleepless nights do not usually have such a profound purpose. If we live in the growing knowledge of God and keep sound wisdom and discretion, our sleep will be sweet. Sleep sounds so unspiritual. But it's important and its absence has an impact on who we are and how we live. Un-confessed sin and the accompanying feelings of guilt can create a restlessness and anxiety in our lives and thus prevent us from achieving sound sleep, but Christ has the answer to both problems and He is available to assist us in our times of need. May you have sweet and peaceful dreams.

~JAMES RUDY GRAY (1953–) SENECA, SC

THE LORD, OUR COMPANION

*Yea, though I walk through the valley of the shadow of death, I will fear
no evil: for thou art with me; thy rod and thy staff they comfort me.*

PSALM 23:4 KJV

Sweet are these words in describing a deathbed assurance. How
many have repeated them in their last hours with intense delight! But
the verse is equally applicable to agonies of spirit in the midst of life.
Some of us, like Paul, die daily through a tendency to gloom of soul.
Bunyan puts the Valley of the Shadow of Death far earlier in the
pilgrimage than the river which rolls at the foot of the celestial hills. We
have some of us traversed the dark and dreadful defile of "the shadow
of death" several times, and we can bear witness that the Lord alone
enabled us to bear up amid its wild thought, its mysterious horrors, its
terrible depressions. The Lord has sustained us and kept us above all
real fear of evil, even when our spirit has been overwhelmed. We have
been pressed and oppressed, but yet we have lived, for we have felt the
presence of the Great Shepherd and have been confident that His crook
would prevent the foe from giving us any deadly wound. Should the
present time be one darkened by the raven wings of a great sorrow, let
us glorify God by a peaceful trust in Him.

~C. H. SPURGEON (1834–1892)

THE CHOSEN PATH

PUTTING GOD FIRST

"But seek first the kingdom of God."
MATTHEW 6:33 NKJV

This, my life verse, has sustained me through difficult times. I became a Christian at age sixteen. We had made a difficult move to Washington, D.C., because my father was an aide to President Richard Nixon. Moving pulled the rug out from under me, but I began a new journey of faith. As I grew in the Lord, I began to change in many ways. My father called me a fanatic. When I felt led to transfer to Columbia International University to study the Bible, he told me that I would never be a success in this world. To him it was the "forbidden place." Quite frankly, although he loved me dearly, he did everything he could to dissuade me from going, including cutting the purse strings. My first day at CIU, I cried the whole way there. I felt torn between my earthly father and my heavenly Father, but I knew I must follow the leading of my heavenly Father. It was this verse that gave me comfort that day. If I put God first and was faithful to what He wanted me to do—He would take care of the rest of the things that were troubling me. And He did! Four years later, my father gave his heart to the Lord. He left his legal and political career and entered fulltime Christian lay ministry with my mother. The Lord went way beyond this little girl's heartfelt prayers and He does have a sense of humor! To prepare for his ministry, my father went to the "forbidden place"—Columbia International University! God calls His people to be faithful first. He is not interested in "worldly success."

~GINNY DENT BRANT (1955–) SENECA, SC

THE CHOSEN PATH

PSALM 23 KJV

The LORD is my shepherd; I shall not want.
He maketh me to lie down in green pastures:
he leadeth me beside the still waters. He restoreth my soul:
he leadeth me in the paths of righteousness for his name's sake.
Yea, though I walk through the valley of the shadow of death,
I will fear no evil: for thou art with me;
thy rod and thy staff they comfort me.
Thou preparest a table before me in
the presence of mine enemies: thou
anointest my head with oil; my cup runneth over.
Surely goodness and mercy
shall follow me all the days of my life:
and I will dwell in the house of the LORD for ever.

A PSALM OF DAVID

ALL THE WORLD

FROM MARK 16:14–16 NKJV

After His resurrection, Jesus Christ met with His disciples before ascending into heaven. He rebuked the "unbelief and hardness of heart" of the eleven apostles. Why? Because they had not believed the report that Jesus had risen from the dead. Remember that even the apostles struggled with this. When Jesus commissioned the apostles, He made His expectations very clear. He showed that the field in which His disciples are to labor is "all the world." There is no nation where the gospel of Jesus Christ should not be proclaimed. But it must be remembered that maps and boundaries are man-made lines. Within a country, there may be different ethnic groups who speak different languages. So "all the world" means every people group in the world. If we are to be obedient to Christ's commands, we must be committed to taking the gospel to all the world. Jesus Christ made the goal of His missionary commission clear—namely, to "preach the gospel to every creature." The gospel must be proclaimed to every person on the planet—not because every person (or any person, for that matter) deserves to hear the gospel. Rather, the gospel must be preached to every person on the planet because the Lord Jesus Christ is so precious and His grace so amazing that He is worthy to be proclaimed to every person made in the image of God. Do you believe this about Jesus Christ? Is He this precious to you? If so, who are you sharing with about His preciousness? What are you doing to see to it that the gospel is being preached to "every creature" on the planet?

~**BILL ASCOL (1952–) SHREVEPORT, LA**

FROM AUTHORIZATION TO AUTHORITATIVE

The fear of the LORD is the instruction of wisdom;
and before honour is humility.

PROVERBS 15:33 KJV

When an individual's life is at stake, obedience is vital. That's why military personnel are taught through discipline that commands are to be obeyed and not questioned. This is clearly ingrained from the beginning so that in the heat of battle, when there's no time for explanations and the sergeant says, "Move it out!" the troops will do so with confidence and without hesitation. One of the more enduring truths is that "the huge door of opportunity often swings open on the tiny hinges of obedience." You must learn to obey in order to learn to command. In the process, respect is established. First you give it, then you get it—because you've earned it. You expect to obey orders, and you pass that expectancy to those you are leading. Initially, the approach is authoritarian, but as you move up the ranks in the military and in life, the style changes from authoritarian to authoritative. You've learned the rules of the game; your commander or boss knows the rules, and he or she also knows that intelligent people respond more to an authoritative person than they do to an authoritarian one. The authoritarian person says, "You do it because I said to do it." The authoritative person says, "We are going to take this step because . . ." or "We're going to move in this directions because . . ." I saw a classic example of the authoritative approach in a family setting, but the principle and procedure work in any environment. Are they at work in your family?

~ZIG ZIGLAR (1926–) ADDISON, TX

THE CHOSEN PATH

THE WEAPON OF PRAYER

Ask of me, and I shall give thee the heathen for thine inheritance,
and the uttermost parts of the earth for thy possession.

It is greatly feared that much of the work of the Church is being done by those who are perfect strangers to the closet. Small wonder that the work does not succeed. While it may be true that many in the Church say prayers, it is equally true that their praying is of the stereotyped order. Even this sort of praying is done by a few straggling men to be found at prayer-meetings. Those whose names are to be found bulking large in our great Church assemblies are not men noted for their praying habits. Yet the entire fabric of the work in which they are engaged has, perforce, to depend on the adequacy of prayer. This fact is similar to the crisis which would be created were a country to have to admit in the face of an invading foe that it cannot fight and has no knowledge of the weapons whereby war is to be waged. In all God's plans for human redemption, He proposes that men pray. The men are to pray in every place, in the church, in the closet, in the home, on sacred days and on secular days. All things and everything are dependent on the measure of men's praying. Prayer is the genius and mainspring of life. We pray as we live; we live as we pray. Life will never be finer than the quality of the closet. The mercury of life will rise only by the warmth of the closet. Persistent non-praying eventually will depress life below zero.

~E. M. BOUNDS (1835–1913)

MIND OVER MATTER

I will take refuge in the shadow of your wings until the disaster has passed.

PSALM 57:1 NIV

No one is sure what causes mental disorders. A few are connected to physical imbalances. Some may be tied to genetic makeup. Others stem from learned attitudes such as low self-esteem, perfectionism, or the failure to give or receive forgiveness. In all these areas, Christians are not exempt. In times of crisis, we may find ourselves battling depression or struggling to retain a rational outlook. The problem is then compounded when we become burdened by guilt because we aren't totally and constantly "victorious." We aren't alone. Many biblical characters fought the same battles that we do—with varying measures of success. David at times felt submerged in problems. After Samuel anointed him the future king of Israel, Saul repeatedly tried to kill him. David fled to the wilderness and moved into the cave of Adullam. When his relatives heard about it, they joined him. Then the cave became really crowded: "All those who were in distress or in debt or discontented gathered around him, and he became their leader. About four hundred men were with him" (1 Samuel 22:2). With a price on his head, live-in relatives, and the responsibility of commanding four hundred distressed, discontented debtors, David could have had a nervous breakdown. But instead of fleeing to the recesses of a muddled mind, he fled to the source of stability. David cried out to God and discovered the secret of a sound mind. He cried out to God instead of withdrawing into himself. And he realized that God was fulfilling his purpose for him—not only in spite of but through troubles.

~VICKI HUFFMAN (1946–) MT. JULIET, TN

USE MONEY WISELY

There is one who scatters, yet increases more: And there is one
who withholds more than is right, but it leads to poverty.

PROVERBS 11:24 NKJV

An excellent branch of Christian wisdom is here inculcated by our Lord on all his followers, namely, the right use of money—a subject largely spoken of, after their manner, by men of the world; but not sufficiently considered by those whom God hath chosen out of the world. These, generally, do not consider, as the importance of the subject requires, the use of this excellent talent. Neither do they understand how to employ it to the greatest advantage; the introduction of which into the world is one admirable instance of the wise and gracious providence of God. It has, indeed, been the manner of poets, orators, and philosophers, in almost all ages and nations, to rail at this, as the grand corrupter of the world, the bane of virtue, the pest of human society. But is not all this mere empty rant? Is there any solid reason therein? By no means. For, let the world be as corrupt as it will, is gold or silver to blame? "The love of money," we know, "is the root of all evil;" but not the thing itself. The fault does not lie in the money, but in them that use it. It may be used ill: and what may not? But it may likewise be used well. It is therefore of the highest concern that all who fear God know how to employ this valuable talent; that they be instructed how it may answer these glorious ends, and in the highest degree.

~JOHN WESLEY (1703–1791)

THE CHOSEN PATH

NO SHAME

I am not ashamed of the gospel, because it is the power of God for the
salvation of everyone who believes: first for the Jew, then for the Gentile.

ROMANS 1:16 NIV

Wow . . . what a statement. And Paul meant what he said. The Bible supports Paul's assertion of "no shame." Paul brought the gospel to everyone he possibly could: kings, zealots, people of differing faiths, crowds in the public square, even to his own guard holding him prisoner. Why would Paul do such a thing? First of all, the gospel changed his life. Paul was one of the strongest critics of Christianity until he met Jesus on the road to Damascus. He was present at the first recorded death of a Christian martyr and he went "on the road" to Damascus to persecute Christians there. But Christ completely changed his life. Salvation was real to Paul. He could not be ashamed of the One who saved him. He knew he was undeserving of God's love and forgiveness, but God still loved him. Paul could never be ashamed of the One who saved him. Second, Paul could not be ashamed because the gospel needed to be told. The gospel is God's power of salvation to all people. Later, Paul said that "all have sinned and fall short of the glory of God" (Romans 3:23). Paul couldn't be ashamed of the gospel that has the power to change him (and everyone). Christ died for others beside Paul, and he knew that it was his responsibility to take this gospel message to all who he could. Paul knew that there was no other power for salvation but the gospel. Who will you share the gospel with today? Go with "no shame."

~JOE JONES (1964–) GOODYEAR, AZ

THE TRUE VINE

"I am the true vine, and My Father is the vinedresser. You are already clean
because of the word which I have spoken to you. Abide in Me, and I in you.
As the branch cannot bear fruit of itself, unless it abides in the vine, neither
can you, unless you abide in Me. I am the vine, you are the branches. He
who abides in Me, and I in him, bears much fruit; for without Me you can
do nothing. If anyone does not abide in Me, he is cast out as a branch and
is withered; and they gather them and throw them into the fire, and they are
burned. If you abide in Me, and My words abide in you, you will ask what
you desire, and it shall be done for you. By this My Father is glorified, that
you bear much fruit; so you will be My disciples."

JOHN 15:1,3–8 NKJV

I have felt drawn to try to write what young Christians might easily
apprehend, as a help to them to take up that position in which the
Christian life must be a success. It is as if there is not one of the
principal temptations and failures of the Christian life that is not met
here. The nearness, the all-sufficiency, the faithfulness of the Lord
Jesus, the naturalness, the fruitfulness of a life of faith, are so revealed,
that it is as if one could with confidence say, "Let the parable enter into
the heart, and all will be right." May the blessed Lord give the blessing.
May He teach us to study the mystery of the Vine in the spirit of
worship, waiting for God's own teaching.

~ANDREW MURRAY (1828–1917)

PLANTING SEEDS

The revelation of Your words brings light and
gives understanding to the inexperienced.

PSALM 119:130 HCSB

The little five-year-old boy attended our Native outreach Sunday school. He blew into the classroom every evening with his fists clinched tight, daring anyone to cross him. What could I do to reach this angry little boy? In prayer, I thought about great men God had called into the ministry from similar backgrounds. I met him in the hall before he entered the classroom. I talked to him about what we were going to do and what he might enjoy doing. I gave him what love he would allow while telling him that Jesus loved him and wanted him to be happy in church. He became my best helper. He was exceptionally bright but bored with class in general. "Would you like to learn Scripture verses?" I asked. He agreed, so I invited him to my home to do just that. He lived nearby. He came the next day and every day that week. My goal was to teach him a verse from every book of the Bible. When he learned to read, I would give him a Bible of his very own. I started planting seeds from Genesis, Exodus, and Leviticus. As the Eskimo boy's family moved often, I didn't get to complete all sixty-six books of the Bible. However, the time spent with him made a difference in his attitude at church and how he dealt with his circumstances. Fifteen years later, he called me while visiting in Fairbanks. He didn't identify himself but quoted his first memory verse. I knew him immediately. I know God has called me to be a sower of His Word. God can be trusted to provide the increase.

~DAVID BALDWIN (1943–) ANCHORAGE, AK

PRAISE GOD, I'M IN HIM

(EPHESIANS 1, PSALM 23, ROMANS 5, JOHN 10)

In Him there's no condemnation
In Him Spiritual blessings abound
In Him sealed by His Spirit
Praise God I'm in Him.
In Him delivered from evil
In Him I'm justified
In Him I've been adopted
Praise God I'm in Him.
In Him I have a Shepherd
In Him green pastures I find
In Him He leads by still waters
Praise God I'm in Him.
In Him when in the valley
In Him I will not fear
In Him mercy shall follow
Praise God I'm in Him.
In Him life's overflowing
In Him abundance I've found
In Him joy everlasting

THE TEN COMMANDMENTS (PART 1)

Remember ye the law of Moses my servant.

MALACHI 4:4 KJV

Some people seem to think we have got beyond the commandments. What did Christ say? "Think not that I am come to destroy the law and the prophets; I am not come to destroy but to fulfill. For verily I say unto you, Till heaven and earth pass away, one jot or one title shall in no way pass from the law, till all be fulfilled." The commandments of God given to Moses in the Mount at Horeb are as binding today as ever they have been since the time they were proclaimed in the hearing of the people. The Jews said the law was not given in Palestine (which belonged to Israel), but in the wilderness, because the law was for all nations. Jesus never condemned the law and the prophets, but He did condemn those who did not obey them. Because He gave new commandments, it does not follow that He abolished the old. Christ's explanation of them made them all the more searching. In His Sermon on the Mount, He carried the principles of the commandments beyond the mere letter. He unfolded them and showed that they embraced more, that they are positive as well as prohibitive. The Old Testament closes with these words: "Remember ye the law of Moses my servant, which I commanded unto him in Horeb for all Israel, with the statutes and judgments. Behold, I will send you Elijah the prophet before the coming of the great and dreadful day of the LORD: and he shall turn the heart of the fathers to the children, and the heart of the children to their fathers, lest I come and smite the earth with a curse" (Malachi 4:4–6).

~ D. L. MOODY (1837–1899)

THE TEN COMMANDMENTS (PART 2)

Remember ye the law of Moses my servant.
MALACHI 4:4 KJV

These are the only messages to men that God has written with His own hand. He wrote the commandments out twice, and spoke them aloud in the hearing of Israel. If it were known that God Himself were going to speak once again to man, what eagerness and excitement there would be! For nearly nineteen hundred years He has been silent. No inspired message has been added to the Bible for nearly nineteen hundred years. How eagerly all men would listen if God should speak once more. Yet men forget that the Bible is God's own Word, and that it is as truly His message today as when it was delivered of old. The law that was given at Sinai has lost none of its solemnity. Time cannot wear out its authority or the fact of its authorship. I can imagine someone saying, "I won't be weighed by that law. I don't believe in it." Now men may cavil as much as they like about other parts of the Bible, but I have never met an honest man that found fault with the Ten Commandments. Infidels may mock the Lawgiver and reject Him who has delivered us from the curse of the law, but they can't help admitting that the commandments are right.

~ D. L. MOODY (1837–1899)

WORSHIP IN SPIRIT AND IN TRUTH

FROM JOHN 4:4–24

The Bible says you have to be working on applying the truth that you know. Worshiping in spirit and in truth is our only true worship. All worship is not true worship. The parameters for true worship are not set by custom, culture; tradition, times; race, religion, region; art, achievements; your opinion, my opinion, or public opinion. God sets the parameters for true worship. Jesus says you sum it up this way: "Love the Lord your God with all your heart and with all your soul and with all your mind and with all your strength." If you can remember that and walk and live by that, you've got it. The third thing in the text is it says worship in spirit and truth; it is that for which we are sought of God. Jesus says to the woman, "For they are the kind of worshipers the Father seeks." Now, understand something about the seeking of God. He knows you! God is seeking in the sense of a suitor in love. Love doesn't always happen to both people at the same time. So the one who falls in love first has to seek the affection of the other. God does this as He seeks His people. He seeks to win your love through His wonderful words, kind deeds, precious gifts. Where did God have to seek in order to win your affections? Or has He won them yet? Have you been playing coy or hard to get? He's seeking. The devil seeks too. The devil seeks whom he may devour. But the Son of Man came to seek and to save what was lost.

~**MARK A. CROSTON, SR.** (1959–) SUFFOLK, VA

CHRIST'S RELATIONSHIP TO CHRISTIANS

Sanctify them through thy truth: thy word is truth.

JOHN 17:17 KJV

No one can too fully understand, or too deeply feel, the necessity of taking home the Bible with all it contains, as a message sent from Heaven to him; nor can too earnestly desire or seek the promised Spirit to teach him the true spiritual import of all its contents. He must have the Bible made a personal revelation of God to his own soul. It must become his own book. He must know Christ for himself. He must know him in his different relations. He must know him in his blessed and infinite fullness, or he cannot abide in him, and unless he abide in Christ, he can bring forth none of the fruits of holiness. "Except a man abide in me, he is cast forth as a branch, and is withered" (John 15:6).

~CHARLES FINNEY (1792–1875)

THE CALL

A certain man had two sons; and he came to the first, and said, Son, go
work to day in my vineyard. He answered and said, I will not: but
afterward he repented, and went. And he came to the second, and said
likewise. And he answered and said, I go, sir: and went not. Whether of
them twain did the will of his father? They say unto him, The first.

MATTHEW 21:28–31 KJV

Each one of us must ask ourselves which son are we. You see, every
single one of us has been called to work in the vineyard of lost souls in
one capacity or another. Or perhaps you are like I was. You received the
call and simply told God you would not go. Once you do that you must
bury yourself in the field of endeavor you have chosen. It keeps you
from having to listen to that still, small voice all the time. The problem,
of course, is it makes you miserable. However, there is one thing that I
learned about pain compliance techniques in law enforcement: when
you stop resisting, the pain goes away. So one dark night, about two
a.m., with tears in my eyes I stopped resisting, repented, and
surrendered to the call that God had placed on my life. That was in
1992, and I've been working in the vineyard ever since at peace with
God and myself, being the good son. The work is hard; you do a lot of
watering, hoeing, weeding, and pruning. You have to contend with the
heat, cold, and storms that come your way, and the insects are always
trying to destroy the crop, but every now and then you get to pick a few
grapes!

~RUSSELL C. LAMBERT (1955–) AIRWAY HEIGHTS, WA

IN CHRIST JESUS: THE SPHERE OF THE BELIEVER'S LIFE

Those three short words, in Christ Jesus, are, without doubt, the most important ever written, even by an inspired pen, to express the mutual relation of the believer and Christ. They occur, with their equivalents, over one hundred and thirty times. Sometimes we meet the expression, in Christ or in Christ Jesus, and again in Him, or in whom. And sometimes this sacred name, or its equivalent pronoun, is found associated with other prepositions—through, with, by; but the thought is essentially the same. Such repetition and variety must have some intense meaning. When, in the Word of God, a phrase like this occurs so often, and with such manifold applications, it can not be a matter of accident; there is a deep design. God's Spirit is bringing a truth of the highest importance before us, repeating for the sake of emphasis, compelling even the careless reader to give heed as to some vital teaching. We shall see a further evidence of the vital importance of the phrase, in Christ, in the fact that these two words unlock and interpret every separate book in the New Testament. Here is God's own key, whereby we may open all the various doors and enter all the glorious rooms in this Palace Beautiful, and explore all the apartments in the house of the heavenly Interpreter, from Matthew to the Apocalypse, where the door is opened into heaven. The more we study the phrase and the various instances and peculiar varieties of such recurrence, the more shall we be convinced of its vital importance to all practical holy living.

~A. T. PIERSON (1837–1911)

JUSTIFICATION

Much more then, being now justified by his blood,
we shall be saved from wrath through him.

ROMANS 5:9 KJV

Under the gospel, sinners are not justified by having the obedience of Jesus Christ set down to their account, as if He had obeyed the law for them, or in their stead. It is not an uncommon mistake to suppose that when sinners are justified under the gospel they are accounted righteous in the eye of the law, by having the obedience or righteousness of Christ imputed to them. I can only say that this idea is absurd and impossible, for this reason, that Jesus Christ was bound to obey the law for himself, and could no more perform works of supererogation, or obey on our account, than anybody else. Was it not His duty to love the Lord his God, with all His heart and soul and mind and strength, and to love His neighbor as himself? The only work of supererogation He could perform was to submit to sufferings that were not deserved. This is called His obedience unto death, and this is set down to our account. It is not required that the obedience of another should be imputed to us. All we owe is perpetual obedience to the law of benevolence. And for this there can be no substitute. If we fail of this we must endure the penalty, or receive a free pardon.

~**CHARLES FINNEY (1792–1875)**

A NEW CREATION

*Therefore if any man be in Christ, he is a new creature: old things
are passed away; behold, all things are become new.*

2 CORINTHIANS 5:17 KJV

I have thought what I could possibly do to secure that my little
book should not draw away attention from the word of God, but rather
help to make the word more precious. I resolved to furnish the work
with marginal references, so that, on every point that was treated of, the
reader might be stirred up still to listen to the Word itself, to God
Himself. I am hopeful that this arrangement will yield a double benefit.
Many a one does not know, and had nobody to teach him, how to
examine the Scriptures properly. This book may help him in his
loneliness. If he will only meditate on one and another point, and then
look up the texts that are quoted, he will get into the way of consulting
God's word itself on that which he wishes to understand.

~ANDREW MURRAY (1828–1917)

MY COMMISSION

"Therefore go and make disciples of all nations, baptizing them in the name of the Father and of the Son and of the Holy Spirit."
MATTHEW 28:19 NIV

Although He called me to ministry and I am eager to do His work, I seemed unable due to illness. I prayed to God, saying, "Lord, I love You. You called me and I am willing to do any work You would have me do. But I can't. I am too sick and hardly able to leave the house. Please give me a job, a ministry, something that I can do to glorify You." The next morning I awoke with this thought at the forefront of my mind. It was "start an Internet church." Ironically, for several years I had considered starting an Internet website named "Godfocus." So I created Godfocus Internet Church, then tried to make it as much like a land-based church as possible by establishing basic ministries that people could access through the Internet. The church began receiving visitors to its ministry pages from people around the world. Especially gratifying were the visits from people located in non-Christian countries. Some were westerners, but others were native born. Many took great risks worshiping, seeking spiritual counsel, and submitting prayer requests through the Internet. I was grateful that people were coming to Godfocus for their spiritual needs and quite surprised that many of them were native to countries that were anti-Christian or had oppressive regimes. Through all this I have learned once again that God will help us in every situation if we ask Him in prayer, listen for His answer, and then follow His directions.

~ DAVID SCHOLTON (1951–) SANFORD, NC

WHY DOES GOD DELAY AN ANSWER TO PRAYER?

I give myself unto prayer.

PSALM 109:4 KJV

You let the musician play a great while ere you throw him down money, because you love to hear his music. God may delay prayer when he will not deny it, that he may humble us. He has spoken to us long in his word to leave our sins, but we would not hear him; therefore he lets us speak to him in prayer and seems not to hear us. He may delay to answer prayer when he will not deny it, because he sees we are not yet fit for the mercy we ask. Perhaps we pray for deliverance when we are not fit for it; our scum is not yet boiled away. We would have God swift to deliver, and we are slow to repent. God may delay to answer prayer, that the mercy we pray for may be more prized, and may be sweeter when it comes. The longer the merchant's ships stay abroad, the more he rejoices when they come home laden with spices and jewels; therefore be not discouraged, but follow God with prayer. Though God delays, He will not deny. Prayer conquers the invincible, it overcomes the Omnipotent (Hosea 12:4). The Syrians tied their god Hercules fast with a golden chain, that he should not remove. The Lord was held by Moses' prayer as with a golden chain. "Let me alone;" why, what did Moses? He only prayed (Exodus 32:10). Prayer ushers in mercy. Be thy case never so sad, if thou canst but pray, thou needest not fear (Psalm 10:17). Therefore, give thyself to prayer.

~THOMAS WATSON (1620–1686)

LETTING GO

He who did not spare His own Son, but delivered Him up for us all,
how shall He not with Him also freely give us all things?

ROMANS 8:32 NKJV

In my early days as a dad, I remember someone saying that "parenting is a long process of letting go of your children." That sage advice was not enough to prepare me for what I would feel for years to come! I probably felt it initially when our first little girl waved good-bye one last time before whirling around and heading confidently into her first day of kindergarten. In the ensuing years, there were lots of good-byes. I had to let go for summer camps, for band trips, and for dates with boys. And, of course, while all this was going on, I was having to repeat it all over again with her younger brother and sister. I cried at graduations, I cried when my son went to serve our nation in the military, and so far I've choked twice on the words "Her Mother and I" when the pastors asked, "Who gives this woman to be married to this man?" They were asking, "Are you ready to let go of these little who have now become beautiful young women—one last time?" Well, I'll tell you a little secret—I'll never completely let go! The sweet memories of each of my three children will always be fixed in my heart. Perhaps that's the reason I stand in awe of my heavenly Father, who "spared not His own Son, but delivered Him up for us all." Imagine that! God let go of His own Son in order to get me! That's enough to make a grown man cry!

~JIM DOWNS (1950–) GREEN BAY, WI

ONE MEDIATOR

For there is one God and one mediator between
God and men, the man Christ Jesus.

1 TIMOTHY 2:5 KJV

Just as there can be no gospel without the atonement as the reason for the Incarnation, so also there can be no Christian life without it. Without the atonement, the Incarnation theme easily becomes a kind of deification of the human and leads to arrogance and self advancement. With the atonement the true message of the life of Christ, and therefore also of the life of the Christian man or woman, is humility and self sacrifice for the obvious needs of others. The Christian life is not indifference to those who are hungry or sick or suffering from some other lack. It is not contentment with our own abundance, neither the abundance of middle class living with home and cars and clothes and vacations, nor the abundance of education or even the spiritual abundance of good churches, Bibles, Bible teaching or Christian friends and acquaintances. Rather, it is the awareness that others lack these things and that we must therefore sacrifice many of our own interests in order to identify with them and thus bring them increasingly into the abundance we enjoy. We will live for Christ fully only when we are willing to be impoverished, if necessary, in order that others might be helped.

~J. P. BOYCE (1827–1888)

GO FISH!

(LUKE 5:1–11 NKJV)

When Jesus told us to go, He assumed we would go;
That His disciples would be willing to let the world know
The good news of His dying to save us from sin
He saved us so that we would go fish!
You know Jonah decided not to follow his Lord
with a hateful rebellion he ran from His Word.
But the Lord convinced Jonah to tell the good news
He saw the light in the gut of a fish!
When Simon had finished a dull fishing trip the
Lord Jesus said, "Simon, get back in your ship"
"Drop your nets in the water and see what I do."
And the boat nearly sank—full of fish!
Saul of Tarsus was hunting down Christians one day
when Jesus showed up and He stood in his way
When the Lord finished speaking, Saul was a new man.
He stopped hunting and started to fish!
He said, "Come and I'll make you a fisher of men.
Follow Me and life won't be the same again."
Will you drop what you're doing and follow the Lord?
He called you so that you would go fish!
Go fish! Tell the world Jesus saves Go fish!
That He's risen from the grave
Go fish! And He's coming again.
He saved us so that we would go fish!
Go fish! Tell the world Jesus lives.
Go fish! Show the love that He gives
Go fish! Share His love with your world.
He loved you so that you would go fish!
He sought you so that you would go fish!
He bought you so that you would go fish!
He caught you so that you would go fish!

~BILL ASCOL (1952–) SHREVEPORT, LA

PRAYER POWER

If my people . . . shall humble themselves, and pray . . .
then will I hear from heaven.

2 CHRONICLES 7:14 KJV

The church never stands taller than when she kneels to pray. She never progresses faster, than when she is on her knees. Prayer is not an option for the church; prayer is absolutely essential if she wants to be a world-changing force. A prayerless church is a powerless church dependent on human thought and methods to create a reason for existing. Jesus said that His house should be called a "House of prayer for all nations." The scriptures are clear. He intended that our sacred service to Him should center in prayer. In many churches, the business of the church takes precedence over prayer. Sometimes the church becomes a "den of robbers" instead of a "house of prayer." We place too much attention on the budget and how to get money to run the buildings and pay the staff instead of on prayer and ministry to the poor and needy, the orphans and the widows. If prayer is to be the central work of the church, there must be the strong belief that Jesus has told us what the central work of the church must be. As we pray, we turn our hearts toward the Lord and receive from Him, thus "fueling" the vision and the work. Without a strong focused prayer life for the church, the people soon burn out, leaving a tired pastor with ill and ornery sheep to try to lead. We must pray. We must call upon Him to enter our churches and our lives with His presence so that we can co-labor with Him in the Vineyard. If we want to have churches that transform society. We must pray!

~GLENN SHEPPARD (1943–) GREENWOOD, MO

THE LORD'S PRAYER

MATTHEW 6:5–13 HCSB

Whenever you pray, you must not be like the hypocrites, because they love to pray standing in the synagogues and on the street corners to be seen by people. I assure you: They've got their reward! But when you pray, go into your private room, shut your door, and pray to your Father who is in secret. And your Father who sees in secret will reward you. When you pray, don't babble like the idolaters, since they imagine they'll be heard for their many words. Don't be like them, because your Father knows the things you need before you ask Him.

The Model Prayer

Therefore, you should pray like this:
Our Father in heaven, Your name be honored as holy.
Your kingdom come.
Your will be done on earth as it is in heaven.
Give us today our daily bread.
And forgive us our debts, as we also have forgiven our debtors.
And do not bring us into temptation,
but deliver us from the evil one.
Or For Yours is the kingdom and the power and the glory forever.

Amen

HONOR YOUR FATHER AND YOUR MOTHER

Do not cast me away when I am old; do not
forsake me when my strength is gone.

PSALM 71:9 NIV

The Bible says, "Do not cast me away when I am old; do not forsake me when my strength is gone." Yet statistics from the American Association of homes for the Aging show that 60 percent of nursing home residents do not have regular visitors. Many are lonely and despondent and could use a friend. Visiting a person in a nursing home requires no special skills or talents. All that is needed is a desire to reach out in Christian love to a special person. Anyone who can read, listen, and share some time is qualified. A conversation about a resident's childhood, family, former occupation, past church involvement, or school may reveal an interesting life. Nursing homes provide an opportunity for churches to make a difference in the community. Christians can bring spiritual encouragement through Scripture reading, hymn singing, preaching, and prayer. This is a ministry families can do together. Some can play instruments, some sing, and others help pass out large print songbooks and sit next to residents to help them find the right page. Children and young adults blend in with the elderly to give more of a church feel. "Gray hair is a crown of splendor; it is attained by a righteous life" (Proverbs 16:31 NIV). Our elders should be treated as a treasure and a precious resource for the wisdom their years have brought them and venerated for the contributions they have made. In our fast-paced, youth-worshipping culture, the church should move against the current and show that God values the elderly.

~JORGE ZAYASBAZAN (1959–) ROUND LAKE BEACH, IL

COMFORTABLE? (PART 1)

Then Jesus said to his disciples, "If anyone would come after me,
he must deny himself and take up his cross and follow me."

MATTHEW 16:24 NIV

I'd like to talk with you about a little known and seldom talked about disease that is at what I believe an epidemic proportion in the church today. The disease that I'm talking about could be called the disease of ease, a comfortable Christianity. Jesus didn't call us to a couch, but to a cross. You know what it's like to be comfortable. When you get home from work, you've had a hard day, and you plop down in your favorite chair. You don't want to get up for anything; you are tired and you just want to relax. (That's often when your wife asks you to do something.) A DISCIPLE NEEDS TO: DENY HIMSELF—What matters is not whether we are comfortable; in fact when we really deny ourselves, it is no longer about us, but rather about Jesus and reaching others for Christ. It's not about us, it's about Him, It's not about us, it's about them. TAKE UP HIS CROSS—When we take up our cross that means we are willing to die for Christ. Paul the apostle said, "I die daily" and "I am crucified with Christ, nevertheless I live, yet not I but Christ who lives within me." FOLLOW JESUS—Wherever He leads I'll go . . . Do we really mean that when we sing it? Will we go across the street to a neighbor that needs Jesus, or on a mission trip to reach an un-reached people group? There are times we won't even go across the church aisle to welcome a newcomer and make them feel like we really want them here.

~DR. DONALD T. SATTERWHITE (1953–) BALTIMORE, MD

COMFORTABLE? (PART 2)

Then Jesus said to his disciples, "If anyone would come after me,
he must deny himself and take up his cross and follow me."

MATTHEW 16:24 NIV

How can we cure the disease of ease? Fall in love with Jesus all over again. Do you love Jesus just like you once did? I'm afraid many are in love with the world more than they are in love with Jesus. We are told to love not the world or the things that are in the world. Do you remember when you first met Him? Are you more in love with Jesus every day? Jesus said, "If you love me, keep my commandments." Don't be content with being an average Christian. On a scale of one to ten, with one being furthest from God and ten being closest, how would you rate yourself today? Those who are average make God sick! Their greatest problem is that they have no sense of need. Get hot for God—on fire for Him—in love with Him.

~DR. DONALD T. SATTERWHITE (1953–) BALTIMORE, MD

ALL TO JESUS, I SURRENDER

(LUKE 22:42)

All to Jesus, I surrender; all to Him I freely give;
I will ever love and trust Him, in His presence daily live.
I surrender all, I surrender all,
all to Thee, my blessed Savior, I surrender all.

All to Jesus I surrender; humbly at His feet I bow,
Worldly pleasures all forsaken; take me, Jesus, take me now.
I surrender all, I surrender all,
all to Thee, my blessed Savior, I surrender all.

All to Jesus, I surrender; make me, Savior, wholly Thine;
Let me feel the Holy Spirit, truly know that Thou art mine.
I surrender all, I surrender all,
all to Thee, my blessed Savior, I surrender all.

All to Jesus, I surrender; Lord, I give myself to Thee;
Fill me with Thy love and power; let Thy blessing fall on me.
I surrender all, I surrender all,
all to Thee, my blessed Savior, I surrender all.

All to Jesus I surrender; now I feel the sacred flame.
O the joy of full salvation! Glory, glory, to His Name!
I surrender all, I surrender all,
all to Thee, my blessed Savior, I surrender all.

~JUDSON W. VAN DEVENTER (1855–1939)

LAPTOPS, LIFE, AND THE LORD

His divine power has given us everything we need for life and godliness
through our knowledge of him who called us by his own glory and goodness.

2 PETER 1:3 NIV

When it comes to twenty-first-century technology, I am not the most advanced of my work-force friends. To say the least, I am not a computer expert. It is often difficult for me to perform some of the simplest of tasks without someone looking over my shoulder. You can ask any of my colleagues, and they will gladly affirm the validity of these statements. I am personally secure in my ignorance of the technological world. When I am experiencing difficulties with my laptop, there are a couple of things that are "no-brainers" to check—one of which sticks out in my mind above others. When I push the power button and nothing happens, I check the power cord. You see, if nothing is happening, it is far easier to check the power source before unscrewing the entire hard drive. The laptop has everything inside for it to work properly, but it must be connected to its proper source of power. Thinking about the Christian life, it is very easy to find ourselves in similar situations. Often times, we are asking God for the special key to live a godly life or to overcome certain struggles. How ironic it is that we already possess everything we need to live a godly life because of our relationship with Jesus Christ. We are simply not relying on our source of power. So, why do we tear our personal hard drives apart seeking something else? A more fitting prayer would be to ask God to help us utilize the power and resources He has already given us through Christ.

~CHRIS JAMES (1978–) LOWELL, MA

DIVINE APPOINTMENTS

*"If you abide in Me, and My words abide in you,
ask whatever you wish, and it will be done for you."*

John 15:7 NASB

On my sixth trip to this Asian country, I heard a familiar voice call, "Andy?" Just days before, I had mentioned to my group that I had not seen Ay-toe-may. Ay-toe-may was a lady that many of us had gotten to know by frequenting her business on our first four trips. We really wanted her to meet the Lord but had never gotten a chance to share with her. I had not seen her for two years because her business had moved, and in a city of four hundred thousand, it was hard to find her. As we were leaving a restaurant, I was surprised to hear my name called in an Asian accent. It was Ay-toe-may! I don't know why I should be surprised; I had asked God for divine appointments while I was there and God is faithful. The same afternoon Michael, one of my team members, had been looking for a man whom he had met two years before and with whom he had lost contact. On the chance that someone might know him, Michael approached a group of older ladies sitting in the town square. He asked if anyone spoke English, and a young college girl replied that she did. Michael requested the college student to ask the ladies if they knew his friend. One lady said, "Yes, he's my brother!" In both cases, we were able to minister to these folks and introduce them to local missionaries. God desires, even more than we do, to do great and mighty things. If we, as God's people, will just get out of the way and let God work, He will!

~Andy Dietz (1950–) Borger, TX

MANUFACTURING ARROWS

As arrows are in the hand of a mighty man; so are children of the youth.

PSALM 127:4 KJV

When God gives a husband and a wife a child, He expects that the child be developed into a mature disciple of Christ. These verses use the analogy of an arrow when we think of raising our children. Our task is to develop our children to be mighty arrows that God can use in spiritual battle. To do this we must consider three basic qualities of a good arrow. First, the arrow must be straight. A crooked arrow will not hit the target. As parents, we must realize that the only thing that will straighten out a little sin-crooked life is salvation in Christ. Therefore, we must do all we can to lead our children to Christ. A second quality of a good arrow is balance. Arrows must be intricately balanced if they are going to fly straight. Once again, parents must work hard to see our children live well-balanced lives. The best way to bring balance into their lives is to make sure that God's Word is woven into every fabric of their being from their early years on. Finally, an arrow must be razor sharp. Without this quality an arrow may fly straight but will have no impact. Our children must become razor sharp if they are going to be able to cut through the false philosophies that permeate our culture. This is accomplished when we demonstrate and teach them to live under the total control of God's Holy Spirit. Parents are in the arrow-making business. We must strive to produce straight, balanced, and sharp arrows. When our task is done, we must turn these arrows over to Christ and allow Him to use them in spiritual warfare.

DR. GLEN SCHULTZ (1947–) HENDERSONVILLE, TN

WHAT DOES IT MEAN TO HAVE VISION FROM GOD?

Without revelation people run wild,
but one who keeps the law will be happy.

PROVERBS 29:18 HCSB

Helen Keller, perhaps the most recognized blind person who has ever lived, was asked what would be worse than being born blind. She responded, "To have sight without vision." Many people have physical sight, but lack true vision for their life, their family, or for their church. Vision may be defined as the ability to see, awareness, or unusual foresight. Vision is seeing things God's way. It involves trusting God enough to say yes to the seemingly impossible. God is a God of vision. God saw in Abraham the father of many nations. He saw in David the shepherd boy, a king. He saw in Mary, a humble virgin girl, the mother of the Savior of the world. The same God sees in you what nobody else can see. He desires to give you a vision for your life, family, and church. We receive a clear vision for our life by humbling ourselves before God and coming before Him with no agenda other than a desire to hear from heaven. We receive a clear vision by listening to God as He speaks to our hearts. God desires to fill your heart with a passion to become more than you are, to do more than you have ever done, and to live a kingdom focused life. If you have committed your life to Jesus Christ and yet you still lack vision, you are missing out on God's best. Seek God with passion and He will give you the vision to live a fulfilling life for His glory!

~SETH POLK (1971–) POKA, WV

PRAYER AND THE HOUSE OF GOD

Israel, return to your tents.

1 KINGS 12:16 HCSB

Prayer is always in place in the house of God. When prayer is a stranger there, then it ceases to be God's house at all. Our Lord put peculiar emphasis upon what the Church was when He cast out the buyers and sellers in the Temple, repeating the words from Isaiah, "It is written, My house shall be called the house of prayer." He makes prayer preeminent, that which stands out above all else in the house of God. They, who sidetrack prayer or seek to minify it, and give it a secondary place, pervert the Church of God, and make it something less and other than it is ordained to be. Prayer is perfectly at home in the house of God. It is no stranger, no mere guest; it belongs there. It has a peculiar affinity for the place, and has, moreover, a Divine right there, being set, therein, by Divine appointment and approval. The inner chamber is a sacred place for personal worship. The house of God is a holy place for united worship. The prayer-closet is for individual prayer. The house of God is for mutual prayer, concerted prayer, united prayer. Yet even in the house of God, there is the element of private worship, since God's people are to worship Him and pray to Him, personally, even in public worship. The Church is for the united prayer of kindred, yet individual believers. As prayer distinguishes Christian from unchristian people, so prayer distinguishes God's house from all other houses. It is a place where faithful believers meet with their Lord.

~E. M. BOUNDS (1835–1918)

THE CHOSEN PATH

SOVEREIGN, DIVINE GRACE

Thine is the kingdom, O LORD, and thou art exalted as head above all.
1 CHRONICLES 29:11 KJV

In a remarkable manner, divine grace was exercised at the time of the Savior's birth. The incarnation of God's Son was one of the greatest events in the history of the universe, and yet its actual occurrence was not made known to all mankind; instead, it was specially revealed to the Bethlehem shepherds and wise men of the East. And this was prophetic and indicative of the entire course of this dispensation, for even today Christ is not made known to all. God could have readily attracted the attention of all mankind to the "star"; but He did not. Why? Because God is Sovereign and dispenses His favors as He pleases. Note particularly the two classes to whom the birth of the Savior was made known, namely, the most unlikely classes—illiterate shepherds and heathen from a far country. No angel stood before the Sanhedrin and announced the advent of Israel's Messiah! No "star" appeared unto the scribes and lawyers as they, in their pride and self-righteousness, searched the Scriptures! They searched diligently to find out where He should be born, and yet it was not made known to them when He was actually come. What a display of Divine Sovereignty—the illiterate shepherds singled out for peculiar honor, and the learned and eminent passed by! And why was the birth of the Savior revealed to these foreigners, and not to those in whose midst He was born? See in this a wonderful foreshadowing of God's dealings with our race throughout the entire Christian dispensation—sovereign in the exercise of His grace, bestowing His favors on whom He pleases, often on the most unlikely and unworthy.

~A. W. PINK (1886–1952)

THE CHOSEN PATH

WHAT? ME WORRY?

"Therefore do not worry about tomorrow, for tomorrow will worry about its own things. Sufficient for the day is its own trouble."

MATTHEW 6:34 NKJV

My mother-in-law, who raised eight children, some of them having been born during the Depression, had a small plaque over her stove. It said, "Today is the Tomorrow you worried about Yesterday." That was a good reminder not to worry nor be anxious over things that she could not control, and it was much like Jesus' words about worry and anxiety in Matthew 6:19–34. In His cure for anxiety, He begins with an important reference: "For this reason . . .," teaching that a divided heart of wrong priorities cause deep insecurities. Jesus had warned his listeners not to lay up treasures on earth, but in heaven. He wanted their focus to be on the right priorities. Once, when I was in University and becoming stressed about writing long papers, my professor said, "You are worrying about a huge load and it is making you feel heavy. Divide your work into small parts, just enough for the day. Your focus will then be on each day's worries, and not on the worries of the days or weeks ahead." He then directed me to focus on Matthew 6:34, "Therefore do not worry about tomorrow, for tomorrow will worry about its own things. Sufficient for the day is its own trouble." Practically speaking this verse tells us: 1) Evaluate your priorities. 2) By faith, choose to focus on what is really important. 3) Continue to believe in God's priorities for your life. 4) Stay focused, seeking His Kingdom first. 5) Let God order your life according to His timing. The result: Your heart will be at rest as you accomplish the needed work.

~JANET MILLER (1943–) WHEAT RIDGE, CO

THE CHOSEN PATH

GOD'S SILENCE, THEN WHAT?

*So, when He heard that he was sick, He stayed
two more days in the place where He was.*

JOHN 11:6 NKJV

Has God trusted you with His silence, a silence that has great meaning? God's silences are actually His answers. God will give you the very blessings you ask if you refuse to go any further without them, but His silence is the sign that He is bringing you into an even more wonderful understanding of Himself. Are you mourning before God because you have not had an audible response? When you cannot hear God, you will find that He has trusted you in the most intimate way possible, with absolute silence, not a silence of despair, but one of pleasure, because He saw that you could withstand an even bigger revelation. If God has given you a silence, then praise Him, He is bringing you into the mainstream of His purposes. The actual evidence of the answer in time is simply a matter of God's sovereignty. Time is nothing to God. For a while you may have said, "I asked God to give me bread, but He gave me a stone instead" (Matthew 7:9 KJV). He did not give you a stone, and today you find that He gave you the "bread of life" (John 6:35 KJV). A wonderful thing about God's silence is that His stillness is contagious—it gets into you, causing you to become perfectly confident so that you can honestly say, "I know that God has heard me." His silence is the very proof that He has. If Jesus Christ is bringing you into the understanding that prayer is for the glorifying of His Father, then He will give you the first sign of His intimacy, silence.

~OSWALD CHAMBERS (1874–1917)

THE CHOSEN PATH

FLOODS ON THE DRY GROUND

Open thy mouth wide, and I will fill it.

PSALM 81:10 KJV

I believe there are many in our churches who do not make a habit of secret prayer, who ever pour out their heart to God, neither in their closet nor in a private place outdoors. I believe there are many who are dropping into hell who never so much as said: "God, be merciful to me a sinner." Ah! These are the dry grounds. It is sad to think that the souls that are nearest to hell are the souls that pray least to be delivered from it; they do not want a work of grace in their souls. I believe many of you came to the house of God today who would rather lose house, and home, and friends, than have a work of grace done in your heart. Nothing would terrify you so much as the idea that God might make you a praying Christian. Ah! You are the dry ground, you love death; they do not attend to the preached Word. I have heard persons concerned for their souls declare that they never heard a sermon in all their life until they were awakened. They say they regularly thought about something else all the time. I believe this is the way with many of you. You are the dry ground. What will God pour out on you? Floods—floods of wrath? No; floods of grace, floods of the Spirit, floods of blessing. Oh, the mercy of God—it passes all understanding! You deserve the flood that came on the world of the ungodly, but He offers floods of blessing. You deserve the rain of Sodom, but, behold, He offers flood of His Spirit.

~R. M. McCheyne (1813–1843)

THE CHOSEN PATH

THE LORD OF THE RING

*I have been crucified with Christ and I no longer live, but Christ
lives in me. The life I live in the body, I live by faith in the
Son of God, who loved me and gave himself for me.*

GALATIANS 2:20 NIV

Back in the days when I had two small children and a third on the
way, the question of whether God was taking care of my family had to
be answered. I was living by faith as a full-time missionary, and that
summer we had very scant provisions. My boys weren't aware of our
situation and begged me to take them swimming. My heart cried out to
God as I drove to the lake, "Lord, I don't want to come home until you
speak to me." Soon my little boys were splashing happily, while I sat
down in the shallow water next to them. I leaned back and felt
something pop up into my right hand. There, glistening in the sunlight,
lay a gold ring! I knew that Jesus had heard my cry. He would provide
for me, even if it meant pulling a coin out of a fish's mouth like He did
with His disciples. The gold ring could be sold . . . but His message to
me was too important. Engraved on that ring were two crosses. One was
the cross of Christ. But the other? Mine! To be crucified with Christ is
not painless. My trials are born out of this fallen world, but are being
used by Him to develop my faith. To this day, on my finger, remains a
gift from the true Lord of the Ring. It is a perfect fit, and always a
reminder of His great love . . . and great sacrifice.

~BRIAN KEAY (1963–) ASHEVILLE, NC

TRUST–DELIGHT–COMMIT

(PSALM 37)

Oh trust in the Lord and do good
Just feed upon His righteousness
Always delight in Him
He'll give the desire of your heart
Commit everything to the Lord
Trust Him to always help you
Rest and wait patiently
Forsake you He never will do
The meek shall inherit the earth
Peace shall be their delight
Our steps are ordered by Him
He watches over each one of them
The law of God is in his heart
None of his steps shall slide
Watches over each one of them
Beside us He'll always abide
Salvation is from the Lord
Our strength along the Way
Delivers us from evil men
Saves us because we trust in Him

~LINDA K. SMITH (1948–) SENECA, SC

R. G. LEE SPEAKS

The Bible . . . Wondrous Book! Book above and beyond all books as a river is beyond a rill in reach, as the sun is above and beyond the tallow dipped in brightness, as Niagara is above and beyond a mill pond in power . . . Book against which infidelities has thrown its sharpest shafts and strongest spear of scorn and ridicule! Book at which the dissecting knives of modernistic intellectuals have whacked at like butchers . . . Book against which some snipers from behind some pulpit stands and some college chairs have aimed their ill-grounded propositions. But withal, all its enemies have neither torn one hole in its holy vesture nor stolen one flower from its wondrous garden nor diluted one drop of honey from its abundant hive . . . nor stayed its triumphant progress so much as one brief hour! It is still the pilgrim's staff, the pilot's compass, the soldier's sword and much more besides! Jesus expresses the entire being of God with entire precession, finality, and perfection. In Him the silence of God breaks into full voice; without Him, the revealer of God, as Savior and Lord, man is a failure, the world is a carcass, eternity is a vast horror. So Jesus in His character reveals God—exegetes God. To know Jesus is to know God. What Jesus was to prodigal and publican, to mother and child, to harlot and hypocrite, to saint and sinner, to rich and poor, to devils and disciples, that is God always, everywhere, to all people. There is a Hell, I don't want to believe there is, but I would rather believe and preach unpleasant truth than to believe and preach pleasant error.

~R. G. Lee (1886–1978)

YOUTH

. . . nor for the destruction that wasteth at noonday.

PSALM 91:6 KJV

Young men dream dreams like Joseph dreamed. Little children dream dreams. But after we get to be men and women and out into the thick of the fight and the years come on with all their battles and burdens, the peril is we shall lose sight of visions and look downward and become muck rakers, with our eyes not "toward the hills from whence cometh our help." Oh the peril when idealism is lost, when a man does not dream dreams anymore, when he can not behold great visions any more, when his hands and his brain and his heart are tired, when he quits dreaming, hoping, planning, building! How perilous his plight is when his idealism is gone! The loss of idealism will make a man say: "I have no time for dreaming. I am a practical man; my business is to make a living." Your primary business is not to make a living. Your primary business is to make a life. Getting enough bread and meet for your household is incidental, but important I will grant you, and quite comfortable and convenient; but making a life is what you and I are in the world for. Making a living is just a passing incident, that is all. Before we are to pray for our daily bread and meat, we are to pray that the kingdom of God may come and that the will of God may be done throughout all the earth even as it is done in Heaven above. Making a life is our real business, a compassionate life, reverent toward God and obedient to His revealed will; the right kind of life, true, fearless, humanity helping and sympathetic.

~G. W. TRUETT (1867–1944)

THE CHIEF END OF PRAYER

And whatsoever ye shall ask in my name, that will I do,
that the Father may be glorified in the Son.

JOHN 14:13 KJV

That the Father may be glorified in the Son: it is to this end that
Jesus on His throne in glory will do all we ask in His Name. Every
answer to prayer He gives will have this as its object: when there is no
prospect of this object being obtained, He will not answer. It follows as
a matter of course that this must be with us, as with Jesus, the essential
element in our petitions: the glory of the Father must be the aim and
end, the very soul and life of our prayer. It was so with Jesus when He
was on earth. The ground on which He asks to be taken up into the
glory He had with the Father, is the twofold one: He has glorified Him
on earth; He will still glorify Him in heaven. What He asks is only to
enable Him to glorify the Father more. It is as we enter into sympathy
with Jesus on this point, and gratify Him by making the Father's glory
our chief object in prayer too, that our prayer cannot fail of an answer.
There is nothing of which the Beloved Son has said more distinctly that
it will glorify the Father than this, His doing what we ask; He will not,
therefore, let any opportunity slip of securing this object. Let us make
His aim ours: let the glory of the Father be the link between our asking
and His doing: such prayer must prevail.

~ANDREW MURRAY (1828–1917)

FLAME OF THE LORD

*And the angel of the LORD appeared unto him in
a flame of fire out of the midst of a bush.*

EXODUS 3:2 KJV

The High Priest bore the names of the twelve tribes upon his heart, each name being engraved as a seal in the costly and imperishable stone chosen by God, each seal or stone being set in the purest gold; he likewise bore the same names upon his shoulders, indicating that both the love and the strength of the High Priest were pledged on behalf of the tribes of Israel. The bride would be thus upborne by Him who is alike her Prophet, Priest, and King, for love is strong as death; and jealousy, or ardent love, retentive as the grave. Thus the Psalmist prayed, "Bind the sacrifice with cords, even unto the horns of the altar." It is comparatively easy to lay the sacrifice on the altar that sanctifies the gift, but it requires divine compulsion—the cords of love—to retain it there. So here the bride would be set and fixed on the heart and on the arm of Him who is henceforth to be her all in all, that she may evermore trust only in that love, be sustained only by that power. Do we not all need to learn a lesson from this? and to pray to be kept from turning to Egypt for help, from trusting in horses and chariots, from putting confidence in princes, or in the son of man, rather than in the living God? How the Kings of Israel, who had won great triumphs by faith, sometimes turned aside to heathen nations in their later years! The Lord keeps His people from this snare.

~J. HUDSON TAYLOR (1832–1905)

LOVER OF THE WORD

O how love I thy law! it is my meditation all the day.

Psalm 119:97 kjv

A godly man delights to walk in this garden and sweetly solace himself. He loves every branch and part of the Word: He loves the counseling part of the Word, as it is a directory and rule of life. The Word is the direction sign which points us to our duty. It contains in it things to be believed and practiced. A godly man loves the directions of the Word. He loves the threatening part of the Word. The Scripture is like the Garden of Eden: as it has a tree of life in it, so it has a flaming sword at its gates. This is the threatening of the Word. It flashes fire in the face of every person who goes on obstinately in wickedness. "God will wound the head of His enemies, the hairy scalp of the one who still goes on in his trespasses" (Psalm 68:21). The Word gives no indulgence to evil. It will not let a man halt half-way between God and sin. The true mother would not let the child be divided (1 Kings 3:26), and God will not have the heart divided. The Word thunders out threats against the very appearance of evil. It is like that flying scroll full of curses (Zechariah 5:1).

~J. P. Boyce (1827–1888)

NO CONDEMNATION

There is therefore now no condemnation to them which are in Christ Jesus.
ROMANS 8:1 KJV

In the second half of Romans 7, the apostle treats the power of sin, which operates in believers as long as they are in the world; in the opening verses of chapter eight, he speaks of the guilt of sin from which they are completely delivered the moment they are united to the Savior by faith. Hence in 7:24 the apostle asks, "Who shall deliver me" from the power of sin, but in 8:2 he says, "Hath made me free," i.e. hath delivered me, from the guilt of sin. "There is therefore now no condemnation." It is not here a question of our heart condemning us, as in 1 John 3:21, nor of us finding nothing within which is worthy of condemnation; instead, it is the far more blessed fact that God condemns not the one who has trusted in Christ to the saving of his soul. We need to distinguish sharply between subjective and objective truth; between that which is judicial and that which is experimental; otherwise, there is no condemnation to them who are in Christ Jesus. "In Christ" is the believer's position before God, not his condition in the flesh. "In Adam" I was condemned (Romans 5:12), but "in Christ" is to be forever freed from all condemnation. "There is therefore now no condemnation." The qualifying "now" implies there was a time when Christians, before they believed, were under condemnation. This "now" then distinguishes between two states or conditions. By nature we were "under the sentence of law," but now believers are "under grace" (Romans 6:14). As believers in Christ, we have everlasting life, and because of this we "shall not come into condemnation."

~A. W. PINK (1886–1952)

THE CHOSEN PATH

SUPREME CLIMB

*Take now thy son . . . and offer him there for a burnt offering
upon one of the mountains which I will tell thee of.*

GENESIS 22:2 KJV

A person's character determines how he interprets God's will (Psalm 18:25–26). Abraham interpreted God's command to mean that he had to kill his son, and he could only leave this traditional belief behind through the pain of a tremendous ordeal. God could purify his faith in no other way. If we obey what God says according to our sincere belief, God will break us from those traditional beliefs that misrepresent Him. If the devil can hinder us from taking the supreme climb and getting rid of our wrong traditional beliefs about God, he will do so. But if we will stay true to God, God will take us through an ordeal that will serve to bring us into a better knowledge of Himself. The great lesson to be learned from Abraham's faith in God is that he was prepared to do anything for God. He was there to obey God, no matter what contrary belief of his might be violated by his obedience. Abraham was not devoted to his own convictions or else he would have slain Isaac and said that the voice of the angel was actually the voice of the devil. That is the attitude of a fanatic. If you will remain true to God, God will lead you directly through every barrier and right into the inner chamber of the knowledge of Himself. But you must always be willing to come to the point of giving up your own convictions and traditional beliefs.

~OSWALD CHAMBERS (1874–1917)

THE CHOSEN PATH

A HOUSE OF PRAYER
FOR ALL NATIONS

After this I looked and there before me was a great multitude.

REVELATION 7:9 NIV

The SBC church I attended as a teenager was a sharp contrast to the city that surrounded it. Miami in the '70s was a mix of African-Americans, Haitians, Cubans, Jews, Anglos, and other groups that usually kept to themselves and were often at odds. That was what the world looked like. My church was different. We were small but we represented a cross section of our changing neighborhood. Smiling faces of different shades sang of Jesus' love of in a fusion of accents. The local church is God's answer to racial and ethnic strife, an agent of healing in a divided world. Didn't Jesus pray for the unity of all believers? (John 17:20–23). And wasn't the church's first public sermon broadcast so Jews of many nations heard Peter's message each in his own language? (Acts 2). Is heaven not multicultural? "After this I looked and there before me was a great multitude that no one could count, from every nation, tribe, people and language, standing before the throne and in front of the Lamb" (Revelation 7:9 NIV). One New Orleans church I planted was a beautiful picture of this. Seminary students worked across barriers of language and culture. The Spanish language church started an English language mission to share both its building and its ministry. My fondest memories of that church revolve around Christmas Eve, when we shared a meal representing the various cultures, a piñata, and some bilingual caroling. Christians from different cultures can work together when the spiritual needs and biblical values take priority over cultural differences.

~JORGE ZAYASBAZAN (1959–) ROUND LAKE BEACH, IL

THE CHOSEN PATH

THE GREAT COMMISSION

(FROM MATTHEW 28)

The eleven disciples traveled to Galilee, to the mountain where Jesus had directed them. When they saw Him, they worshiped him, but some doubted.

Then Jesus came near and said to them,

"All authority has been given to Me in heaven and on earth.
Go, therefore, and make disciples of
all the nations, baptizing them in the name of the Father and
of the Son and of the Holy Spirit, teaching them to observe all
things that I have commanded you; and lo, I am with you always,
even to the end of the age." Amen.

Father, You have blessed us with every opportunity so that
we will make right decisions in this life here on earth. I pray that
we, Your children, will decide for You, which means life eternal.
Help us, Lord God, as we trod the Chosen Path, to prepare
ourselves according to the instructions You have given us in Your Holy
Word, that we might be workmen who are not ashamed of the gospel
of Jesus Christ. Help us, too, Lord, to allow the Holy Spirit to guide us
in our daily lives that we will bare witness of You everywhere we go
and in everything we do, for Your glory and honor, and because we
love You, our Lord and Savior, Jesus Christ.

Amen

THE CHOSEN PATH

ASSURANCE

And we know that all things work together for good to them that love God, to them who are the called according to his purpose.

ROMANS 8:28 KJV

How wonderful is the providence of God in over-ruling things most disorderly, and in turning to our good things which in themselves are most pernicious! We marvel at His mighty power which holds the heavenly bodies in their orbits; we wonder at the continually recurring seasons and the renewal of the earth; but this is not nearly so marvelous as His bringing good out of evil in all the complicated occurrences of human life, and making even the power and malice of Satan, with the naturally destructive tendency of his works, to minister good for His children. This must be so for three reasons. First, because all things are under the absolute control of the Governor of the universe. Second, because God desires our good, and nothing but our good. Third, because even Satan himself cannot touch a hair of our heads without God's permission, and then only for our further good. Not all things are good in themselves, nor in their tendencies; but God makes all things work for our good. Nothing enters our life by blind chance: nor are there any accidents. Everything is being moved by God, with this end in view, our good. Everything being subservient to God's eternal purpose, works blessing to those marked out for conformity to the image of the Firstborn. All suffering, sorrow, loss, are used by our Father to minister to the benefit of the elect. There is nothing in God, and there is nothing from God, for which the saints do not love Him. And of this they are all assured, "We love Him because He first loved us."

~A. W. PINK (1886–1952)

"NO I DIDN'T"

You may be sure that your sin will find you out.

NUMBERS 32:23 NIV

A little boy decides all by himself that he wants a cookie, the ones with white frosting and blue and red sprinkles. Eyeing the exact coordinates that his mommy has placed the objects of his desire and while no one is around, he devises a fail-safe plan in order to have his cookie. He slides a chair from the dinning room table across the kitchen floor up and places it right against the cabinets. Once the target is identified and the best cookie is in his grasp, he goes off to a S.A.F.E. (Safe Area For Evasion) zone and enjoys the spoils of his plan. The boy, all pumped up from the thrill of victory, decides to venture down to the basement of his home where his mommy is working. She spies a little boy with somewhat of a cheesy grin on his face and asks, "What are you doing?" "Nufing," he says. She notices on at the corners of his mouth the evidence of a cookie and then asks, "Did you eat something?" Confident of his testimony the boy offers his answer, "No I didn't!" Assured that his answer meets the approval of his mommy, he then proceeds to provide iron-clad evidence that no food was taken by him by opening his mouth and asking his mommy to "See!" Surprised by the act of her child, she looks closely to find blue and red sprinkles in his teeth. Shocked to receive a guilty verdict, that boy, my beloved son, taught me how Christians often justify sin or downplay their behavior toward God with regard to their sin.

~MILES ROHDE (1972–) MARSHALL, MN

WHO IS YOUR GLORY AND JOY?

We loved you so much that we were delighted to share with you not only the gospel of God but our lives as well, because you had become so dear to us.

1 THESSALONIANS 2:8 NIV

I can remember the first time I met Jack. It was late afternoon and I was finishing up some tasks in our campus ministry office. He dropped by to find out more information about Christian involvement on campus. He had just recently committed his life to Christ and desired to go deeper in his newly found faith. Since that spring afternoon, Jack and I have met consistently in discipleship. Many lunches and walks have been spent talking about the Bible and how it applies to life. Trust has been built through mutual transparency and honesty. My heart has been encouraged as I hear of how God has transformed his thought-life and worldview through Scripture and prayer. It has been an honor to walk along side of this young disciple of Christ and share my life with him (and his with me) as he grows to be more like Jesus. Relationships like this must have been what Jesus had in mind when He commissioned His disciples to "go and make disciples" (Matthew 28:20). After all, He had shared His entire life and ministry with His chosen few. This commission is not just for the pastor or missionary and there are certainly no age limitations or caps. This is the call of discipleship to every follower of Christ—invest the gospel and your life into other people. Then, those whom we disciple can truly become our "glory and joy" (1 Thessalonians 2:20).

~CHRIS JAMES (1978–) LOWELL, MA

THE CHOSEN PATH

THE GLASS IS HALF FULL

Thou wilt shew me the path of life: in thy presence is fulness of joy;
at thy right hand there are pleasures for evermore.

PSALM 16:11 KJV

As I look back on my life, I have to conclude that I have lived a charmed life. I can point to wonderful parents, and particularly to my mother who was the most positive and optimistic person I have ever known. I remember Sunday school teachers and others in my church who cared enough about a teenage boy to encourage me to follow the ways of the Lord. I attended good schools surrounded by caring teachers and loyal friends. The blessings of a wonderful family and of meaningful work have been showered upon me. However, I have known other people, Christians and non-Christians, with an equal or better heritage who are negative and bitter about life. Why do some people "always look on the sunny side of life"? Is the glass half full or half empty? Is the reason we look at life positively or negatively the result of nature or nurture? The answer is probably a combination of the two. But the key is found in the last verse of our psalm. "Thou wilt show me the path of life; in thy presence is fullness of joy; at thy right hand there are pleasures for evermore." David, the author of this psalm, had his share of hardships and, like all of us, was a sinful human being. Yet his relationship with God was the most fundamental fact of his life, and it produced a profound gratitude for the goodness he experienced in life. May it be so for us.

~DR. JOHN A. WOOD (1938–) WACO, TX

JUST IN THE NICK OF TIME

"My friends, do not be afraid of those who kill the body."

LUKE 12:4 NKJV

My doctor husband, Jim, and I were in Kediri, Java, Indonesia, during President Sukarno's 1956 unsuccessful Communist coup. Muslims rose up and killed hundreds of thousands of communists who had tricked them. November 5th, a band of Muslims almost butchered a Communist to death. He was brought into the emergency room with his throat was cut through the trachea down to the carotid arteries. His jaw and tongue were chopped, and his arm was deeply lacerated and two bones broken. This man was terrified as Jim moved toward him for treatment. What would this white Christian doctor do to him—he who wanted all Christians dead? During two hours of medical care, suturing and setting the bones, Jim shared the love of Jesus and His salvation. A calm and peace came over his patient. Even though he couldn't speak, it was obvious the Lord had touched him as tears rolled down his face. Because there was no law in Indonesia at that time, the Muslims came in and took Jim's Communist patient and killed him. Weeks later we found out that same man was head of the Communist village across the road from us. He had volunteered to bring a band of Muslims to our house and kill Jim, our three young girls, and me on November 8th, three days after his murder. God not only saved our family but He brought that wicked Communist murderer to heaven, saved and whole. Isn't it amazing, our gracious, Awesome God saved this man just in the nick of time. How wonderful to have given Jim the opportunity to be in the right place at the right time.

~JOYCE S. CARPENTER (1931–) SENECA, SC

CHRIST, OUR ADVOCATE

*And if any man sin, we have an advocate with the
Father, Jesus Christ the righteous.*

1 JOHN 2:1 KJV

If God had not been mercifully disposed towards sinners, no
Advocate had been appointed, no question of forgiveness had been
raised. It implies also that the exercise of mercy on certain conditions is
possible. Not only is God mercifully disposed, but to manifest this
disposition in the actual pardon of sin is possible. Had not this been the
case, no Advocate had been appointed. It implies that there is hope,
then, for the condemned. It implies that there is a governmental
necessity for the interposition of an advocate; that the sinner's relations
are such, and his character such, that he can not be admitted to plead
his own cause in his own name. He is condemned, he is no longer on
trial. In this respect he is under sentence for a capital crime;
consequently be is an outlaw, and the government cannot recognize
him as being capable of performing any legal act. His relations to the
government forbid that in his own name, or in his own person, he
should appear before God. So far as his own personal influence with the
government is concerned, he is as a dead man—he is civilly dead.
Therefore, he must appear by his next friend, or by his advocate, if he
is heard at all. He may not appear in his own name and in his own
person, but must appear by an advocate who is acceptable to the
government.

~CHARLES FINNEY (1792–1875)

GRACE ABOUNDING

*It is a night to be much observed unto the L*ORD *for bringing them
out from the land of Egypt: this is that night of the L*ORD *to be
observed of all the children of Israel in their generations.*

EXODUS 12:42 KJV

It is profitable for Christians to be often calling to mind the very
beginnings of grace with their Souls. When God had brought the
children of Israel through the Red Sea, far into the wilderness, yet they
must turn quite about thither again, to remember the drowning of their
enemies there (Numbers 14:25). For though they sang His praise before,
yet "they soon forgat his works" (Psalm 106:11–13). In this discourse of
mine you may see much; much, I say, of the grace of God towards me.
I thank God I can count it much, for it was above my sins and Satan's
temptations too. I can remember my fears, and doubts, and sad months
with comfort; they are as the head of Goliath in my hand. There was
nothing to David like Goliath's sword, even that sword that should have
been sheathed in his bowels; for the very sight and remembrance of
that did preach forth God's deliverance to him. Oh, the remembrance
of my great sins, of my great temptations, and of my great fears of
perishing for ever! They bring afresh into my mind the remembrance of
my great help, my great support from heaven, and the great grace that
God extended to such a wretch as I.

~JOHN BUNYAN (1628–1688)

LIGHT AFFLICTIONS

For our light affliction, which is but for a moment, worketh
for us a far more exceeding and eternal weight of glory.

2 CORINTHIANS 4:17 KJV

Afflictions are not light in themselves for often times they are heavy and grievous; but they are light comparatively! They are light when compared with what we really deserve. They are light when compared with the sufferings of the Lord Jesus. But perhaps their real lightness is best seen by comparing them with the weight of glory which is awaiting us. As said the same apostle in another place, "For I reckon that the sufferings of this present time are not worthy to be compared with the glory which shall be revealed in us" (Romans 8:18). Should our afflictions continue throughout a whole lifetime, and that life be equal in duration to Methuselah's, yet is it momentary if compared with the eternity which is before us. At most, our affliction is but for this present life, which is as a vapor that appears for a little while and then vanishes away. Oh that God would enable us to examine our trials in their true perspective. Our light affliction, which is but for a moment, "worketh for us a far more exceeding and eternal weight of glory." The present is influencing the future. It is not for us to reason and philosophize about this, but to take God at His Word and believe it. Experience, feelings, observation of others, may seem to deny this fact. Often times afflictions appear only to sour us and make us more rebellious and discontented. But let it be remembered that afflictions are not sent by God for the purpose of purifying the flesh: they are designed for the benefit of the "new man."

~A. W. PINK (1886–1952)

THE CHOSEN PATH

GIVER OR TAKER

Now this I say, he who sows sparingly will also reap sparingly,
and he who sows bountifully will also reap bountifully.

2 CORINTHIANS 9:6 NASB

Recently, several of the churches in our community had been broken into and robbed. Within weeks, the thieves were apprehended, only to find out that the churches that had been robbed had ministered to the men in many ways. One of the thieves had had several hundred dollars worth of medical bills paid by one of the churches, and another had his marriage restored by the counseling he'd received from a church. People today just don't want to hear about giving. They complain about the pastor who preaches on giving, they complain about the amount the church might spend on certain items, and yet these folks are usually the ones who don't even tithe! To be honest, I have never been able to out-give God. In fact, it is so much fun to give and watch God bless your giving. Several years ago, God convicted my wife and I about our debt so we decided to sell the house that we loved so much. We had been faithful in our tithe to the church, but we were unable to bless others as we wanted. The next day, a couple rang our doorbell and asked if we would sell the house. They made an offer of exactly what we needed for the house, so we sold it. Today, God has given us back the house at even a lower cost than when we first bought it, and we are now able to bless others. When we don't give, we are not only robbing God, but we are robbing ourselves of a blessing!

~ANDY DIETZ (1950–) BORGER, TX

A CURE FOR "POOR ME"

Nor height, nor depth, nor any other creature, shall be able to separate us from the love of God, which is in Christ Jesus our Lord.

ROMANS 8:39 KJV

"Nobody likes me, everybody hates me; I'm going to eat some worms." Remember that? We used to say it as kids. We've grown up now and don't say these words, but instead use adult expressions that have the same meaning: "Poor me—everything is going wrong, God doesn't care how bad things are, etc., etc." It is unfortunate that many Christians believe that once they are saved they are somehow exempt from misfortune. God does want us to prosper in every aspect of life; however, His primary concern is for our spiritual health and well-being. He sent Jesus to redeem our spirits from sin and make us right with God, not to save us from all life's physical and material woes. In the Scriptures before the above reference, Paul asks four questions, then provides the answers. The last question is "who shall separate us from the love of Christ?" Notice he says "who" not "what." The "who" that desires man be separated from Jesus is Satan. Next Paul lists the things, physical and emotional, that Satan uses to torment Gods children; "tribulation, distress, persecution, famine, nakedness, peril, or sword." When we suffer these things it's often "poor me," but we need to keep reading because even though our bodies may be hurting, our spirits can soar from His promise of everlasting love that nothing can diminish. Poor me? No way! How can we not be in a constant state of praise and joy when we remember this promise of our loving Lord?

~G. W. STROTHER (1933–) CLAYTON, GA

YOURS FOR THE ASKING

I rejoice in your promise like one who finds great spoil.
PSALM 119:162 NIV

A newspaper carried a picture of a man arduously searching through his city's garbage dump. According to the caption he was "Looking for Lost Millions." He had purchased a lottery ticket, put it in a kitchen cabinet, and forgotten about it. His wife threw it away while cleaning the kitchen. When the winners were announced, he was one of them. If he could find the discarded ticket, he would be able to claim $2.9 million. The camera caught him looking down, totally intent and oblivious to the needle-in-a-haystack task it would be to rake through the tons of garbage around him. His face told the story—frustration and disappointment mingled with a touch of hope that the ticket might not have been destroyed yet. He was so close to something he really wanted, but he had to have that ticket in order to claim it. Like him, but with less reason, many people search through the trash of the world desperately seeking something to make them happy. Those of us who know Christ don't have to wait for our ships to come in. The world offers grand prizes to only a few, God offers His prizes to all who believe. But as Corrie ten Boom said, "Too often we are like people who stand in front of the show window of a jewelry store. We admire the beautiful watches, rings, and bracelets, but we do not go in and pay the price in order to possess them. We just walk away! It is through Jesus that God's greatest and most precious promises have become available to us." God's precious promises are available, and they are yours for the asking.

~VICKI HUFFMAN (1946–) MT. JULIET, TN

LOVE, ULTIMATE LOVE

For God so loved the world, that he gave his only begotten Son, that whosoever believeth in him should not perish, but have everlasting life.

JOHN 3:16 KJV

"God so loved the World," meaning the whole race of men. Not only the Bible, but the nature of the case, shows that the atonement must have been made for the whole world. For plainly if it had not been made for the entire race, no man of the race could ever know that it was made for himself, and therefore not a man could believe on Christ in the sense of receiving by faith the blessings of the atonement. There being an utter uncertainty as to the persons embraced in the limited provisions which we now suppose to be made, the entire donation must fail through the impossibility of rational faith for its reception. . . . All having an equal claim and none any definite claim, none can inherit. If the atonement were made in this way, no living man would have any valid reason for believing himself one of the elect, prior to his reception of the Gospel. Hence he would have no authority to believe and receive its blessings by faith. In fact, the atonement must be wholly void—on this supposition—unless a special revelation is made to the persons for whom it is intended. As the case is, however, the very fact that a man belongs to the race of Adam—the fact that he is human, born of woman, is all-sufficient. It brings him within the pale. He is one of the world for whom God gave His Son, that whosoever would believe in Him might not perish, but have everlasting life.

~CHARLES FINNEY (1792–1875)

THE CHOSEN PATH

DON'T HAVE TO, BUT GET TO

Thus Noah did; according to all that God commanded him, so he did.

GENESIS 6:22 NKJV

Chapter 6 is a very pivotal chapter in the book of Genesis. In this chapter, God decides that He has had enough of the corruption, violence, and lawlessness of mankind. In the decision to judge man by sending a world-wide flood (yes, I do believe it . . . the evidence is there!), God finds that Noah is a righteous man. God then gives Noah a God-size task. In addition to building the ark which was 450 feet long, 75 feet wide, and 45 feet high, Noah was to have an incredible array of animals on board that he would be caretaker to for one year. If that wasn't enough, Noah would then preach a message of judgment for 120 years, while building this "monstrosity" with his sons. If Noah had been a Baptist, the committee selection process would have used up half the time it took to build the boat! But just as all great saints of God, Noah looked at this God-size task with the right perspective—he didn't have to, but he got to! Because Noah did all that God commanded him, he got to build the first cruise ship in history! Because Enoch did what God commanded him to do, he got to walk with God right into God's house. Because Moses did what God commanded him to do, he got to part the Red Sea. Because Elijah did what God commanded him to do, he got to take a ride on a chariot of fire. Why not do what God commands you to do and GET TO!

~KEVIN KING (1962–) STEAMBOAT SPRINGS, CO

THE CHOSEN PATH

THEY SHALL BE COMFORTED

Blessed are they that mourn: for they shall be comforted.

MATTHEW 5:4 KJV

This refers first of all to the removal of the conscious guilt which burdens the conscience. It finds its fulfillment in the Spirit's application of the Gospel of God's grace to the one whom He has convicted of his dire need of a Savior. It issues in a sense of free and full forgiveness through the merits of the atoning blood of Christ. This Divine comfort is the peace of God which passes all understanding filling the heart of the one who is now assured that he is "accepted in the Beloved." God wounds before healing, abases before He exalts. First there is a revelation of His justice and holiness, then the making known of His mercy and grace. "They shall be comforted" also receives a constant fulfillment in the experience of the Christian. Though he mourns his excuseless failures and confesses them to God, yet he is comforted by the assurance that the blood of Jesus Christ His Son cleanses him from all sin. Like the Apostle, the believer who is in communion with his Lord can say, "As sorrowful yet always rejoicing." Yes "mourning" Christians are comforted even now by the Divine Comforter, by the ministrations of His servants, by encouraging words from fellow Christians, and when these are not to hand, by the precious promises of the Word being brought home in power to his memory and heart. "They shall be comforted." The best wine is reserved for the last. Sorrow may endure for a night, but joy cometh in the morning.

~A. W. PINK (1886–1952)

CHRIST'S ATONING WORK

For both he that sanctifieth and they who are sanctified are all
of one: for which cause he is not ashamed to call them brethren,
Saying, I will declare thy name unto my brethren, in the midst
of the church will I sing praise unto thee.

HEBREWS 2:11–12 KJV

The atoning work of Christ was not sufficient for the salvation of man. That work was only Godward, and removed only all the obstacles in the way of God's pardon of the sinner. But the sinner is also at enmity with God, and must be brought to accept salvation, and must learn to love and serve God. The first step here is to make known to man the gospel, which contains the glad tidings of this salvation, under such influences as ought to lead to its acceptance. The Gospel is, therefore, commanded to be proclaimed to every creature, inasmuch as there is in the work of Christ a means of redemption for every one. This is the external call of the Gospel. This proclamation, however, meets with no success because of the willful sinfulness of man, although, in itself, it has all the elements which should secure its acceptance. God knowing that this is true, not only of all mankind in general, but even of the elect whom he purposes to save in Christ, gives to these such influences of the Spirit as will lead to their acceptance of the call. This is called Effectual Calling.

~J. P. BOYCE (1827–1888)

THE CHOSEN PATH

ALL THE WAY MY SAVIOR LEADS ME

*For the Lamb who is in the midst of the throne will shepherd
them and lead them to living fountains of waters.*
REVELATION 7:17 NKJV

All the way my Savior leads me What have I to ask beside?
Can I doubt His tender mercy, Who through life has been my Guide?
Heav'nly peace, divinest comfort, Here by faith in Him to dwell!
For I know, whate'er befall me, Jesus doeth all things well;
For I know, whate'er befall me, Jesus doeth all things well.
All the way my Savior leads me Cheers each winding path I tread,
Gives me grace for every trial, Feeds me with the living Bread.
Though my weary steps may falter And my soul athirst may be,
Gushing from the Rock before me, Lo! A spring of joy I see;
Gushing from the Rock before me, Lo! A spring of joy I see.
All the way my Savior leads me O the fullness of His love!
Perfect rest to me is promised In my Father's house above.
When my spirit, clothed immortal, Wings its flight to realms of day
This my song through endless ages: Jesus led me all the way;
This my song through endless ages: Jesus led me all the way.

~ **FANNY CROSBY** (1820–1915)

DOES LIFE MAKE ANY SENSE?

FROM ECCLESIASTES 1:2 KJV

The book of Ecclesiastes is unique in all of Scripture. The writer says over and over again, "All is vanity." That is, all is meaningless, futile, and senseless. He bemoans the fact that life hasn't really repaid him for all his hard work. He concludes that no matter how hard he works and how wisely he plans, life remains uncontrollable and unpredictable. Death hangs over the book like a dark cloud. His basic theology is that God is unknowable and, consequently, life is shrouded in mystery. He is one of the sages, or wise men, who has come to the painful conclusion that wisdom cannot achieve its goal of understanding the meaning and purpose of life. Why then was this book included in sacred Scripture? On the surface it appears to be totally opposite from biblical faith. On the contrary, it is fortunate that the book was included in the Bible. The author challenges his fellow wise men that think they can answer every mystery in life with a simple proverb. As valuable and practical as the book of Proverbs is, he knows that you cannot reduce every question to an easy two-line answer. There is genuine mystery in the universe, so one shouldn't be smug and think that he or she has a neat and rational answer to every problem. There is undeserved suffering and tragedy in the world, which tends to lead people to either despair or to the easy answers of popular religion. This book forces the reader to embrace an honest faith that accepts paradoxes and ambiguities, but which knows that there is a sovereign God who ultimately brings meaning to it all.

~DR. JOHN A. WOOD (1938–) WACO, TX

MANSIONS

In my Father's house are many mansions.

JOHN 14:2 KJV

Heaven is God's house. A house of public worship is an house where God's people meet from time to time to attend on God's ordinances, and that is set apart for that and is called God's house. The temple of Solomon was called God's house. God was represented as dwelling there. There he has his throne in the holy of holies, even the mercy seat over the ark and between the cherubim's . . . the highest heaven is especially represented in Scripture as the house of God. As to other parts of the creation, God hath appointed them to inferior uses; but this part he has reserved for himself for his own abode. We are told that the heavens are the Lord's, but the earth he hath given to the sons of men. God, though he is everywhere present, is represented both in Old Testament and New as being in heaven is a special and peculiar manner. Heaven is the temple of God. Solomon's temple was a type of heaven. The apostle Paul is his epistle to the Hebrews does from time to time call heaven the holy of holies, as being the antitype not only of the temple of Solomon, but of the most holy place in that temple, which was the place of God's most immediate residence: Hebrews 9:12, "He entered in once into the holy place;" "For Christ is not entered into the holy places made with hands, which are the figures of the true, but into heaven itself." As in houses of public worship here there are assemblies of Christians meeting to worship God, so in heaven there is a glorious assembly, or Church, continually worshipping God.

~JONATHAN EDWARDS (1703–1758)

MINISTRY NEEDS

The earth is the LORD's, and all the fulness thereof.

PSALM 24:1 KJV

In the fifth and sixth centuries, Gildas and Salvian arose to alarm and arouse a careless church and a stuffy ministry. In the sixteenth century, that task fell to the Reformers. In the seventeenth century, Richard Baxter, among others, took a major part in stimulating the godliness and idle energies of his fellow ministers. In the eighteenth century, God raised up some choice and noble men to awaken the church and lead the way to higher and bolder career of ministerial duty. The present century stands no less in need of some stimulating influence. We have experienced many symptoms of life, but still the populace is not revived. We require a new Baxter to awaken us by his voice and his example. It is depressing to see the amount of ministerial apathy and incompetence that still over spreads our land. How long, O Lord, how long! The injecting of new life into the ministry ought to be the object of more direct and special effort, as well as of more united and fervent prayer. The prayers of Christians ought to be more largely directed to the students, the preachers, the ministers of the Christian church. It is a living ministry that our country needs; and without such a ministry it can no longer expect to escape the judgments of God. We need men that will spend and be spent—that will labor and pray—that will watch and weep for souls. Are you one who can be counted?

~HORATIUS BONAR (1808–1889)

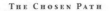

THE CHOSEN PATH

FRIENDLY CHURCHES
ARE NOT OUT OF STYLE

Don't neglect to show hospitality.

HEBREWS 13:2 HCSB

Most churches consider themselves friendly, but in reality, few are truly friendly to visitors. Churches believe themselves to be friendly because members are friendly to each other. I doubt that faithful church members intentionally avoid or ignore Sunday visitors. It's just that it is much easier to be friendly to people they know. I remember one church I visited where an usher handed me a bulletin without making eye contact or even saying, "Good morning." He was too busy talking to the other usher! People tell me about churches where they walked in and, an hour later, walked out without anyone saying a word to them. Is that rude? What would Jesus do? The Bible teaches, "Don't neglect to show hospitality, for by doing this some have welcomed angels as guests without knowing it" (Hebrews 13:2 HCSB). Being friendly to Sunday visitors is more than a technique to make your church grow. In the Bible, offering hospitality is a moral imperative. God's people remember that they were once strangers and refugees who were taken in by God (Deuteronomy 10:19). That first-time visitor may be weighed down by a great emotional burden. A kind word from you can lift that person's spirit. Even people who don't attend church see church as a source of comfort and consolation and will seek out a church in time of deep need. That trust can be shattered by a cold, indifferent reception from a cliquish church. First impressions are strong and will no doubt determine people's attitude toward the church as a whole. Go out of your way to make guests feel at home.

~JORGE ZAYASBAZAN (1959–) ROUND THE LAKE BEACH, IL

A SOLDIER'S LOVE FOR HIS BRIDE

*That their hearts might be comforted, being knit together in love,
and unto all riches of the full assurance of understanding, to the
acknowledgement of the mystery of God, and of the Father, and of Christ.*

COLOSSIANS 2:2 KJV

Being a pastor in a military town is rewarding. You get to know the soldiers in unexpected ways. A young soldier in our church gleefully returned from the first deployment to Iraq in 2003 with much more than war stories. He brought other young soldiers into our fellowship that had became believers in Jesus Christ while in the heated battles in the distant desert. One of these new soldier converts, in particular, came home excited about sharing his newfound faith with his wife. She was reluctant but appreciated new character traits developing in her husband. At a planned lunch with the soldier and his unconvinced wife, shortly after the soldier joined our church, the young man made clear his intent. The reason was specific: "To share with my wife how she can be born again." Lunch came and went as I shared with this young woman the love God had for her. At the point when she was ready to ask Christ to be her Lord, I turned to her husband and said, "You lead her in prayer." The two bowed in this crowded restaurant and became one, not just in marriage, but also in spirit. At that moment she came into the kingdom of God and now knows that she, like her husband, will spend eternity in heaven, "forever." That same "forever" is available to you . . . right where you are!

~**TOMMY HENSCHEL (1947–) ELLERSLIE, GA**

THE CHOSEN PATH

MANY STILL LACK THE FIRE!

And when he is come, he will reprove the world of sin, and of righteousness and of judgment: Of sin, because they believe not on me.

JOHN 16:8–9 KJV

It is true that Pentecost, historically, took place once for all. So did Calvary. But each individual must personally appropriate the blood by faith and so must each believer receive by faith the Spirit for power. It is an experience of spiritual thirst, then coming to Christ, drinking of the Spirit by faith, believing and overflowing (John 7:37–39). So the blood and bread must be accompanied by fire. We have fundamentalism and facts; we have activity and earnestness and sincerity; we even have blood-washed and blood-nourished Christians, well-taught in the Word, WHO STILL LACK FIRE. Some are prejudiced against it, identifying any definite experience of the Spirit with fanaticism. Some see nothing but a gradual growth in grace. Some mistake the indwelling of the Spirit for the infilling. Some have "received" with a cheap and easy "believism" who somehow did not receive after all. For many reasons the church is largely behind closed doors as before Pentecost, and believers try to stir up a fire from their own sparks instead of being set on fire of God. We are not here advocating some wild and weird emotional experience, but we do hold that he who seeks to burn out for God will have to go deeper than sentence prayers and occasional wishful thinking. There must be a holy burning and a consuming longing for the fullness of the Spirit. Tears and fastings and all night prayers have no value of themselves, but God will reward the man who forgets all else seeking the double portion of "power with God and men."

~VANCE HAVNER (1901–1986)

THE CHOSEN PATH

REJOICE IN THE LORD ALWAYS

And again I say, Rejoice.
PHILIPPIANS 4:4 KJV

Why should I, who am by nature no different from the careless and godless throngs all around, have been chosen in Christ before the foundation of the world and now blest with all spiritual blessings in the heavenlies in Him? Such grace, such love, "passeth knowledge." But if my mind is unable to discern a reason, my heart can express its gratitude in praise and adoration. But not only should I be grateful to God for His grace toward me in the past, His present dealings will fill me with thanksgivings. What is the force of that word "Rejoice in the Lord alway" (Philippians 4:4)? Mark it is not "Rejoice in the Savior," but we are to "Rejoice in the Lord," as "Lord," as THE MASTER OF EVERY CIRCUMSTANCE. Need we remind the reader that when the apostle penned these words he was himself a prisoner in the hands of the Roman government. . . . He had been persecuted by those within the church as well as by those Without. . . . And still he writes, "Rejoice in the Lord alway." But how did he, and how do we, "know," that all things work together for good? The answer is, Because all things are under the control of and are being regulated by the Supreme Sovereign, and because He has naught but thoughts of love toward His own, then all things are so ordered by Him that they are MADE TO MINISTER TO OUR ULTIMATE GOOD.

~A. W. PINK (1886–1952)

WARFARE

For I delight in the law of God after the inward man: But I see another
law in my members, warring against the law of my mind, and bringing
me into captivity to the law of sin which is in my members. O wretched
man that I am! who shall deliver me from the body of this death?
I thank God through Jesus Christ our Lord. So then with the mind
I myself serve the law of God; but with the flesh the law of sin.

ROMANS 7:22–25 KJV

Truly, we are more than conquerors through Him that loved us; for we can give thanks before the fight is done. Yes, even in the thickest of the battle we can look up to Christ, and cry, Thanks to God. The moment a soul groaning under corruption rests the eye on the Lord Jesus, that moment his groans are changed into songs of praise. In Christ you discover a fountain to wash away the guilt of all your sins. In Christ you discover grace sufficient for you—grace to hold you up at the end—and a sure promise that sin shall soon be rooted out altogether. "Fear not, I have redeemed thee. I have called thee by My name; thou art Mine." Ah, this turns our groans into songs of praise. How often a Psalm begins with groans, and ends with praise! This is the daily experience of all the Lord's people. Is it yours? Try yourselves by this. If you know not the believer's song of praise, you will never cast your crowns with them at the feet of the Lamb. Dear believer, be content to glory in your infirmities that the power of Christ may rest upon you.

~R. M. McCHEYNE (1813–1843)

THE GOOD WAY OF COMING BEFORE THE LORD

*Wherewith shall I come before the LORD, and bow myself
before the high God? He hath shewed thee, O man, what is good;
and what doth the LORD require of thee, but to do justly,
and to love mercy, and to walk humbly with thy God?*

MICAH 6:6, 8 KJV

The question of an awakened soul—"Wherewith shall I come before the Lord?" An unawakened man never puts that question. A natural man has no desire to come before God, or to bow himself before the High God. He does not like to think of God. He would rather think of any other subject. He easily forgets what he is told about God. A natural man has no memory for divine things, because he has no heart for them. He has no desire to come before God in prayer. There is nothing a natural man hates more than prayer. He would far rather spend half an hour every morning in bodily exercise or in hard labor, than in the presence of God. He has no desire to come before God when he dies. He knows that he must appear before God, but it gives him no joy. He had rather sink into nothing; he had rather never see the face of God. Ah! my friends, is this your condition? How surely you may know that you have "the carnal mind which is enmity against God." You are like Pharaoh—"Who is the Lord, that I should obey Him?" You say to God, "Depart from me, for I desire not the knowledge of Thy ways." What an awful state it is to be in to have no desire after Him who is the fountain of living waters!

~R. M. McCheyne (1813–1843)

THE CHOSEN PATH

PERSONAL GROWTH VS. SELF-FULFILLMENT

For wisdom is better than rubies, and all the things
one may desire cannot be compared with her.

PROVERBS 8:11 NKJV

The motivation of self-fulfillment creates the Dead Sea Syndrome. It's the pond without an outlet that becomes stagnant, toxic, and unfit for human use. Self-fulfillment is a self-centered approach to life that ultimately prevents us from reaching our full potential. When our thoughts are primarily upon ourselves, our motivation is self-fulfillment. That's looking out for number one. That's a thought pattern that leads to difficulty, hampers our effectiveness, restricts our productivity on the job, and destroys a major portion of our future. This attitude also seriously limits the number of friends and long-term relationships we can build. Very few people are interested in being friends with or establishing long-term relationships with those who are motivated by self-fulfillment. Yes, self-fulfillment is a dead-end street, whereas the motivation of personal growth is the flowing river that gets its water from one source and delivers it to another, watering crops or generating electricity on the way. Self-fulfillment is the perennial student who acquires knowledge primarily for the sake of knowledge so he or she will have the answers. Motivation for personal growth is the teacher who acquires the knowledge so he or she will have the answers to share with others. Where are you in your personal growth?

~ZIG ZIGLAR (1926–) ADDISON, TX

FROM LEPROSY TO LIBERTY

Right away a man with a serious skin disease came up and knelt before
Him, saying, "Lord, if You are willing, You can make me clean."
Reaching out His hand He touched him, saying, "I am willing;
be made clean." Immediately his disease was healed.

MATTHEW 8:2–3 HCSB

Your doctor walks in the exam room and says, "I am sorry to inform you that you have_____." What is the worse thing you can imagine the doctor saying? How would it affect your life? What it would have been like 2,000 years ago? The worse disease you could have imagined would have been leprosy. Throughout the Bible, leprosy represents a physical manifestation of sin. Sin, like leprosy starts small and unstopped will lead to spiritual death. This leper was desperate, one who has lost everything, his family, his friends, his home, he couldn't work, he couldn't worship. But he believed that if he could get to Jesus, he could he cured. He was desperate, devoted, and determined. He was willing to be humiliated as he walked through the crowd yelling, "Unclean! Unclean!" Falling at Jesus' feet, he says, "Lord, if You are willing, You can make me clean." Jesus was willing and healed him. Before we made Jesus Lord of our lives, we were just like this leper. We were lost, alone, and without hope, and needing a miracle. Our cure is Jesus Christ. "Lord, if You are willing, You can make me clean." If you admit, believe, and confess, Jesus will say, "I am willing; be made clean." There is a serious epidemic in this world, we must offer Christ as the cure or people will continue to die. Save a life, share Jesus today. Bring someone from Leprosy to Liberty.

~**TERRENCE ROBERTS (1964–) MERIDIAN, MS**

THE CONCEPT OF DIVINE CONTROL

...how much more shall your Father which is in
heaven give good things to them that ask him?

MATTHEW 7:11 KJV

Jesus is laying down the rules of conduct in this passage for those people who have His Spirit. He urges us to keep our minds filled with the concept of God's control over everything, which means that a disciple must maintain an attitude of perfect trust and an eagerness to ask and to seek. Fill your mind with the thought that God is there. And once your mind is truly filled with that thought, when you experience difficulties it will be as easy as breathing for you to remember, "My heavenly Father knows all about this!" This will be no effort at all, but will be a natural thing for you when difficulties and uncertainties arise. Jesus is laying down the rules of conduct for those people who have His Spirit, and it works on the following principle: God is my Father, He loves me, and I will never think of anything that He will forget, so why should I worry? Jesus said there are times when God cannot lift the darkness from you, but you should trust Him. At times, God will appear like an unkind friend, but He is not; He will appear like an unnatural father, but He is not; He will appear like an unjust judge, but He is not. Keep the thought that the mind of God is behind all things strong and growing. Not even the smallest detail of life happens unless God's will is behind it. Therefore, you can rest in perfect confidence in Him.

~OSWALD CHAMBERS (1874–1917)

GIVE GOD YOUR VERY BEST

"When you present a blind animal for sacrifice, is it not wrong? And when you present a lame or sick animal, is it not wrong? Bring it to your governor! Would he be pleased with you or show you favor?" asks the LORD of Hosts."

MALACHI 1:8 HCSB

In the days of the prophet Malachi, God's people were required to sacrifice an animal, such as a lamb, as a payment for their sin. God required that they bring an unblemished animal to the altar. Yet, in the days of Malachi, the people brought God their worst animal, not their best one. Their worship had become drudgery, and they tried to get through it by giving unto the Lord that which they really did not want in the first place—a blind, sick, or injured animal. Yet there were already Old Testament laws that told them what to do with animals that had been injured or attacked in the field. Exodus 22:31 says, "Be My holy people. You must not eat the meat of a mauled animal found in the field; throw it to the dogs." It appears that these worshippers were presenting dog food to the Lord of Hosts! And if we are not careful, we can follow in their footsteps, giving unto the Lord that which is cheap, convenient, or simply undesirable. The way in which people worship the Lord says a great deal about what they think about Him. If Jesus is not first place in one's life, there will always be other things in the schedule or in the budget that take precedence. But when Jesus is viewed as the One who rescues from sin, death, and hell while giving new life and the promise of heaven—only the very best will do!

~RYAN BOWMAN (1972–) LEE'S SUMMIT, MO

ARE YOU WALKING WITH GOD?

And Enoch walked with God: and he was not; for God took him.
GENESIS 5:24 KJV

Walking with God not only implies that the prevailing power of the enmity of a man's heart be taken away, but also that a person is actually reconciled to God the Father, in and through the all sufficient righteousness and Atonement of His dear Son. "Can two talk together (says Solomon), unless they are agreed?" Jesus is our peace as well as our Peacemaker. When we are justified by Faith in Christ, then, but not till then, we have peace with God; and consequently cannot be said till then to walk with Him, walking with a person being a sign and token that we are friends to that person, or at least, though we have been at variance, yet that now we are reconciled and become friends again. This is the great errand that Gospel Ministers are sent out upon. To us is committed the Ministry of Reconciliation; as Ambassadors for God we are to beseech sinners, in Christ's stead, to be reconciled unto God, and when they comply with the gracious invitation, and are actually by Faith brought into a state of reconciliation with God, then, and not till then, may they be said so much as to begin to walk with God.

~GEORGE WHITEFIELD (1714–1770)

THANKSGIVING DAY

I will praise the name of God with a song,
And will magnify Him with thanksgiving.

PSALM 69:30 NKJV

Thanksgiving is one of the best holidays. It's going to Grandma's house for turkey dinner. It's getting to see your family, and laugh with them and pass the dressing and the cranberry sauce to them. It's the toddler who has changed so much since last year, and the old uncle who hasn't, both making you smile. And it's everyone sharing something you're especially thankful for, and then bowing your heads together and giving thanks. We should do Thanksgiving regularly. Not the turkey dinner, of course, but the giving thanks. In Bible times, whenever believers in God got together, the main thing was to give thanks. Now we have more stuff, more freedom, way more food, better health, and the promises of the whole Bible, and yet when we pray or go to church it seems we are always looking to get more, instead of saying, "Thank You!" This is something we can change, just by giving thanks, every day. Thanksgiving is an attitude of the heart. It's choosing to be grateful for the good things in our lives, for family and friends, for work and rest, for life itself and the beauty that surrounds us. It's thanking Jesus every day for the gift of forgiveness and eternal life, which were not purchased for us at a bargain price. It's deciding that because of all that, there is no room for bitterness, resentment, or any of the things that live in an ungrateful heart. Thanksgiving is, in the highest sense, a way of life. Because if our hearts are truly thankful, then we can only live for the One who has given us so much.

~DAVID F. RASMUSSEN (1952–) GREENCASTLE, PA

BE AMAZED, GOD IS IN CONTROL

Look among the nations and watch—be utterly
astounded! For I will work a work in your days which
you would not believe, though it were told you.

HABAKKUK 1:5 NKJV

After the Communist walls fell in Eastern Europe, my father, Harry Dent, was one of the first to go with Evangelist John Guest to Romania. He immediately formed a bond with our dear Romanian brothers and sisters who had endured great persecution for their faith. He formed a partnership between the city of Columbia, S.C., and Cluj, Romania, to assist their transition from Communism to freedom. He paid a visit to President George H. Bush and Secretary of State James Baker to explain why he thought Romania should receive "Most Favored Treaty Status" from the U.S. It was granted. For years the Romanian Christians prayed through their persecution. After forty years of Communism and the miraculous growth of an underground church through persecution, God answered their prayers. The Communist walls fell like a game of dominos. James Baker told my father that day in Washington that the fall of Communism was clearly the hand of God. The CIA did not predict it—no one saw it coming. My father and I believe that God brought it to be—for such a time as this. It makes me wonder what He will do to bring the Muslim walls down or any wall that hinders His message. Just wait and see!

~GINNY DENT BRANT (1955–) SENECA, SC

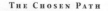

THE CHOSEN PATH

IDENTITY THEFT

For you have died and your life is hidden with Christ in God.

COLOSSIANS 3:3 NASB

Over the past couple of years, there has been much attention placed on the reality of stolen identities as a result of credit card fraud. Credit card numbers are left for the taking whether on an old bank statement or through the Internet. The tempted find the numbers and use them for their own personal gain by spending YOUR money on THEIR luxuries—all in YOUR name, making you look like someone you are not. As I hear of stolen identities in the financial world, I cannot help but think about all of the people in the spiritual world that are just as guilty of identity theft. There are people everywhere who are Bible-believing Christians who simply do not know who they are. Within the secular world, they are quick to label themselves as bankers, lawyers, homemakers, or students. Within the church, it is also easy to be personified through the things done for the church. But identities are not found in professions, family names, wealth, or church service even though they are not necessarily bad things. To claim identity in those things, however, is to steal the ultimate identity God has given you. As Christians, the Bible says that our ultimate identity is found in Jesus Christ alone. The apostle Paul says that our "life is hidden with Christ in God." So, in essence, a relationship with Christ is not simply a moral or religious side of you. Instead, it is the very essence of who you are. It is your ultimate identity. So, the question is simple—have you committed identity theft or are you living in full assurance of who you are in Jesus Christ?

~CHRIS JAMES (1978–) LOWELL, MA

TRUE REPENTANCE

. . . to give repentance to Israel, and forgiveness of sins.

ACTS 5:31 KJV

The seat of true repentance is in the soul. It is not of itself the mere intellectual knowledge of sin, nor the sorrow that accompanies it, nor the changed life which flows from it; but it is the soul's apprehension of its heinous character, which begets the horror and self-loathing which accompany it, and the determination to forsake sin which flows from it. That true repentance is inconsistent with the continuance in sin because of grace abounding. That true repentance consists of mental and spiritual emotion, and not of outward self-imposed chastisements. Even the pious life and devotion to God which follow are described not as repentance, but as fruits meet for repentance. The Scriptures teach that the author of true repentance is God operating by truth upon the renewed heart (Acts 5:31). Christ is said to have been exalted "to give repentance to Israel, and remission of sins" (Acts 11:18). "Then to the Gentiles also hath God granted repentance unto life." The means used is the preaching and other exhibition of the truth. Repentance like faith comes through the hearing of the word. By this, men are exhorted to that duty, and gain the knowledge of the truths taught by God, through spiritual apprehension of which men are led to the truth.

~J. P. BOYCE (1827–1888)

CHANGING THE WORLD
IN JESUS' NAME

*When they observed the boldness of Peter and John and realized
that they were uneducated and untrained men, they were
amazed and recognized that they had been with Jesus.*

ACTS 4:13 HCSB

Peter and John were arrested because they had preached that salvation comes through faith in Jesus alone. The authorities were threatened by the message and the apostles were arrested and brought into court. These men found themselves in trouble for boldly taking a stand for Jesus. We face the temptation of thinking of these men and those who served alongside them as super saints. Often Christians face opposition and ridicule in a secular world. How can we make a difference? How can we be world changers for Jesus? The Galilean fishermen in this passage found themselves in the religious supreme court of the nation facing the rich, able, educated, power brokers of their day. There was nothing outstanding about their persons except that their strength was in God who can take the ordinary and do extraordinary things. They were courageous and were unashamed of the gospel of Jesus. Today the world needs Christians who will stand for Christ in a world that does not honor Him as Lord. It takes courage that the Holy Spirit will provide if we will submit ourselves to Him. They had great faith. They remembered the confidence with which their Lord had stood. They had been with Jesus. That is the defining characteristic of any Christian, whether or not we have been with Jesus. To be with Jesus makes us reflect Jesus. He cannot be concealed. Our faith in Him and deep abiding love for Him will compel us to speak is name!

~SETH POLK (1971–) POKA, WV

FOLLOW THE LAMB

Arise, shine; for thy light is come, and the glory
of the LORD is risen upon thee.

ISAIAH 60:1 KJV

Remember what you are, and what God expects at your hand. Act out your own professions, your own faith, your own prayers. God has had mercy on you; and in His great love He has laid His almighty hand on you that you might be saved. He has "sent from above, and taken, and drawn you out of many waters" (Psalm 18:16); delivering you not only "from the wrath to come" (1 Thessalonians 1:10), but from "a present evil world" (Galatians 1:4). By His gracious power, He has turned you from the error of your ways; and one of the many names by which you are henceforth to be known on earth is that of "converts" or "turned ones." But your "turning" or "conversion" is only a beginning. It is not the whole; it is but the first step. You are a "disciple," that is, one under teaching; but your teaching, your discipleship, has only commenced. Your life is a Book; it may be a volume of larger or smaller size; and conversion is but the title-page or the preface. The Book itself remains to be written; and your years and weeks and days are its chapters and leaves and lines. It is a Book written for eternity; see that it be written well. It is a Book for the inspection of enemies as well as friends; be careful of every word. It is a Book written under the eye of God; let it be done reverently; without levity, yet without constraint or terror.

HORATIUS BONAR (1808–1889)

NIGHT AT A HOMELESS SHELTER

"The poor you will always have with you."
MATTHEW 26:11 NIV

There is a buzz of activity as a team of volunteers transforms the church's fellowship hall into a homeless shelter. Chatter and laughter fill the air as the cooking team mixes, stirs, cuts, tosses, and spreads and the Girl Scouts set up the sleeping mats. The guests arrive, enjoy dinner, and gather around the TV to watch a movie as the volunteers clean up. Volunteers come and go throughout the night attending to different tasks. Tammy is particularly tenderhearted toward the homeless. She has a kind word and a smile for everyone, making sure that each person has enough to eat. She tries to have new socks on hand and long underwear. "If their feet get wet and they can't change their socks, they'll be cold all day," she says. Wake up time is 5 a.m. A breakfast of cold and hot cereal, milk, juice, and coffee is ready as our guests wake up and gather their belongings, taking a sack lunch on their way out. As I leave for work I wonder what they will do today. A few have jobs, others will look for work and others will just find a place to stay warm on the cold November streets of Chicago. They will return tonight. It seems an endless and fruitless task. Jesus said, "The poor you will always have with you" (Matthew 26:11 NIV) He also taught us that that when we feed the hungry and clothe the naked we are ministering to him (Matthew 25:40). And so I will volunteer again and I thank God for churches that open their doors to the "least of these" and the Christians who serve them.

~JORGE ZAYASBAZAN (1959–) ROUND THE LAKE BEACH, IL

NO AGE DISCRIMINATION

*. . . but, the L*ORD* helping me, I will drive them out just as he said.*

JOSHUA 14:12 NIV

Caleb and Joshua were two of the twelve spies who investigated the Promised Land. All the spies said it was a land flowing with milk and honey, but all except Caleb and Joshua advised against trying to conquer the land. They had seen giants in the land and considered themselves mere grasshoppers in comparison. Caleb and Joshua stood against the majority opinion and declared that with God on their side the grasshoppers could beat the giants. Because the people wouldn't listen to Caleb and Joshua and refused to go into the Promised Land, God declared they would die in the wilderness. All except Caleb and Joshua. Caleb was eighty-five when the time finally came to conquer the Promised Land. Did he look for a shady front porch for his rocker? Not him. Instead he said, "I am still as strong today as the day Moses sent me out; I'm just as vigorous to go out to battle now as I was then. Now give me this hill country that the Lord promised" (Joshua 14:11–12). Caleb didn't ask for the mountain area so he could catch the evening breeze. His was the hardest territory to conquer—the land of the giants. "But, the Lord helping me, I will drive them out just as he said" (Joshua 14:12). Not all of us keep our physical strength or a keen mind into our advanced years, but too many concede to the giant of age without any battle at all. Don't discount your abilities because of gray hair. Your life isn't over until its over.

~VICKI HUFFMAN (1946–) MT. JULIET, TN

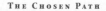

THE CHOSEN PATH

BRIDGE ON THE RIVER CRY

Always be prepared to give an answer.
1 PETER 3:15 NIV

The varsity football quarterback in the little Texas town was public hero number one, but he had problems. Drugs and other teenage distractions had pulled him down and his aunt, a strong Christian, had asked me to try to help him. How could I reach such a popular figure? I needed to build a bridge. I started taking photographs at the games and giving them away to the players. The foundation was laid! I gained access to the athletes, and as the next two seasons progressed, I became the team chaplain and even traveled with them. Lots of girders were going up on my bridge. I was always careful to play it low key. Most of my conversations with the quarterback didn't even have a religious tone. Eventually I asked him about his "spiritual" life and got a pretty positive response, but I didn't want to push it. I waited; half from fear of driving him away, but admittedly, half from fear of rejection. Even so, during the course of my bridge construction, many unintended evangelistic targets were reached. The quarterback's brother, mother, father, and several of his teammates got saved via my back door evangelism. The night I finally presented the gospel he was eager, but the presentation was cut short by the unexpected arrival of a "buddy" of his. We agreed to finish "some time" but time was against us. Two weeks later he and his "buddy" were killed in a car accident. At his funeral, a friend claimed he spoke of a recent life-changing encounter with God, but I wonder to this day if my bridge had too much support and not enough length to reach the other side.

~SCOTT TAYLOR (1960–) MARIETTA, SC

THE HOME'S WELFARE

And the men said unto Lot, Hast thou here any besides?
son-in-law, and thy sons, and thy daughters, and whatsoever
thou hast in the city, bring them out of this place.

GENESIS 19:12 KJV

The chief human institution in the city is the home. To be sure, the Church stands in a class by itself, a Divine institution, fashioned by our Divine, loving Savior and Master, but the first institution that God gave to human society was the home. It is the ultimate basis of human society. As goes the home, so will go the city. And I pause to say that the home is in peril and endangered now as it has not been in modern times. With "society" and worldliness claiming our well-to-do people, with our highly mechanized industrial order, with multitudes of poor and underprivileged people in our larger cities, living in tenement houses, where peaceful home life is well nigh impossible, the sanctity and sacredness of home can be enjoyed only by the very few. The competitive system, the highly industrialized order, the speed, the rush, the restlessness that marks life on every side, imperil and endanger as never before. If the home is lost, all will go down into the maelstrom with the failing and defeated homes. Important indeed are our economic problems, our problems of labor and state craft, our problems of public education, important enough to challenge the worthy attention of all men and women who care for their country— but far more important than any of these, or than all of these put together, is the conservation of the home. More important than all the men we have in the national capitol at Washington, is the conservation of the home life of our American people.

~G. W. TRUETT (1867–1944)

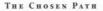

THE CHOSEN PATH

AMOS THE PROPHET

FROM AMOS 5:21–24 KJV

Amos was an eighth-century B.C. businessman from the southern kingdom of Judah who made regular business trips to the northern kingdom of Israel. He saw that while the Israelites were careful to observe all the outward trappings of religion, they were guilty of widespread cheating in the marketplace and of terrible mistreatment of the poor and needy. He concluded that greed, dishonesty, and neglect of the poor fueled Israel's vibrant economy. Amos became the first prophet to argue that social justice is as vital to genuine religion as worship of the one true God. His book is a fire-and-brimstone message about how God despises formal worship when it is not accompanied by a genuine concern for fellow human beings, especially the vulnerable ("widows and orphans") and those unable to fend for themselves. In some of the strongest language imaginable, Amos speaks for God: "I hate, I despise your festivals, and I take no delight in your solemn assemblies. Even though you offer me burnt offerings and grain offerings, I will not accept them; and the offering of well being of your fatted animals I will not look upon. Take away from me the noise of your songs; for I will not hear the melody of your harps. But let justice roll down like waters, and righteousness like an ever-flowing stream" (NRSV). Amos wasn't introducing something new here. He was only reminding the Israelites that love for God and love for humans intersect. Love for God and love for others cannot be separated. True worship of God includes caring for the neighbor.

~Dr. John A. Wood (1938–) Waco, TX

OUR BOLDNESS IN PRAYER (PART 1)

*And this is the confidence that we have in him, that,
if we ask anything according to his will, he heareth us.*

1 JOHN 5:14 KJV

One of the greatest hindrances to believing prayer is . . . they know not if what they ask is according to the will of God. As long as they are in doubt on this point, they cannot have the boldness to ask in the assurance that they certainly shall receive. And they soon begin to think that, if once they have made known their requests, and receive no answer, it is best to leave it to God to do according to His good pleasure. They think of God's will as His hidden counsel—how should man be able to fathom what really may be the purpose of the all-wise God. This is the very opposite of what John aimed at in writing thus. He wished to rouse us to boldness, to confidence, to full assurance of faith in prayer. He says, "This is the boldness which we have toward Him," that we can say: Father! Thou knowest and I know that I ask according to Thy will: I know Thou hearest me. "This is the boldness, that if we ask anything according to His will, He heareth us." On this account He adds at once: "If we know that He heareth us whatsoever we ask, we know, through this faith, that we have," that we now while we pray receive "the petition," the special things, "we have asked of Him."

~ANDREW MURRAY (1828–1917)

OUR BOLDNESS IN PRAYER (PART 2)

And if we know that he hear us, whatsoever we ask, we know
that we have the petitions that we desired of him.

1 JOHN 5:15 KJV

John supposes that when we pray, we first find out if our prayers are according to the will of God. They may be according to God's will, and yet not come at once, or without the persevering prayer of faith. It is to give us courage thus to persevere and to be strong in faith, that He tells us: This gives us boldness or confidence in prayer, if we ask anything according to His will, He heareth us. It is evident that if it be a matter of uncertainty to us whether our petitions be according to His will, we cannot have the comfort of what he says, "We know that we have the petitions which we have asked of Him." Let us yield ourselves unreservedly to the Holy Spirit as He teaches us to abide in Christ, to dwell in the Father's presence, and we shall soon understand how the Father's love longs that the child should know His will, and should, in the confidence that that will includes all that His power and love have promised to do, know too that He hears the petitions which we ask of Him. "This is the boldness which we have, that if we ask anything according to His will, He heareth us."

~ANDREW MURRAY (1828–1917)

ON FAITH

FROM HEBREWS 11:1 KJV

Faith is belief, Hope is expectation. Each involves the idea of trust, but with the use of different prepositions. Faith is trust in or reliance upon any person or thing. Hope is trust of some person or thing, or expectation of the happening of something desirable. Joyful expectation enters into the nature of hope, but not into that of faith. It is only because the things believed beget a joyful hope, that the Christian's trust can be mistaken for hope. Hope is the result or effect of faith and, therefore, not faith itself. They differ in their objects. Faith rests upon Christ and His work for our salvation and upon the promises made of blessings. Hope rests in the blessings resultant from that work and those promises. Its object is salvation, freedom from sin, heaven, glory hereafter. We cannot say we have faith in salvation, but in the Savior and His work; we have not faith in future freedom from sin; but we have it in the promised deliverance. Likewise, we have not faith in heaven or glory; but in these as promised to us.

~J. P. BOYCE (1827–1888)

CHANGE ME LORD

(PHILIPPIANS 3:8)

There are times I feel so all alone, no one to share my pain,
Thoughts of being swallowed up in deep despair.
There's a spirit Lord of hopelessness I know not where it comes
But I know it's not Your will and way for me.
Just thinking all about relationships in life
I'm complaining, murmuring and full of strife.
Crying out "Oh Lord please change me," I know I'm grieving You.
Then the Spirit whispered gently "Look at Me.
Walk not in the flesh My child, it will destroy your joy.
Look to Me. I've prepared a work for you.
I will hold you in My hand and pray the Father's will be done.
It's My spirit that will strengthen and keep you."
Then I saw Your precious face that shines so bright and full of grace
A heart of gratitude returns to me.
You're the lifter of my head, praise You, Lord, You raise the dead
My Redeemer, You are everything to me.

~Linda K. Smith (1948–) Seneca, SC

THE GOD OF SECOND CHANCES

Then the word of the LORD came to Jonah a second time: "Get up!
Go to the great city of Ninevah and preach the message that I tell you."

JONAH 3:1–2 HCSB

When you think of Jonah, what comes to mind? Usually we think of his rebelliousness leading to a divinely appointed trip inside the belly of a great fish. Jonah's journey provides a vivid picture to the familiar description that "sin will take you farther than you want to go, keep you longer than you want to stay, and cost you more than you want to pay!" But the account of Jonah also gives a tremendous picture of God's mercy. From within the fish, Jonah offers a prayer of repentance for disobeying the Lord's call to preach in Nineveh. God hears Jonah's prayer and demonstrates marvelous grace in sparing Jonah's life. But God's forgiveness goes even further than letting Jonah live, for we see in the passage above that God also reinstates Jonah's call to preach in Nineveh. God is truly a God of second chances! Jonah is not put on the shelf and another prophet called to take his place. Jonah gets another opportunity to heed the Word of the Lord. In his second response, we have a picture of Jonah on the move again, but this time he is headed in the right direction! When a second chance comes, we must immediately make the most of the opportunity. Thank God that He is faithful even when we falter, fail, or fall. It should be a priority to make things right with God quickly so that we may get back on track and back in service for the Lord!

~RYAN BOWMAN (1972–) LEE'S SUMMIT, MO

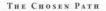

WE SING, IMMANUEL, THY PRAISE

We sing, Immanuel, Thy praise, Thou Prince of Life and Fount of grace,
Thou Flower of heaven and Star of morn,
Thou Lord of lords, Thou Virgin-born. Hallelujah!
For Thee, since first the world was made,
So many hearts have watched and prayed;
The patriarchs' and prophets' throng
For Thee have hoped and waited long. Hallelujah!
Now art Thou here, Thou Ever-blest! In lowly manger dost Thou rest.
Thou, making all things great, art small;
So poor art Thou, yet clothest all. Hallelujah!
From Thee above all gladness flows, Yet Thou must bear such bitter woes;
The Gentiles' Light and Hope Thou art,
Yet findest none to soothe Thine heart. Hallelujah!
But I, Thy servant, Lord, today Confess my love and freely say,
I love Thee truly, but I would That I might love Thee as I should. Hallelujah!
I have the will, the poser is weak; Yet, Lord, my humble offering take
And graciously the love receive
Which my poor heart to Thee can give. Hallelujah!
Had I no load of sin to bear, Thy grace, O Lord, I could not share;
In vain hadst Thou been born for me
If from God's wrath I had been free. Hallelujah!
Thus will I sing Thy praises here With joyful spirit year by year;
And when we reckon years no more, May I in heaven Thy name adore!
Hallelujah!

~Paul Gerhardt (1607–1676)

DO NOT FEAR

It is I, be not afraid.
MARK 6:50 KJV

A little child with a tale of woe on his heart flies to his mother's arms for comfort—intending to tell her the whole story of his trouble. But as soon as that mother takes the child in her arms and expresses her love, the child becomes so occupied with her and the sweetness of her affection that he forgets to tell his story, and in a little while even the memory of the trouble is forgotten. It has just been loved away and the mother has taken its place in the heart of her child. In this same manner, God comforts us. It is I, be not afraid is His reassuring word. The circumstances are not altered, but He Himself comes in their place and satisfies our every need, and we forget all things in His gracious presence as He becomes our all in all. I am breathing out my sorrow On Thy kind and loving breast; Breathing in Thy joy and comfort, Breathing in Thy peace and rest. I am breathing out my longings In Thy listening, loving ear; I am breathing in Thy answer, Stilling every doubt and fear.

~A. B. SIMPSON (1844–1919)

THIS OLD BODY WON'T GO!

*For our light affliction, which is for the moment, worketh for us
more and more exceedingly an eternal weight of glory.*

2 CORINTHIANS 4:17 ASV

Your doctor has run some tests. Your body isn't working like it used to. Something is wrong. You suspect something wrong deep in your bones . . . deep in your soul. Worry begins to rob you of the sweet peace you once enjoyed. Perhaps His Spirit's quiet voice has prepared you along the way. Then you receive the call: "I'm sorry to inform you, but you have cancer." The world seems to pause and let you step off momentarily. How can this happen to me? I've served only You! I've been faithful! Is there some sin present within me? For once in your life you believe you understand Jesus' words, "Why have You forsaken me?" As time passes, His Spirit nurses you back to reality and you rejoin the fray. You realize that this life is temporary. Nothing is news to Him. Thank God He knows! He gently prods you to continue on . . . and faint not! Though the outward man is decaying, the inward man is renewed day by day! We all know that our earthly tabernacle will eventually be dissolved. How and when remains life's great mystery. We have, however, a great home eternal . . . not made with hands. He tenderly reminds us that a more blessed day is ahead! Once we step over into the Sweet Bye and Bye, we will look forward realizing this eternal weight of glory. Clothed in our heavenly habitat we will muse about this light affliction that once passed our way. As for now, let us work more and more exceedingly until that eternal day.

~**DR. W. ALTON BRANT (1953–) SENECA, SC**

THE CHOSEN PATH

CONQUERING FEAR

*Fear not; I am the first and the last, and the Living one;
and I was dead, and behold, I am alive for evermore,
and I have the keys of death and of Hades.*

REVELATION 1:17–18 ASV

Jesus bids us to be unafraid of life. He reminds us that He is "the first and the last, and the Living One." Is the fear of life real? It is poignantly so with many. The liability of fear is constant, and this fact is perhaps the explanation for many a suicide. I asked one who sought in a despondent hour to snuff out the candle of life, and was prevented from so doing: "Why did you wish to end your life?" And the pathetic answer was given: "I was afraid to go on with life." People are afraid, for one thing, because they are so dependent. They are utterly dependent upon God, and greatly dependent upon one another. Sometimes the proud expression is heard: "I am independent." Let such a one tell us of whom he is independent, and how and where and when? We are all bound together in the bundle of life. Are you trusting in Christ as your personal Savior, and do you gladly bow to him as your rightful Master? Your personal relations to Christ will determine your relations to the three vast matters: life, death and eternity, concerning which He would have us put all our fears away, now and forever more. He is our Pilot, our Righteousness, our Savior, our Advocate, our promised and infallible Guide, even unto death, and throughout the vast beyond, forever. Well do we often sing: "He leadeth me." As we sing it now, who wishes openly to confess him and follow him?

~G. W. TRUETT (1867–1944)

DON'T LOOK BACK . . . OR DOWN!

*. . . rooted and built up in him, strengthened in the faith
as you were taught, and overflowing with thankfulness.*
COLOSSIANS 2:7 NIV

My mind wanders as I push the stroller through the reptile section of the zoo while my kids have fun. Things have been piling up lately. Why did I choose this path in my life? I have the Midas Touch in reverse—everything I do turns to dust! I watch two box turtles going about their lives in their landscaped cage with a pond bordered by a rock mountain. There is a low-grade trail which winds around the pond up to the top. God is silent. I thought He led me in this course. One of the turtles has been trying to climb straight up the steep face of the mountain while the other speeds up the trail. Why doesn't the pitiful turtle give up and follow the easy path? His two back feet slip and struggle in slow turtle speed for a footing! God, you have done this to me! A Gideon's fleece test—if the turtle fails, God is telling me that I was wrong and have to start over. If the turtle makes it, God is approving me. The turtle miraculously makes it! I almost cheer when a positive thought breaks through—Everyone has his own path but the turtle who took the mountainous way will be stronger the rest of his life for it! Just then, little hands tug on my sleeve to go see the otters and I tear up at the many blessings I have been given. Has your pain and path really been for nothing? Don't try to compare your life to others but be convinced of His promise to make you strong.

~**BRIAN KEAY** (1963–) **ASHEVILLE, NC**

LET OTHERS SEE JESUS IN YOU

While passing through this world of sin,
and others your life shall view,
Be clean and pure without, within; let others see Jesus in you.
Let others see Jesus in you, Let others see Jesus in you.
Keep telling the story, be faithful and true;
Let others see Jesus in you.

Your life's a book before their eyes,
they're reading it through and through
Say, does it point them to the skies, do others see Jesus in you?
Let others see Jesus in you, Let others see Jesus in you.
Keep telling the story, be faithful and true;
Let others see Jesus in you.

Then live for Christ both day and night,
be faithful, be brave and true,
and lead the lost to life and Christ.
Let others see Jesus in you.

~B. B. McKinney (1886–1952)

FINALLY

Among whom are ye also the called of Jesus Christ . . .
ROMANS 1:6 KJV

If you are saved yourself, be on the watch for the souls of others. Your own heart will not prosper unless it is filled with intense concern to bless your fellow men. The life of your soul lies in faith; its health lies in love. He who does not pine to lead others to Jesus has never been under the spell of love himself. Get to the work of the Lord—the work of love. Begin at home. Visit next your neighbors. Enlighten the village or the street in which you live. Scatter the word of the Lord wherever your hand can reach. Reader, meet me in heaven! Do not go down to hell. There is no coming back again from that abode of misery. Why do you wish to enter the way of death when Heaven's gate is open before you? Do not refuse the free pardon, the full salvation which Jesus grants to all who trust Him. Do not hesitate and delay. You have had enough of resolving, come to action. Believe in Jesus now, with full and immediate decision. Take with you words and come unto your Lord this day, even this day. Remember, O soul, it may be now or never with you. Let it be now; it would be horrible that it should be never. Again I charge you, meet me in heaven.

~C. H. SPURGEON (1834–1892)

THE PATH OF PROGRESS:
BEARING THE CROSS

*I thank God through Jesus Christ our Lord. So then with the mind
I myself serve the law of God; but with the flesh the law of sin.*

ROMANS 7:25 KJV

In Romans 7, the question of holiness of life is in view—a living, personal holiness. There you find a true man of God trying to please God in righteousness, and he comes under the law and the law finds him out. He is trying to please God by using his own carnal power, and the Cross has to bring him to the place where he says, "I cannot do it. I cannot satisfy God with my powers; I can only trust the Holy Spirit to do that in me." There is a great difference between "the flesh," as spoken of in Romans 7 in relation to holiness of life, and the working of the natural energies of the soul-life in the service of the Lord. With all the above being known—and known in experience—there still remains this one sphere more which the death of the Lord must enter before we are actually of use to Him in service. Even with all these experiences, we are still unsafe for Him to use until this further thing is effected in us. We are used in a sense, but at the same time we destroy our own work, and sometimes that of others also, because of there being somewhere something undealt with by the Cross. Now we have to see how the Lord has set out to deal with the soul, and then more particularly how this touches the question of our service for Him.

~WATCHMAN NEE (1903–1972)

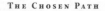

STRENGTH FOR THE JOURNEY

I lift my eyes toward the mountains. Where will my help come from?
My help comes from the LORD, the Maker of heaven and earth.

PSALM 121:1–2 HCSB

Here we find that the Israelites would sing over and over as they made pilgrimages to Jerusalem for the annual feasts and for worship. Jerusalem is approximately 2,400 feet in elevation, and travelers approaching from the north, south, east or west must make an ascent to reach the Holy City. Their journeys were potentially dangerous ones. Though the hills along the way were beautiful and majestic, they could also be treacherous. The psalm expresses anticipation, hope, and strength. Their power for the journey was their hope in God. In this life, we face many dangers. In a sin fallen world, each of us is subject to a multitude of trials and tribulations. We anxiously look with anticipation toward our heavenly home. Our power for the journey rests with our heavenly Father, the one who loves us with an everlasting love. When trouble seems to be the greatest, we can rely on God and rest safely in His arms. Do you have physical problems? Turn to the Great Physician. Do you have emotional problems? Turn to the Great Comforter. Do you have financial problems? Turn to the one who owns the cattle on a thousand hills. Do you have family problems? Turn to the Great Counselor. No matter what your problem is, your answer and hope is in God. The Lord Jesus said, "Come to Me, all of you who are weary and burdened, and I will give you rest" (Matthew 11:28 HCSB). The key is to look beyond yourself and realize your help comes from the Lord. Look beyond the trouble and see Jesus!

~SETH POLK (1971–) POKA, WV

WALK WORTHY

As ye have therefore received Christ Jesus the Lord, so walk ye in him.

COLOSSIANS 2:6 KJV

Let us abide in Him. It is much easier to keep the fire burning than to rekindle it after it has gone out. Let us not have to remove the cinders and ashes from our hearthstones every day and kindle a new flame; but let us keep it burning and never let it expire. Among the ancient Greeks, the sacred fire was never allowed to go out. So, in a higher sense, let us keep the heavenly flame aglow upon the altar of our hearts. It takes much less effort to maintain a good habit than to form it. A true spiritual habit once formed becomes a spontaneous tendency of our being, and we grow into delightful freedom in following it. Let us go on unto perfection; not laying again the foundation of repentance from dead works (Hebrews 6:1); whereto we have already attained, let us walk by the same rule, let us mind the same thing (Philippians 3:16). Every spiritual habit begins with difficulty and effort and watchfulness. But if we will only let it get thoroughly established, it will become a channel along which the currents of life will flow with divine spontaneousness and freedom.

~A. B. SIMPSON (1844–1919)

OH, WORSHIP THE KING

Oh, worship the King All glorious above:
Oh, gratefully sing His power and His love,
Our Shield and Defender, The Ancient of Days,
Pavilioned in splendor And girded with praise!
Oh, tell of His might, Oh, sing of His grace,
Whose robe is the light, Whose canopy space!
His chariots of wrath The deep thunder-clouds form,
And dark is His path On the wings of the storm.
This earth, with its store Of wonders untold,
Almighty, Thy power Hath founded of old,
Hath 'stablished it fast By a changeless decree,
And round it hath cast, Like a mantle, the sea.
Thy bountiful care What tongues can recite?
It breathes in the air, It shines in the light,
It streams from the hills, It descends to the plain,
And sweetly distils In the dew and the rain.
Frail children of dust And feeble as frail,
In Thee do we trust Nor find Thee to fail.
Thy mercies, how tender, How firm to the end,
Our maker, Defender, Redeemer, and Friend!
O measureless Might, Ineffable Love,
While angels delight To hymn Thee above,
Thy humbler creation, Though feeble their lays,
With true adoration Shall sing to Thy praise.

~ROBERT GRANT (1779–1838)

THE CHOSEN PATH

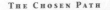

HOW TO GET IT ALL

*"Seek first his kingdom and his righteousness,
and all these things will be given to you as well."*

MATTHEW 6:33 NIV

Several years ago I became disgusted with the materialism of Christmas, so I joined the Kill Santa Clause Coalition. Instead of having a tree, I put up a cross and placed gifts under the cross. Needless to say my family was convinced that I had finally lost my mind. After searching the Scriptures I discovered that God is a gift giver. God is not a mean employer who only pays enough to keep you in poverty. Rather, God has "plans to prosper you and not to harm you, plans to give you hope and a future" (Jeremiah 29:11). God knows all your needs and He wants to meet those needs. Jesus instructs His disciples how to get it all. Pursue God with Passion—Jesus said, "Seek." Passion is a heart totally committed to being in His presence. "You will seek me and find me when you seek me with all your heart" (Jeremiah 29:13). Make God Your Priority—Jesus said, "Seek first." To prioritize is to put first things first. "You shall have no other gods before me" (Genesis 5:7). When God is first he influences and impacts whatever comes after. Obey God to Fulfill Your Purpose—Jesus said, "His Kingdom and His Righteousness." If there is a kingdom then there is a King. In other words, seek to live in the presence of the King. The more I am in His presence, the more I reflect His nature. When I begin to reflect on His nature, then I can be trusted with His blessings. "And all these things will be given to you as well."

~WILLIAM M. BLACKFORD, IV (1969–) LOUISVILLE, KY

THE CHOSEN PATH

FEARING GOD MORE THAN MEN

*"And I say to you, My friends, do not be afraid of those who
kill the body, and after that no more can they do. But I will show
you whom you should fear. Fear Him who, after He has killed,
has power to cast you into hell; yes, I say to you, fear Him!"*

LUKE 12:4–5 NKJV

As a trustee of the International Mission Board, I was privileged to spend several weeks with the IMB workers at the Jibla Baptist Hospital in Yemen in July of 1997. A few weeks before my arrival, one of our missionary doctors was kidnapped by Muslim extremists. Her miraculous escape had brought about a great sense of thankfulness. When I noticed that all the men and boys carried machine guns on their backs and jambeas (knives) across their chests, I became disturbed. When malaria broke out and rumors of threats against the workers of the hospital were whispered, I became alarmed. When I heard machine gun fire outside my door—that was the straw that broke this camel's back. I had reached my FEAR FACTOR! I can remember voicing my fears to a young nurse. "Nothing here appears safe to me. What is your definition of safe?" I asked her. She very confidently answered, "Safety is being in the middle of God's will." I have never forgotten those words. When living became dangerous, the workers would pray and continue working. They simply feared God and not fulfilling His Will more than they feared what any man could do to them. Apparently they understood the words of our Lord in the next verse, "Do not fear therefore; you are of more value than the sparrows" (Luke 4:7).

~GINNY DENT BRANT (1955–) SENECA, SC

THE GIFT GIVERS

On coming to the house, they saw the child with his mother Mary, and
they bowed down and worshiped him. Then they opened their treasures
and presented him with gifts of gold and of incense and of myrrh.

MATTHEW 2:11 NIV

An interesting thing happened after Jesus was born. During this first Christmas, the magi, or wise men, as they are sometimes called, heard that the Savior had been born and came to see Him. They gave baby Jesus presents, then bowed down and worshipped him. This is important because it gives me an example to emulate. I don't have the kind of gifts brought by the magi, but I have other gifts. Do I show gratitude for our Savior in thought and deed? Am I following His teachings and trying to become more like Him? Do I use my life to glorify Him? I try to do all of these things, sometimes well, other times not. The truths that they allude to do not dismiss the secular celebration of Christmas. But for me, they need to be at the core. Christmas isn't about honoring each other with gifts. It's about honoring Jesus and following His teachings. These are our gifts to Him. I'm going to start doing what a friend of mine does every year as a reminder of why we celebrate Christmas. Along with a holiday dinner she makes a white cake. When I first saw it I didn't know what it was as it is not a usual Christmas dessert. After dinner she dimmed the lights and lit candles she had placed on the cake. When she brought it to the table I looked at the sentiment written there. It said, "Happy Birthday, Jesus."

DAVID SCHOLTON (1951–) SANFORD, NC

GOD'S CHRISTMAS

FROM LUKE, CHAPTER 2

This is a season of special joy and love. We try to find the perfect greeting card for friends; we'll spend hours shopping for just the perfect gift for a loved one and families will pick out the perfect tree to decorate. In a sense, this was God's feeling on that first Christmas. He loved us enough to send the perfect greeting, to select the perfect gift, and to choose the only tree that would benefit mankind. The greeting came by angelic messenger first to Zacharias, the soon to be father of John the Baptist, then to Mary the mother of Jesus. The long awaited Promise was fulfilled in Jesus the Savior of the world. God could have sent us any number of gifts, but the only perfect gift was Himself. What greater, more perfect gift could God have given than the gift of eternal life, and the right to be called children of God? Our trees are beautiful, well shaped, and green. The tree God selected was just a plain, rough pole. Anything would do to hold a crossbeam. It was stained red, perhaps from earlier executions, but certainly from the blood of Jesus. Our trees are covered with beautiful ornaments, but God's tree only had one— God's indescribable gift. We take down our ornaments and decorations till next year, but when God took Jesus down from His tree, He never hung on another. God took Him down and gave Him life, so our Christmas will go on forever.

~G. W. STROTHER (1933–) CLAYTON, GA

GUIDE ME, O THOU GREAT JEHOVAH

Guide me, O Thou great Jehovah,

Pilgrim through this barren land.

I am weak but Thou art mighty;

Hold me with Thy powerful hand.

Bread of heaven,

Feed me till I want no more.

Open now the crystal fountain

Whence the healing stream doth flow;

Let the fiery, cloudy pillar

Lead me all my journey through.

Strong Deliverer

Be Thou still my Strength and Shield.

When I tread the verge of Jordan,

Bid my anxious fears subside;

Death of death and hell's Destruction,

Land me safe on Canaan's side.

Songs of praises

I will ever give to Thee.

~WILLIAM WILLIAMS (1717–1791)

GOD WANTS HOLY MEN

*And the very God of peace sanctify you wholly; and I pray
God your whole spirit andsoul and body be preserved
blameless unto the coming of our Lord Jesus Christ.*

1 THESSALONIANS 5:23 KJV

Holiness is wholeness, and so God wants holy men, men whole-hearted and true, for His service and for the work of praying. These are the sort of men God wants for leaders of the hosts of Israel, and these are the kind out of which the praying class is formed. . . . Man is one in all the essentials and acts and attitudes of piety. Soul, spirit and body are to unite in all things pertaining to life and godliness. The body, first of all, engages in prayer, since it assumes the praying attitude in prayer. Prostration of the body becomes us in praying as well as prostration of the soul. The attitude of the body counts much in prayer, although it is true that the heart may be haughty and lifted up, and the mind listless and wandering, and the praying a mere form, even while the knees are bent in prayer. . . . The entire man must pray. The whole man, life, heart, temper, mind, are in it. Each and all join in the prayer exercise. Doubt, double-mindedness, division of the affections, are all foreign to the closet character and conduct, undefiled, made whiter than snow, are mighty potencies, and are the most seemly beauties for the closet hour, and for the struggles of prayer.

- EDWARD M. BOUNDS (1835–1913)

CHOSEN AND CALLED BY CHRIST

*I pray also that the eyes of your heart may be enlightened
in order that you may know the hope to which he has called you.*

EPHESIANS 1:18 NIV

When I think of all the great Bible characters, the lessons they learned, the praise and service they gave to God, I often feel that I don't measure up. God worked through many great people. What do I have to offer that could make a difference in today's world? Matthew was chosen by Jesus to be one of the disciples. To carry on spreading the gospel after Christ ascended to heaven. But Matthew was a tax collector with a reputation for cheating people for his own personal gain. He was an outcast, despised because of his dishonest career. The responsibility of disciple was given to one who was not good enough, but was simply willing to be changed by God. We see in the story that Matthew responded immediately to Jesus' call on his life. Following Jesus was more important than leaving behind his previous lifestyle. Without hesitation, he accepted not knowing where he would be called to go, what he would be asked to do, when or if he would ever return. This story reminds me that God is in the business of changing lives and using them for His service. God has a purpose for each of us and we should respond immediately to His calling. Following Christ often involves stepping out in faith without knowing what lies ahead. Have you been chosen and called of God? Have you turned your life over to Christ allowing Him to change you? Are you willing to leave your comfort zone and step out in faith following Christ down His Chosen Path?

~TERESA N. SHAW (1966–) ALABASTER, AL

STEPS TO PEACE WITH GOD (PART 1)

STEP 1—GOD'S PURPOSE:

Peace and Life. God loves you and wants you to experience peace and life—abundant and eternal.

The Bible says . . . "We have peace with God through our Lord Jesus Christ" Romans 5:1 (NIV). "For God so loved the world that He gave His only begotten Son, that whoever believes in Him should not perish but have everlasting life" ~John 3:16 (NIV). "I have come that they may have life, and that they may have it more abundantly" John 10:10 (NIV). Why don't most people have this peace and abundant life that God planned for us to have?

STEP 2—THE PROBLEM:

Our Separation. God created us in His own image to have an abundant life. He did not make us as robots to automatically love and obey Him. God gave us a will and a freedom of choice. We chose to disobey God and go our own willful way. We still make this choice today. This results in separation from God.

The Bible says . . . "For all have sinned and fall short of the glory of God" ~Romans 3:23 (NIV). "For the wages of sin is death, but the gift of God is eternal life in Christ Jesus our Lord" ~Romans 6:23 (NIV). Our Attempts to Reach God. People have tried in many ways to bridge this gap between themselves and God . . . *The Bible says . . . "There is a way that seems right to a man, but in the end it leads to death" ~Proverbs 14:12 (NIV). "But your iniquities have separated you from your God; your sins have hidden his face from you, so that he will not hear" ~Isaiah 59:2 (NIV). No bridge reaches God . . . except one.*

THE CHOSEN PATH

STEPS TO PEACE WITH GOD (PART 2)

STEP 3—GOD'S BRIDGE:

The Cross. Jesus Christ died on the Cross and rose from the grave. He paid the penalty for our sin and bridged the gap between God and people.

The Bible says . . . "For there is one God and one mediator between God and men, the man Jesus Christ" ~1 Timothy 2:5 (NIV). "For Christ died for sins once for all, the righteous for the unrighteous, to bring you to God" ~1 Peter 3:18 (NIV). "But God demonstrates his own love for us in this: While we were still sinners, Christ died for us." ~Romans 5:8 (NIV) God has provided the only way. Each person must make a choice.

STEP 4—OUR RESPONSE:

Receive Christ. We must trust Jesus Christ as Lord and Savior and receive Him by personal invitation.

The Bible says . . . "Here I am! I stand at the door and knock. If anyone hears my voice and opens the door, I will come in and eat with him, and he with me" ~Revelation 3:20 (NIV). "Yet to all who received him, to those who believed in his name, he gave the right to become children of God" ~John 1:12 (NIV). "That if you confess with your mouth, 'Jesus is Lord,' and believe in your heart that God raised Him from the dead, you will be saved" ~Romans 10:9 (NIV).

Where are you? Will you receive Jesus Christ right now? Here is how you can receive Christ: (1) Admit your need (I am a sinner). (2) Be willing to turn from your sins (repent). (3) Believe that Jesus Christ died for you on the Cross and rose from the grave. (4) Through prayer, invite Jesus Christ to come in and control your life through the Holy Spirit. (Receive Him as Lord and Savior.)

THE CHOSEN PATH

STEPS TO PEACE WITH GOD (PART 3)

STEP 5—PRAYER:

How to Pray: Dear Lord Jesus, I know that I am a sinner and need Your forgiveness. I believe that You died for my sins. I want to turn from my sins. I now invite You to come into my heart and life. I want to trust and follow You as Lord and Savior. In Jesus' name. Amen.

God's Assurance: His Word. If you prayed this prayer,

The Bible says . . . "Everyone who calls on the name of the Lord will be saved" ~Romans 10:13 (NIV). Did you sincerely ask Jesus Christ to come into your life? Where is He right now? What has He given you? "For it is by grace you have been saved, through faith—and this not from yourselves, it is the gift of God—not by works, so that no one can boast" ~Ephesians 2:8–9 (NIV).

Receiving Christ, we are born into God's family through the supernatural work of the Holy Spirit who indwells every believer. This is called regeneration, or the "new birth." This is just the beginning of a wonderful new life in Christ. To deepen this relationship you should: (1) Read your Bible everyday to know Christ better. (2) Talk to God in prayer every day. (3) Tell others about Christ. (4) Worship, fellowship, and serve with other Christians in a church where Christ is preached. (5) As Christ's representative in a needy world, demonstrate your new life by your love and concern for others.

~Dr. Billy Graham (1918–) Charlotte, NC

BIOGRAPHIES

(With Special Permission by the Authors)

Dr. Dextral D. 'D.D.' Alexander (1945–) b. Marvell, AR; Sr P Holy Tabernacle of God (An IMB Global Priority Ch), B Ch Inglewood, CA; S, Paulette; 4 children; Ed: Philander Smith Col, Little Rock, AR -Early Childhood Development & Child Psychology; U of AR, Little Rock, AR-Business Adm and Public Adm; El Camino C, Torrance, CA-Psychology & Child Psychology; CA St U, Dominguez, Hills CA- Religious Anthropology & Psychology; P, St Luke Missionary B Ch, N Little Rock, AR; Staff Minister Greater Ebenezer Missionary B Ch, Los Angeles, CA; Moderator, Crescent Bay/West Los Angeles SBA; Mission Team Leader; Stewardship Team Leader; Cmte Member CA SBC; Cmte on Committees; Consultant: Lifeway Ministry Multiplier; NAMB - Next Level Leadership Training; IMB – Cross Cultural Training; CA SBC; Healthy Chs /Discipleship Training; Facilitator: LifeWay Conf Ctrs (Ridgecrest/ Glorietta); Crescent Bay/West Los Angeles SBA Ch Leadership Training Inst; Served on assignments to Kenya, South Africa, Mozambique, Swaziland, and Brazil.

Rev. Almer (Andy) Anderson (1964–) S, Cheryl; 3 sons; Bi-vocational Sr P Emmanuel B Ch Belle Fourche, SD; Sr P Rangeland Ministries Alzada, MT.

Dr. William Wallace (Bill) Ascol (1952–) P Heritage B Ch, Shreveport, LA; Chai, Bd of Dir for Founders Ministries, Inc; Founder, Saved By Faith Yth Challenge; B.S. Lamar U in Beaumont, TX; M.Div and D. Min. S B T S in Fort Worth, TX; S, Karen; Five Children; Pres LA B Ps' Conf; VP Exec Bd of the LA B Conv; Cmt Nominations LA B Conv; Assoc Editor Founders Journal, quarterly magazine of Founders Ministries, Inc; Editor LifeLine, newsletter of the LA B conservative resurgence; written periodicals and journals; contributed chapters in the following two books: *Reclaiming the Gospel* and *Reforming Churches*, Founders Press; Corrective Church Discipline and Biographical Sketch of John A. Broadus; Dear Timothy: Letters on Pastoral Ministry, Founders Press; Be Courageous http://www.hbcshreveport.org; Founders Ministries, Inc. is committed to bringing about reformation in the S B C through the recovery of the gospel of God's grace and the renewal of local churches. We are grateful for the rich spiritual and theological heritage that has been handed down to us by those precious saints who founded the SBC in the mid-nineteenth century. Committed to the same vision of church life as were they, believing as they did that truth is unchanged and unchanging. For more information,

contact: editor@founders.org; Saved By Faith Yth Challenge, ministry to discipline young people with a view to helping them become Great Commission Christians so that they discover their part in sending and/or being sent out as missionaries. Contact: SBFYC Mr. Bill Ascol, Coordinator c/o 457 Mohican Lane Shreveport, LA 71106 klascol@bellsouth.net © May 8, 2004; Words by Bill Ascol. All rights reserved.

REV. DAVID NELSON BALDWIN, SR. (1943–) Exec Dir/Treasurer, AK B C; Master of Religious Ed, SB TS, Fort Worth, TX; M DIM, NOB S, New Orleans, LA; S, Nancy; 2 children; spent twenty years as a Home Missionary with the NAMB, SBC; served in AK since 1981.

WILLIAM M. BLACKFORD, IV (1969–) b. Buffalo, NY; Resides, Louisville, KY; S, Felice; Three children; BA, Psychology, U of Louisville, KY (Pres of United B Fellowship BS, U of Louisville, KY (Member Fiesta Bowl Championship Team, Awarded Outstanding Defensive Back, Outstanding Player Award, Pres Omega Psi Phi Frat, Inc.) ; M Ed/Sports Adm; Consumer Rep, General Electric, Louisville, KY; MDiv S B T S, Louisville, KY (Martin Luther King, Jr. Garret Fellow, Nat'l Minority Leadership Award, Sr Class Pres) V-Pres of the NAACP Chapter at U of L; Sr P/Founder, More Than Conquerors Christian Ch; Former Sr P, Greater Salem B Ch; Exec Dir, B Fellowship Ctr; M LK Jr. Fellow, S B T S; Former Dir, Family Life Ctr, St. Stephen B Ch, M Evan, St. Stephen B Ch, Exec Dir of the KY Minority AIDS Council, Louisville, KY, Consumer Rep, G E, Hamilton Tigercat Football Club, Summer Missionary, Ghana, West Africa; Leadership Louisville, Business First Foremost Young Leaders Under Forty; Leadership Network.

RYAN BOWMAN (1972–) P of Summit Woods Bt Ch, Lee's Summit, MO; Degrees: B.A. U of Central AK; M Div. M B T S; S, Karen; 2 Children; Member of the Resolutions Committee for the MO B Con.

DR. W. ALTON BRANT (1953–) S, Ginny; 3 sons; teaches American Sign Language at Clemson U, in Clemson, SC; Served at the SC School for the Deaf and the Blind and 10 years as the Dir of the Sch for the Deaf. His first language is American Sign Language. His parents, Francis and Mollie Brant of Columbia, SC, are both deaf; B.A. in Biblical Ed from Columbia Int'l U; M.Ed. in Learning Disabilities from the U of SC; Ed.D. in Special Ed Adm USC; mission trips to Gaza, Russia, and The Czech Republic speaking on deafness. He currently serves on the Tri-State School of Theology Board which prepares deaf men and women for ministry; involved in deaf ministry for 29 years; member Utica B Ch of Seneca, SC.

GINNY DENT BRANT (1955–) S, Dr. W. Alton; 3 sons; elementary counselor, Oconee County Schools, SC; serves on his ministry board; adjunct prof of child growth and development and Christian speaker and singer; B.A. in Biblical Ed from Columbia Int'l U and two Masters degrees from the USC in Ed and Counseling; trustee of the Int'l Mission Board; short term mission trips to Yemen, Gaza, Russia, The Czech Republic, and Romania; member-Utica B Ch; SS teacher, choir member, on mission committee in several churches; daughter of Harry and Betty Dent of Columbia, SC; father gave up his legal and political career at age 48 and went into full-time Christian Lay Ministry. Known for his mission work in Romania.

DR. JIMMIE H. CARPENTER, M.D. (1927–) b. in LA; MD; BS LA Tech; MS LSU; MD at Tulane U, Pres. LSU-Tulane Med BSU; Interned at McLeod Med Ctr, SC; Residency, Huey P. Long Charity Hospital, LA; SB T S, TX; S B Med Missionary, Indonesia; FP Physician, Grace Family Practice, SC; County Chairman Republican Party; SC Human Affairs Commission; SC B Hospital Board; Int'l Mission Board, Richmond VA; Med Mission Volunteer, Jordan, Bangladesh, Gaza, Yemen, Suriname; SC B Exec Board; Missions Impact Team, Teacher, Deacon, Utica B Ch, Seneca, SC; Former Moderator, Beaverdam B Association; SC St Republican Exec Committeeman; Indonesian Bible Study and Worship Group, Anderson, SC; S, Joyce; 4 children.

JOYCE CARPENTER (1931–) Raised in China to SB missionary parents; S, Dr. Jim Carpenter, MD; 4 children; Served with husband as SB med missionaries to Indonesia; involved in ch and community organizations. Bible teacher/ public speaker; B.S. from Louisiana B C.

DR. MARK A, CROSTON, SR. (1959–) DMIN b. Phila, PA; S, Karen; 2 children; DMin, VA Union U, Richmond, VA; M Div, SBTS, Louisville, KY; BS and Engineering, UP, Phila, PA; East End B Ch, Suffolk, VA; M of Yth, First B Ch, Jeffersontown, KY; Dir of Christian Ed, Christian Mission Fellowship B Ch, Phila, PA; Systems Engineer, IBM Corp; Licensed/ordained by Christian Mission Fellowship B Ch, Phila, PA; VP, Nat'l African American Fellowship of the SBC; Second VP, B Gen Assoc of VA; Moderator, Portsmouth B Assoc; V Moderator, Portsmouth B Assoc; Bd Member, Prest, VP, African American Fellowship of VA, SBC; Trustee, Children's Home of VA B; Missions Promotion Dir,

Portsmouth B Assoc; Member, Christian Life Cmte, B Gen Assoc of VA, Town & Country Cmte, B Gen Assoc of VA; VP, United B Fellowship, SB T S; Chair, Yth Acti Cmt, Greater Phila B Assoc; Chair of Visita, Phila B Evangelistic Support Thrust; Chair of Yth Involvement, Phila B Evangelistic Support Thrust; St. Maarten Mission Trip; St. Croix Mission Trip; Jamaican Mission Trip, St. Mary's, Jamaica; Antigua Mission Trip, St. John's, Antigua; PA/South Jersey Evangelism Conf, Harrisburg, PA; B Gen Assoc of VA, 21st Century Evang Conf, Richmond, VA/ PA; Doctrine Sty Ldr, Black Ch Leadership Week, Ridgecrest, NC; Keynote Speaker, TN P's Conf, Nashville, TN; Bible Study Ldr, Family Missions Conf, B Gen Assoc of VA, Eagle Eyrie B Conf Ctr; Keynote Spker, East Coast Missions Conf; Nat'l Sdt Conf, Ridgecrest, NC; B SS and BTU Congress of VA, Lynchburg Col; AL BSU State Conv, Shocco Spgs, AL; E Regional Meeting of BSU Dirs, Wilmington, NC; VA Blk BSU Conv, Eagle Eyrie, VA; AL Blk BSU Conv, Shocco Spgs, AL; Spea, Glorietta, NM.

ANDY DIETZ (1950–) P of Missions and Evangelism, First B Ch, Borger TX; Bachelors in communications from West TX A&M U, Canyon, TX; S, Becky; 4 children; Traveled in Music Evangelism for twelve years: five with gospel quartet The Royalheirs, seven with his twin brother as The Dietz Brothers. Has ministered in three SBC churches: Second B Ch, Amarillo, TX, First B Ch, Broken Arrow, OK, and First B Ch, Borger, TX.

REV. JAMES (JIM) ALAN DOWNS (1950–) Sr P at Highland Crest B Ch , Green Bay, WI; served in Shawnee, OK, Konawa, OK, Crossett, AK, and Olney, TX; Associate of Arts, Hannibal LaGrange College, Hannibal, MO; BA, Oklahoma B Um History/Social Studies Shawnee, OK; M Div 1983 S B T S; S, Vonna; 3 children.

REV. JACK R. ELLIOTT (1941–) P, New Bethel B Ch Tobaccoville, NC; BB Theology from Int'l Bible Institute & S, Orlando, FL; Master of Bible Theology, Clarksville Theological S, Clayton, NC; P for over 20 years; S, Carolyn; 2 children; finance committee of the Pilot Mtn B Assoc.

REV. TODD FUEHRER (1967–) Sr P Riverwood B Ch, Bismarck, ND; Master of Arts in Biblical Study from Trinity; S, Robin; 3 Children; State Music Consultant for the Dakota B Conv.

MIKE GOODE (1958–) SBC ch member; S, Kim; Two children; Founder and President, Goode Games International, Inc. Nicholasville, KY; SS teacher; Radio announcer.

DR. BILLY GRAHAM (1918–) Reared on a dairy farm in Charlotte, North Carolina. Ordained by a church in the Southern Baptist Convention, Mr. Graham received a solid foundation in the Scriptures at Florida Bible Institute (now Trinity College in Florida) and graduated from Wheaton College, IL. Mr. Graham's Los Angeles crusade in 1949 launched him into international prominence. Since that time he has preached the Gospel of Jesus Christ to more people in live audiences than anyone else in history—over 210 million people in more than 185 countries and territories. Mr. Graham has authored 24 books, many of which have become top sellers. His autobiography, *Just As I Am*, achieved a "triple crown," appearing simultaneously on the three top best-seller lists in one week. Mr. Graham's counsel has been sought by presidents. Recognitions include the Congressional Gold Medal (1996) and an honorary knighthood, Honorary Knight Commander of the Order of the British Empire (KBE), in December 2001. Mr. Graham is regularly listed by the Gallup organization as one of the "Ten Most Admired Men in the World," whom it described as the dominant figure in that poll since 1948-making an unparalleled 47th appearance and 40th consecutive appearance. He and his wife, Ruth, have three daughters and two sons, 19 grandchildren, and numerous great-grandchildren. Used with special permission from the Billy Graham Evangelistic Association.

DR. JAMES RUDOLPH "RUDY" GRAY (1953–) Graduated-Anderson Col (editor of sch newspaper, Denmark Honor Society, Who's Who); attended USC , jr yr; BA Bible Southern Wesleyan U; Th.M, D.Min. Luther Rice S; M.A. Counseling Liberty U; post graduate studies, S B T S; Utica B Ch; S, Anne; 3 children; Pastored four SC SBC chs; author of three books; "The Please Principle" and "Boundaries and Blessings" marriage enrichment seminars; Certified, Nt'l Board for Certified Counselors; Charter Mem of the American Assoc of Christian Counselors, Assoc For Psychological Type; American Counseling Assoc; Counseling Referral Resource for Rapha and FOF; Seminar Facilitator on personality type and team building using MBTI; Certified Instructor for "Listening and Loving"; Outstanding Young Men of America; Who's Who Among Human Service Professionals; Who's Who In Religion; Trustee of the B Courier; Chairman, Resolutions Committee SCBC; Member General Bd, S.C. B C; Trustee, N O B T S; Trustee, Anderson Col.

MARSHA ANN GRAY (1953–) Services Mgr, NW B Convention, Vancouver, WA; Attended Washington State U, Pullman, WA; S, Donald; 2 children; Past Ch Secretary for First B Ch of Lakewood, Lakewood, WA, and Metropolitan B Ch, Portland, OR; Communications Department Secretary, Northwest B Conv; Secretarial Mgr, NW B Conv.

Rev. Steven Grose (1959–) Graduated from Wollongong Teacher's College (Australia) with a Diploma of Teaching; Graduated from The B\ Theological Col of N.S.W. (Australia) with Bachelor of Theology, and a Diploma of Ministry degree; Kiama BC; Church planting pastor; Glen Innes B Ch; Sr P East Hills B Ch and Wattlegrove B Ch; Ch planting pastor The Newcastle B Tabernacle, Newcastle, New South Wales; Sr P; LifeWay Int'l Representative; S, Lorelle; 3 children.

Dr. Tommy A. Henschel (1947–) Dr. of Ministry Degree. Ordained; Pastored ches throughout GA; Sr P of Cornerstone Bt Ch in Ellerslie, GA. Cornerstone is a phenomena in itself, since it is the result of two B Chs merging to become one growing and healthy fellowship of believers; S, Carol; 4 children; Exe Dir of the Columbus, GA Crisis Preg Ctr.

Carol Henschel (1951–) Exe Dir of the Columbus Crisis Preg Ctr in Columbus, GA and has held similar positions throughout GA; Bible Study Ministry in the ch and conducts women's conferences in the Columbus, GA area; Spouse, Dr. Tommy Henschel, SB pastor in Ellerslie, GA; Four children.

Vicki Huffman (1946–) Freelance writer/editor; served as an editor for Thomas Nelson Publishers and Cook Communications; Author of hundreds of newspaper columns and magazine articles; Authored Applying the Lesson section for Broadman Comments; author of two books: *The Best of Times* (Broadman 1986), and *Plus Living: Looking for Joy in All the Right Places* (Harold Shaw 1989); Former SS teacher and Women's Bible studies; S, Richard; Two children; Member First B C in Nashville, TN. Attended the U of IL.

Rev. Chris James (1978–) Evangelical Campus Minister at UMASS in Lowell, MA for 3 years; served in ch in Mississippi as MM and Students; Chaplain for the Lowell Spinners, a minor league affiliate of the Boston Red Sox; Graduate of U of Southern MS with a BA in music; finishing MDiv at the SB Theological S in Louisville, KY; frequent youth and collegiate speaker.

Rev. Brian Keay (1963–) Ordained; Masters in Marriage and Family Ministry, Talbot Sch of Theology; BA in Organizational Behavior, Covenant Col; Counselor to families and married couples; Served with Freedom In Christ for seven years. Pres, Truth Action, Inc.

The Chosen Path

Grew up in the Children's home where his parents served for thirty years: a home for children whose parents were incarcerated long term. S, Anne; 3 children.

Rev. Russell C. Lambert (1955–) Pa & Chaplain; Liberty Bible Institute-Bible; Certificate- Ctr for Biblical Counseling, American Assoc of Christian Counselors; S, Bonnie May; 3 children; Guest Soloist; Music Leader; P, Sunset Hill B Ch; Life Services of Spokane, WA; Spokane County Sheriff's Dept, Associate Chaplain; supply P; Discipleship Pr, Divine Design Community Ch; Community Chapl, Clallam Bay, WA; Lay Minister, Prison Fellowship, Salem, OR; Licensed Chapl, Nt'l Chaplain's Assoc; Licensed SBC Minister; Ordained; Certified Chaplain, Int'l Conf of Police Chaplains; Certificate of Achievement, AZ Depart of Corrections, SCAT Team (aka SWAT); NRA Police Firearms Inst; Certificate of Appreciation, Class Advisor AZ Dept of Cor; Hazardous Material Technician; Career Level Supervisory Certif, WA St Criminal Justice Comm; Emergency Response Instructor-Office of Correctional Operations, WA; Inland Empire B Assoc Finance Committee.

Rev. Joseph Anthony Jones (1964–) S, Rebecca; 3 children; P/Ch Planter, Goodyear B Ch; BGS in P Ministries, N O B T S, N.O. LA; Presently enrolled in M Div at GGB TS, Arizona Campus, Phoenix, AZ; Vice Moderator for Pearl River B Assoc, Pearl River, MS; Served 12 years (combined) in the U.S. Navy and U.S. Army as an electronics technician.

Rev. Randolph (Randy) Alan McCollum (1952–) S, Pattie Ann; 2 children; Licensed, New Hope B Ch, Glencoe, AL; Ordained, Eastside B Ch, Gadsden, AL; Missionary, HMB of SBC, Atlanta, GA; MDiv, SBTS, Louisville, KY; BA, Jacks'ville St U, Jacks'ville, AL; Certi, Basic Leadership for Dir of Missions; HMB, SBC; Certi: Basic Leadership Dir of Missions, HMB, SBC, Christian Training, Samford U, Birmingham, AL; Reality Thrpy, William Glasser, MD, UA Birmingham, AL, Short-Term Counseling, U A-Birmingham, SE Regional Spt Ctr (Nat'l Institute on Drug Abuse), Rational Emotive Therapy, Albert Ellis, UA-Birmingham, AL, Drug Counseling, "The Bridge Drug Alert Center," Gadsden, AL; Gadsden St Jr. Col, Gadsden, AL; P, Bloomington B Ch, Bloomington, IN; mission activities, Brazil; H M B, SBC, Atlanta, GA; Dir of Missions, Miami B Assoc; NCentral IN B Assoc; East Ctl IN B Assoc; P, Creekwood B Ch, Muncie, IN, First B Ch, Hartsville, IN and Pleasant Grove Hospital, Louisville, KY; Psychiatric Technician; Spring Meadows Children's Home, Louisville, KY H'parent; P, Reece City B Ch, Reece City, AL; "The

Bridge" Drug Alert Cter - Eastside B Ch, Gadsden, AL; H'parent/Counselor -Reality House; P, Mt. Olive B Ch, Reece City, AL; Westminster Christian Sch, Gadsden, AL, Music Dir/teacher; Eastside B Ch, Gadsden, AL, Ass P, MM, Ed/Yth; New Hope B Ch, Glencoe, AL, MM and Yth; contributor -WMU Website, Adults On Mission Plan Bk, WMU; HMB, SBC; Serve White River A Personal Committee; Campus Ministry Council, White River Assoc, IN; Assoc SS Dir, White River Assoc, IN; Served Adult Advi Group nat'l WMU 2-year term; Ministry- Rio de Janeiro, Brazil; Evangelistic Crusade; Chair, Std Work Cmt, Metro B Assoc, Indianapolis, IN; Cons, B Campus Min (BCM) IN U, Bloomington, IN; Std Wk Consu, BSU ,Notre Dame U, S Bend, IN, and Ball St U, Muncie, IN; St Cons, Music Team, St Conv of Bt, IN; ASSIST Cons, St level, St Conv of B, IN; Alumni Pres IN; S S Alumni Advi Council; Music-Annual Conv of Dir of Missions, SBC in Indianapolis, IN; Assoc Dir of Discipleship Training, East Cent'l B Assoc, IN; Assoc Dir of SS, Discipleship Training, S Ctrl B Assoc, IN; Moderator, S Ctrl B Assoc, IN; Chaplain, Brown Cty Dive Rescue Team, and Bloomington Township Dive Rescue Team (Monroe County) Jail Ministry, Teach classes and other ministry services at Monroe Cty Correctional Facility, Bloomington, IN; Prof /Dir S Ext of the Exec Bd of SBC, Nashville, TN; Prof/Dir Boyce B Col Ext Prog; Established Boyce B Col, Ext Pro; Prof Boyce B Col Ext Prog; Registrar/Sub Teacher, Howard Ext Prog Samford U, Birmingham, AL.

JANET MILLER (1943–) B.A. in Biblical Studies, COChristian U; S, Roy; 3 children; Lay Ministry, Applewood B Ch; Bible teacher to children, teens, and young adults for over 25 years; Women's Ministry: Teacher, Retreat Speaker, Christian Women's Club speaker; 11 years as missionary with IMB (1993-2004), working with Internationals on the Cote d'Azur, France; helped to plant and minister in Int'l B Ch, Nice, France; helped to plant and minister in Int'l B Ch, St. Paul de Vence, France; taught English classes and bible classes to Int'ls; organized Women's Ministry, hospitality ministry; Summa cum Laude (CO Christian U); Recipient of American Bible Society award in Biblical Studies and Theology; Who's Who in American Cols and U; Delta Chi Epsilon Honor Society; Home Mission Bd Literacy Award; Water Color Exhibition, Rocky Mt Ntl WaterColor Show, Golden, CO.

REV. ROY MILLER (1935–) IMB Missionary; Team Leader of Cote d'Azur English Language Ch Planting Team until May 2004, when I came to the States for final stateside assignment before my upcoming retirement on December 31, 2004; B.S. in Geology, TX

Technological Col, Lubbock, TX; M.A. in Counseling, Denver Cons B S, Denver, CO; S, Janet; 3 children; 25 years as a layman: 1st B Ch, Lafayette, LA: ordained as deacon; Applewood B Ch, Wheat Ridge, CO; served in various teaching and lay-leadership capacities; including the Lay Renewal movement in the 70's; participated in several volunteer partnership mission trips; 5 years as ordained minister in Applewood B Ch as Associate P in charge of adm. and counseling; 11 years as missionary with IMB; ch planter for English-speaking Internationals on the Cote d'Azur, France; planted and pastored Int'l B Ch, Nice, France; planted and pastored Int'l B Ch, St. Paul deVence, France; Team Leader for Cote d'Azur English Language Church Planting Team.

Rev. Timothy Ray Pittman (1959–) Born again 1976; S, Linda; 4 children; Missionary P; Bachelor of Theology, Andersonville B S; Master of Biblical Study, Andersonville B S; Attended Blue Mountain Col and Sanford U taking courses in Theology Biblical Study while Ministering in S B Ch; MM/ Youth; P: Bivocational for almost 25 years: MS, AL, VT; Current P of two Ches in VT, Sheffield Federated Ch and South Wheelock Bt, through Green Mtn B Association. Six years at both Chs; Current Principal/ Teacher/ Administrator for a B Christian School in VT.

Rev. Seth N. Polk (1971–) b. FL; S, Emilee; 3 children; Liberty U Lynchburg, VA; Working on DrM degree; SBTS- Wake Forest, NC; Mdiv, Pastoral Track with Biblical Languages; NOBTS-Orlando FL, Ext Ctr Mdiv Studies; FL Southern College- Lakeland, FL; BS, Business Adm; Honors: Graduated Magna Cum Laude; South FL Community Col, Avon Park, FL; Undergraduate; Honors: Phi Theta Kappa Honor Fraternity; Frostproof HS- Frostproof, FL; Graduated High Honors; Ordained, First B Frostproof, FL; Licensed, First B, Frostproof, FL; Present: Sr P, Cross Lanes B Ch, Cross Lanes, WV; F P, Red Mtn B Ch, Rougemont, NC; F Assoc P, First B Frostproof, FL; Mgr, Polk Citrus Groves; Supply Preacher numerous ches; S FL; AWANA Ministry Advisory Bd; Ch Council, First B Frostproof, FL; AWANA Commander, First B Frostproof, FL; Young Married Adult Bible Study Teacher, First B Frostproof; Youth Dir, First B Frostproof, FL; Yth Discipleship Leader, First B Frostproof, FL; Evangelism/Ch Growth Council, Yates B Assoc; Durham, NC; General Bd Rep Region IV- B St Conv of NC; SS Dirr, Pioneer B Assoc, Charleston, WV; Moderator, Pioneer B Assoc, Charleston, WV; Exe Bd, WV Conv of SB; Evangelism Committee, WV Conv of S B VP of the Pastors Conf, WV Conv of S B; Selected as alternate preacher for 2005 Conv Sermon, WVCSB; Certified in F.A.I.T.H. SS Evangelism

Strategy; Certified with Prison Fellowship Ministries for Prison Ministry; Mission Trip to Jamaica, 2004, Trip to War, WV; Trip to Coahuila, Mexico; Trips to Littleton, NH to support NAMB Ch Plant.

REV. DAVID F. RASMUSSEN (1952–) b. Holland, MI; served as p of Greencastle B Ch (http://www.greencastlebaptist.org/) Greencastle, PA since 1998. Previously served S B ches in Mi, ND; graduated from Michigan St U and Southwestern B Theological S; S, Ann L. from 1973 until her death late 2002. He has one son.

REV. TERRENCE ORLANDO ROBERTS (1964–) P/Developer; B.A. Communications MS St U; S, Terrey; 3 children; Terrence, a native of Flint MI, served as an AM, S S Superintendent, and currently is serving as pr/developer of New Wine Ministries, in Meridian MS a MS B Conv Bd sponsored ch plant.

DR. JON RALEIGH ROEBUCK (1960–) Sr P, Woodmont B Ch, Nashville, TN; D Min , The SB Theological S, Louisville, KY; M Div, SB Theological S, Louisville, KY; B.A., Samford U, Birmingham, AL; S, Linda; 3 children; Bd of Trustees, Belmont U, Nashville; Member of the Ed Comm, AL B Conv; Prog Chairman, Birmingham Ministers Conference, Birmingham B Association; Chair of the Campus Ministry Committee, Nashville B Association; Camp P, Summer Children's Choir Camp, TN B Conv; Recipient of the E.Y. Mullins Humanitarian Award, A B T S; Participant in Mission Trip Experiences in Brazil and Ecuador; Contributor to Proclaim Magazine; Recipient of a Top 100 Award, Lottie Moon Christmas Offering.

REV. MILES ROHDE (1972–) Senior Pastor, Calvary B Ch, Marshall, MN; Assoc. of Applied Science—Community College of the Air Force; BS/Biblical Studies —Moody Bible Institute; Spouse, Pamela; 1 son.

DR. DONALD T. SATTERWHITE (1953–) Sr P, Middle River B Ch, Baltimore, MD; S, Marie; 3 children; served as P for over 20 years in SC, NC, and PA prior to coming to MD; served as pres of the Pastor's Conf in the Lexington B Association, Robeson B Association and Saluda B Association. served on the Resolutions Committee for the B St Conv of NC; graduate of FL Bible College and New Orleans B Theological S with an MDiv and DMin.

REV. DAVID SCHOLTON (1952–) P of Godfocus Internet Ch, http://godfocus.net; missionary for the B Ch of Beaufort, SC, having just returned from 3 yrs in Italy; S, Trudi;

He and his wife grew up in military families and have lived much of their life abroad; retired from the US Army Medical Service; worked in military journalism, substance abuse counseling, preventive medicine and other areas. Because of severe chronic illness his pastoral and missionary efforts have been unconventional and creative. David started an Internet ch that he manages from home and assists military chaplains when possible. He also visits patients and their families at military and civilian hospitals during his frequent medical trips. David holds a Bachelors Degree in Psychology from the U N Y and is a Masters Degree Candidate at Liberty B Theological S in Lynchburg, VA. David has applied and is currently being considered for ordination as a Hospital Chaplain.

DR. GLEN SCHULTZ (1947–) Dir of Christian School Resources, LifeWay Church Resources of the SBC, Nashville, TN; completing his 36th year of involvement in edu ministry; prior to position at LifeWay was Southeast Regional Dir Assoc of Christian Schs Int'l.; 7 years developed and coordinated services for approximately 600 Christian schs with a combined student population of 120,000 in eight sts, conducting conventions, conferences and seminars as well as overseeing accreditation and certification among other administrative functions; teaching career includes five years as a public high school chemistry teacher, one year as a Christian sch science teacher, six years as a Christian sch secondary principal and nine years as superintendent of a Christian sch. While serving in the administrative positions, continued to teach science and Bible to high school students; conducted professional seminars for teachers, administrators and chu leaders throughout the US and seven foreign countries. He is the author of Kingdom Education: God's Plan for Educating Future Generations and A Parent's Greatest Joy; active in chu work ; served as an associate pastor at Thomas Road B Ch, Lynchburg, VA, for 9 years; taught an adult SS class at First B Snellville GA; conducted seminars for ch leaders/parents in conjunction with Josh McDowell as well as conducting marriage and parenting seminars at a number of chs. Ordained at First B Ch, Snellville, GA.; married with three children; BA, Roberts Wesleyan Col, Rochester, NY; MEd UV, Charlottesville. Permission given to use Excerpts taken from Kingdom Education by Glen Schultz, LifeWay Press, Nashville, TN 1998.

TERESA N. SHAW (1966–) Preschool M at Westwood B in Alabaster, AL; s, Kenneth; 2 children; As a family they enjoy serving in many ministries, from teaching babies to leading youth to Student Praise Band. Teresa has a real love for sharing God's love with children and states, "The Lord has blessed Westwood with many young families. I am very thankful to be a part of His ministry partnering with parents to make a difference in the life of a child."

Jacquelyn Sheppard (1943–) Educator, Counselor and Bible Teacher, and international speaker. Southern B Minister's wife and mother of three missionary children; S, Glenn Sheppard.

Rev. Glenn Sheppard (1943–) M.Div. Southern S; B.A. Valdosta St U; Ordained S B Minister; P, twenty-two years; Founding Dirof the Office of Prayer for Spiritual Awakening for NAMB of the SBC; Founder and Presi of Int'l Prayer Ministry; Founding member of American Nat'l Prayer Committee; Former Sr Associate for Prayer for Lausane Committee. S, Jacquelyn; 3 children.

Linda K. Smith (1948–) Spouse, Marvin; Three children; Former bookkeeper; Course study on lay counseling with The American Association of Biblical Counseling; Public speaker; Mentor hurting/wounded women struggling from abusive childhoods. Community Bible Study Core Leader, Seneca, SC.

Earlene R. Strother (1933–) BA LA College; MA LA Tech U; graduate study UG; S, Dr. Joseph; Son: Joey deceased; Retired Ed: Public schools of NC, Maryland, GA, and LA: China Experiences: Xi'an Jiatong University, Xian, PRC English majors, U of Science and Technology, Beijing, PRC English to Ph.D. candidates-Chinese Academy of Sciences, Beijing, PRC. English to Ph.D. candidates; Distinguished Alumni in 2002, Louisiana College.

Dr. J. W. Strother (1933–) BA LA College; MA U G Ed.D UG; S, Earlene; Son: Joey, deceased 1980; Retired U Adm; Professor Emeritus; Forty years in public ed; retired as Dir of School of Art and Architecture, LA Tech U; Raised in China, son of SB missionaries, Dr. Greene and Martha Krause Strother, who served 40 years in China and Malaya; Paintings exhibited in 50 Nat'l Art Exhibitions and One-Man Shows; China Teaching Experiences at Xi'an Jiatong U, Xian; Uof Science and Technology and Chinese Academy of Sciences, Beijing; Distinguished Alumni of LA College.

Bill Sumners (1950–) Dir and Archivist, S B Historical Library and Archives Nashville, TN; Archivist, E.C. Dargan Research Library; Assistant Archivist, Auburn U Archives; B.A. Samford U; M.A. History and Archival Administration, U of TX at Arlington;

Published articles in Baptist History and Heritage, Alabama Baptist Historian, Christian Media Journal, Church Media Magazine, Quarterly Review, Provenance, Journal of Florida Baptist History, Baptist Peacemaker, Church Administration, Journal of African American SB History and Inside the Auburn Tigers; Resident of Franklin, TN; Sp, Donna; Three adult children; SS teacher at Oak Valley B Ch, Franklin.

Rev. Scott H. Taylor (1960–) S, Carolyn; 2 sons; Ordained at Perryton, TX; Bachelor of Music/Ch Music; Hardin Simmons U, Abilene, TX; Served full-time Yth Ministry or Yth Ministry in combination with music, discipleship and evangelism in chs in TX and SC; Served in the MM at New Hope B Ch, Seneca, SC; Franklinton B Ch, Franklinton, NC; Calvary B Ch, Rocky Mt, NC; Immanuel B Ch, Rogers, AR; Six years with touring choir, Hardin Simmons U, Abilene, TX ; Voice coach, HSU; Assoc Yth Min, Exe Bd, Canadian B Assoc; Camp Dir, Panfork B Yth Camp, Beaverdam Assoc-wide Yth Camp; Dir, Perryton Community Choir, Perryton, TX; Soloist with Amarillo Symphony; Regular substitute - All-level public sch music; Clinician for HS choir contest music and area choir festival judge; Kenya evangelistic crusade team ldr; Evangelism/building mission trip to Kigali, Rwanda; Trinidad mission trip; Seminary choir soloist in Elijah and Amahl and the Night Visitors; Member of Faithful Men representing Southeastern S; Sang at SBC in New Orleans; Atlanta; Assist Dir - Male Chorale, Southeastern S; Regularly lead chapel worship at SE S; Contest Clinician, Middle Sch band, Rogers, AR; Directed fully staged, 200 cast, Resurrection Dramas, Rogers AR; Directed premier of Genovox Christmas cantata, Branson, MO; Composer and arranger of Sovereign God; General Mger, KBNV, 90.1 FM, American Family Radio; Dir premier of Christmas cantata,, Gatlinburg, TN; P & W Leader, S C B Conv; Continuing Witness Training (CWT) certification; Yth Ministry U; St Key Leader Training Conf; Yth Minister's Convention/Workshops; Stu Discipleship Ministries Certification; Precept Ministries Level 1 Training; Music/Choral wkshops; FAITH evangelism strategy ldr; M Div/Ch Music; SBTS.

Rev. Willian Wojcicki (1957–) b. São Paulo - SP – Brazil; S, Sonia Reginai; 2 children; Graduated Bacharel in Theology by the Theological B S of the S of Brazil - Rio de Janeiro; Study of Brazilian Problems by the Mackenzie U - São Paulo - went until the 5th period of Philosophy by the U of Rio de Janeiro, he also graduated by the United Chaplains Int'l - being a voluntary Chaplain register in NY - USA by the certificate of Incorporation #

F010709000515. Ordained, Evangelical B Ch in Praça do Carmo - Rio de Janeiro - (25 years on Pastoral Ministry and 25 years of Marriage); S, Gleidson Sant'anna; two children.

Dr. John A. Wood (1938–) Prof of Religion (retired), Baylor U; B.A. Columbia Bible College; B.D. Southwestern BTheological S; Ph.D. Baylor U; Public speaker; S, Suzanne (deceased 1993). 4 sons; S, Karen; Dir, Christian Social Ministries, Waco B Association (in connection with the Home Mission Board); Dir of Prog Dev, Christian Life Commission, SBC, Nashville, TN.

Rev. Jorge Zayasbazan (pastor_jz@yahoo.com) Pastor, Grace Chapel of Round The Lake Beach, IL; S, Tracy; 4 children; Jorge has worked on Spanish & English language ch starts across the US and overseas and is the founding p of four churches.

Zig Ziglar (1926–) b. Hilary Hinton Ziglar in Alabama, one of 12 children. At school in MS in the 1930s, he was nicknamed "Zig." His father died in 1932 in the midst of Depression, leaving the family in financial hardship, but he managed to go to college in Jackson, MS, and the USC. He walked away from a record-setting sales career to help other people become more successful in their personal and professional lives. Has been featured in the *NY Times*, *The Washington Post*, *The Dallas Morning News*, *Fortune*, *Success* and *Esquire* magazines, and has appeared on the *Today Show*, *20/20*, *60 Minutes*, and *The Phil Donahue Show*. He has that rare ability to make audiences comfortable and relaxed, yet completely attentive. Author of nine books; Recognized in the Congressional Record of the US for his many contributions to the American way of life. Shared the platform with such distinguished Americans as Presidents Ford, Reagan, and Bush, Generals Norman Schwarzkopf and Colin Powell, Dr. Norman Vincent Peale, Paul Harvey, and Dr. Robert Schuller, as well as numerous U.S. congressmen and governors; Chairman of the Board of Ziglar Training Systems; Spouse, Jean; Four children, one gone to be with the Lord; Special Recognition Award, Religious Heritage of America; Communications and Leadership Award, Toastmasters; Honorary Doctor of Law, Criswell Center for Biblical Studies; MS of the Year, MS Broadcasters Association; Communicator of the Year Award, Sales and Marketing Executives International; Wilbur M. McFeely Award, National Management Council; Elected to Advisory Council, Boy Scouts of America; Alumnus of the Year, Hinds Community College, Raymond, Mississippi; Sales & Marketing Executives International Academy of Achievement Ambassador of Free Enterprise;

The Chosen Path

Honorary Doctor of Humanities, OK Christian University of Science and Arts; Recognized as one of the Toastmasters International Five Outstanding Speakers of 1997 for Contributions to the Art of Public Speaking; Harry S. Truman Distinguished Service Award for support for and belief in community colleges across the nation, given to people outside the field of education who have made major contributions to community colleges, American Association of Community Colleges; Sales & Marketing Executives Marketing Leadership Award; Honorary Doctor of Letters Degree for Contribution to Literature on Human Potential, Southern Nazarene U; National Speakers Association Master of Influence Award; Toastmasters International Golden Gavel Award; Cavett Award, National Speakers Association; Silver Buffalo Award, Boy Scouts of America.